Hatfield Polytechnic

Wall Hall Campus
Aldenham, Watford
Herts WD2 8AT

This book must be returned or renewed
on or before the last date stamped below.
The library retains the right to recall
books at any time.

ll Campus
RY

THEMES IN DRAMA

An annual publication

Edited by James Redmond

4

DRAMA
AND
SYMBOLISM

CAMBRIDGE UNIVERSITY PRESS

CAMBRIDGE

LONDON   NEW YORK   NEW ROCHELLE

MELBOURNE   SYDNEY

Published by the Press Syndicate of the University of Cambridge
The Pitt Building, Trumpington Street, Cambridge CB2 IRP
32 East 57th Street, New York, NY 10022, USA
296 Beaconsfield Parade, Middle Park, Melbourne 3206, Australia

First published 1982

Printed in Great Britain at the
University Press, Cambridge

Library of Congress
catalogue card number:
81-10250

British Library cataloguing in publication data
Themes in drama. – Vol. 4
1. Drama – History and criticism – Periodicals
809.2′005   PN1601

ISBN 0 521 22181 1

Contents

BOOKS

FORUM: SYMBOLISM IN CHEKHOV

Themes in Drama Conferences

Annual conferences are held at the University of London and at the University of California. The subject each year is the theme of the volume in preparation:

> Drama and the Actor 1982
> Drama, Sex and Politics 1983
> Historical Drama 1984
> The Theatrical Space 1985
> Farce 1986

Further information may be obtained from

> James Redmond
> Editor *Themes in Drama*
> Westfield College
> University of London
> London NW3 7ST

Contributors

Geoffrey Arnott, *School of Classics, University of Leeds*
Dennis Bartholomeusz, *Department of English, Monash University*
Virginia Bennett, *Department of Russian, University of California, Davis*
A. R. Braunmuller, *Department of English, University of California, Los Angeles*
Martin Esslin, *Department of Drama, Stanford University*
John Fletcher, *School of Modern Languages and European History, University of East Anglia*
Peter Holland, *Fellow of Trinity Hall, Cambridge*
Kathleen Hulley, *Department of English, University of North Dakota*
Linn B. Konrad, *Department of French and Italian, Rice University*
Ben Maddow, *writer and director*
Dana Sue McDermott, *Department of Theater, University of California, Riverside*
Arthur E. McGuinness, *Department of English, University of California, Davis*
Michael Neill, *Department of English, University of Auckland*
Leonard C. Pronko, *Department of Modern Languages, Pomona College*
John Ripley, *Department of English, McGill University*
Laurence Senelick, *Department of Drama, Tufts University*
Leigh Woods, *Department of Theater and Drama, Indiana University*

Illustrations

Editor's preface

This is the fourth volume of *Themes in Drama*, which is published annually. Each volume brings together reviews and articles on the theatrical activity of a wide range of cultures and periods. The papers offer original contributions to their own specialised fields, but they are presented in such a way that their significance may be appreciated readily by non-specialists. The review section is unusually important, since reviewers have much more than customary scope to give detailed critical accounts of drama in performance, and to discuss in depth the most significant contributions to scholarship and criticism. The section entitled 'Forum' provides an opportunity to debate questions of general interest, including those raised in earlier volumes of *Themes in Drama*.

Each volume indicates connections between the various national traditions of theatre by bringing together studies of a theme of central and continuing importance. The annual international conferences (see p. vii) provide an opportunity for scholars, critics and theatrical practitioners to exchange views, and many of the papers in the volumes are revised versions of papers read and discussed at the conferences. The present volume reflects the range and quality of the 1980 conference on 'Drama and Symbolism'.

Contributions are invited for the main body of the text and for the Forum section; they should follow the style of presentation used in this volume, and be sent to

James Redmond
Editor *Themes in Drama*

Westfield College
University of London
London NW3 7ST

The stage: reality, symbol, metaphor*

MARTIN ESSLIN

All the world's a stage.
(Shakespeare)

Sehn wir doch das Grosse *aller* Zeiten
Auf den Brettern, die die Welt bedeuten,
Sinnvoll, still an uns vorübergehn.
(Schiller)

Alles Vergängliche
Ist nur ein Gleichnis.
(Goethe)[1]

Symbolism in the theatre: before embarking on the subject we must attempt to clear up some of the almost impenetrable confusion that surrounds the term. What are symbols? If we take the term as it is employed, for example, by Ogden and Richards in their *The Meaning of Meaning*,[2] it will comprise the whole of language; all of linguistics becomes what they call a 'science of symbolism'. Now it is true that in the theatre there is a specific language that has its own system of signs and significations (which includes the whole of the field of linguistics as well as a lot of other sign systems), yet clearly the term 'symbolism' when applied to the theatre is not directly relevant in that sense. The modern discipline of semiotics, which derives from Saussure and Peirce as well as Ogden and Richards, uses a triple division of signs: 'symbols' are signs arbitrarily linked with their objects or referents; 'icons' are similar to their objects or referents; 'indices' are physically connected with their objects or referents. Clearly, but also somewhat paradoxically, the specific nature of the theatre makes it more concerned with icons (images, representations of people and things) and indices (gestures) than with symbols in this sense. Umberto Eco includes as a fourth category unintentional signs, such as blushing, which are also clearly relevant to the theatre. And then there is another use of the terms 'symbol' and 'symbolism' in mythology, anthropology, and theology. An enormous literature is devoted to the explanation

---

* This paper was read at the *Themes in Drama* International Conference on 'Drama and Symbolism' held at the University of California, Riverside, in May 1980.

and interpretation of conventional symbolic systems. This is also a field of some applicability to the theatre, but it is not the primary sense in which we are dealing with the subject here.

There is also, of course, the specific use of the terms 'Symbolism' and 'Symbolist' to refer to the artistic movement that started in the nineteenth century and had a strong impact on the theatre from Ibsen and Maeterlinck to Strindberg and Hofmannsthal. That movement was characterised by a particular use of theatrical symbols, but here again this is not what I am concerned with in the first instance. My concern is with a connotation of the term 'symbol' which is related to all those previously mentioned, and in a very specific way: the use, that is, of the term to denote a secondary as distinct from a primary meaning, an overtone of meaning by which a given sign or image can carry a deeper, or higher, or more recondite charge of significance than the sign or object or image in question could ordinarily carry, a meaning more charged with emotion or insight than the primary signifi-cance could accommodate and by which the mundane, prosaic word or object or image becomes transmuted into something poetic and sublime.

This, after all, is the original meaning of 'symbol', the Greek roots of which denote the 'bringing together' of two disparate things and their recombi-nation into something new which is more valuable because of its greater complexity; this greater complexity allows more profound insights to be communicated in areas of human experience that are multilayered, delicate and beyond the reach of discursive speech. And it is my contention that drama – including the cinema, television and radio drama – is among the principal media for the expression and communication of such complex contents, precisely because of its power to produce symbols in this particular sense, which, to distinguish them from all the other diverse and confusing uses of the term, I propose to call 'dramatic symbols'. These too are *signs* and a good deal of the science of signs, semiotics, is applicable to their under-standing. But they are signs of a peculiar character, which is conferred on them by the very fact that they are incorporated in a new field of force, that of *a stage* (whether a theatrical stage, a cinema or television screen, or the mind of a listener to radio drama). For the stage itself here becomes the primary symbol-producing agent.

Let me illustrate what I mean by a passage from one of the best play-wrights of our time, the Swiss novelist and dramatist Max Frisch. Frisch wrote a novel which aroused the interest of the 'dramaturg' of the Zurich Schauspielhaus, Georg Hirschfeld, who invited him to try to write a play for his theatre. When Frisch objected that he knew too little about the theatre, Hirschfeld invited him to attend any rehearsals at the Schauspielhaus he would care to come to. And so Frisch, at the age of twenty-five, became an ardent rehearsal-watcher. In his published diary he describes an episode which occurred in 1946:

Went again today to attend a rehearsal; and as I was an hour too early I retreated to one of the boxes, where it is dark as in a confessional. The stage was, luckily, open and without a set, and I did not know the play that was to be rehearsed. Nothing is as stimulating as nothingness, at least for a time. Only occasionally a stagehand crossed the stage, a young man in brown overalls. He shakes his head, stops and quarrels with another, whom I cannot see; and it is the most ordinary language that is heard from the stage, anything but poetry. Shortly afterwards an actress appears, eating an apple, while crossing the empty stage in her overcoat and hat; she says 'good morning' to the stagehand, nothing else, and then again there is silence, the empty stage, occasionally a sound when a tram passes outside. This little scene, which happens a thousand-fold outside on the street, why does it here have such a different, such an immensely more powerful effect? The two people who have just crossed the stage had a presence, a being, a destiny which naturally I don't know; yet it was there, albeit as a mystery; it had an existence which filled the whole large space. I have to add that there was only an ordinary working light, a light like ashes, without any magic, any so-called atmosphere, and the whole effect clearly derived from the fact that there was simply nothing else but this little scene; everything around it was night; for the length of a few breaths there was only one thing: a stagehand who is talking angrily, and a young actress who yawns and goes into her dressing room, two human beings who encounter each other in space, who can walk and stand upright and have echoing voices; and then all that is gone again, incomprehensibly, as though someone had died, incomprehensible that it should have stood before our eyes, should have spoken, ordinary and trivial, and yet deeply exciting ...

Something in this little episode seems to me deeply significant. It also reminds one of the experience we have if we take an empty picture frame and hang it, as an experiment, on a bare wall; perhaps it is a room in which we have already been living for years, but now for the first time we notice how the wall is plastered. It is the empty frame that compels us to see. True, my reason tells me that the plaster I have now framed can't look any different here than on the rest of the wall, indeed, it is no different, not a whit. But it has become apparent, it is here, it is speaking to me. Why are pictures framed? Why do they look different when we take them out of the frame? They are no longer differentiated from the accidentals of their surroundings; they are, without a frame, suddenly no longer secure; they no longer rest in themselves; one has the feeling that they are falling apart and one is a little disappointed; they look worse suddenly, worse than they really are. The frame when it is there detaches them from nature; it is a window into a different kind of space, a window into the spirit where the flower, the painted flower, is no longer a flower which withers but an interpretation of all flowers. The frame puts it outside time. In that respect there is an immense difference between the space which lies within the frame and space in general which is infinite. Certainly those would be bad painters who believed they could save all by a frame, that everything, merely by being within a frame, would gain the significance of a symbol; but it does get, willy-nilly, at least the claim to such a significance. What does a frame say to us? It says: look here, here you will find something worth looking at, something standing outside mere coincidence and temporality. Here you will find significance that lasts, not just flowers that wither, but the image of flowers, as I said before: the *Sinn-Bild* [the sense-making image which is the German for *symbol*][3]

This passage deserves to be quoted at such length because it is so graphic
and so clear in illustrating a phenomenon which, because we are so ha-
bituated to it, we tend hardly to notice in our daily preoccupation with
drama: the stage itself as a significance-producing phenomenon. As Frisch
says, it is a frame, an area which by its very existence proclaims the special
significance and meaningfulness of everything that happens or can be found
on it. In that, as Frisch observes, it is analogous to the frame of a picture, the
pedestal of a sculpture. It says to the onlooker: what you see in this space is
something you are supposed to look at as being on display, on exhibition,
something that will be worth looking at, that will carry special significance.
But unlike the picture or the sculpture the objects that are displayed on a
stage are not all *representations*. Not only are most objects on the stage now-
adays three-dimensional, they are to a considerable extent *real*: real chairs,
real tables, people wearing real clothes.

The stagehand and the actress whom Frisch observed were totally real
people, yet the stage suddenly endowed them with a special symbolic
significance. They became *representative* of other real people, images of a more
general applicability, because, as Frisch rightly observes, they were being
put into a different context, removed into a different world, the world behind
the frame; and, as such, they were being exhibited as *specimens of humanity*.
Also, because the stage tells us to look out for a universe more ordered, more
meaningful, a universe deliberately created to enhance and interpret the
significance of the real world, a universe of *fiction*, which is to say a universe of
a higher, more permanent order of reality, even their most casual remarks
were turned into a kind of poetry. In that sense anything that is put on the
stage acquires some characteristics of a symbol. It becomes a sign – an icon –
a sign for itself, but one that is pointing beyond itself to a higher significance
transcending itself.

Let us start with the simplest possible case. A chair is a chair. If we see it in
a room with which we are familiar we hardly notice it. It is certainly without
any significance there. It is not a sign. If we see a chair in a room with which
we are not familiar, that chair becomes to a certain degree a sign: for
example, we might deduce the taste of the owner of the room from that chair;
or we might regard a very elegant chair as a sign of affluence in the owner of
the room. Put that chair on the stage and it will immediately become
considerably more meaningful, for now we know that we are meant to
deduce important information from it, from its position on the stage, its style,
its colour, its period, its sumptuousness or shabbiness. And, what is more,
that very real chair, if it is being used in, say, a production of *Hamlet*, at the
same time becomes a *fictional* chair: a chair in Elsinore many hundreds of
years ago, a chair, we may be meant to imagine, that had belonged to
Hamlet's father, that reminds Hamlet of the time his father was alive. That
very ordinary real chair has become an element in a fictional universe and

plays its part as much as the actor who plays Hamlet himself. In other words, the real chair we might have had in our own lodgings the day before has now become a symbol, a sign for a chair in Elsinore and all the associations and significances that such a chair, in its humble way, must carry on the stage during the performance of *Hamlet*. And, of course, the same applies to the actor who plays Hamlet. He is a real person with his real looks, real voice, real style of movement. The audience watching his performance knows his real name, his domestic circumstances, titbits about his private life. But he is also, by virtue of being on the stage, by virtue of his costume and make-up, the fictional character of Hamlet. The real person has turned himself into a sign, a symbol for that fictional person. He is himself, but he is also Hamlet. In the terminology of linguistics and semiotics the actor is both the *signifier* and the *signified* at one and the same time; he is an *iconic* sign in Peirce's sense of being similar to the object that is being signified, but also an index in that he is physically linked with the object being signified and also, being Hamlet, insofar as his gestures and movements are being interpreted by the audience, a carrier of *symptomatic* significance. When he blushes the audience will interpret this as a sign of his embarrassment (an embarrassment which might be an involuntary product of the actor's subconscious identification with the character, or a deliberately produced signal which the actor was able to make appear on cue by a conscious effort). This intensity and richness of simultaneous sign-production and conveyance is surely unique in the field covered by semiotics. All the more surprising is the fact that the theoreticians of semiotics have until recently paid insufficient attention to the theatre. In Umberto Eco's *A Theory of Semiotics*, by far the most comprehensive book on the subject (which is also mercifully free from the obscurantist jargon that disfigures so much work in this field), there is no mention of theatre or drama.[4]

On the most basic level therefore *everything* that is put on a stage is a symbol, a sign, a signifier. And because it is a physical object representing itself, it is also, at least partially, its own referent, the thing that is being signified. But only partially. Take, for example, the famous map of Africa in Uncle Vanya's office in Chekhov's play. It is a map of Africa and it represents a map of Africa in that fictional office. But it also means much more; it indicates the irrationality, the lack of purpose, the casualness of Vanya's life-style; its very lack of discernable function in a Russian estate office tells us that this is a place inhabited by a man who does not care about the functionality of his office's layout or furniture, who puts a map on the wall for no other reason than that he happened to own it and liked its colour or wanted to cover a bad patch of wallpaper. The richness and complexity of the associations that humble object can produce are astonishing. In that sense it becomes a true *dramatic* symbol with the connotations that I have tried to outline. Here the signifier, besides denoting, or referring merely to itself, also evokes a whole universe of related significances, which become overtones, harmonics, whole clusters of associations and images. There is thus a veritable hierarchy of significances that the stage, by its very nature, confers on the objects, persons and events that appear on it.

Take a simple object such as a crown, made of paper and painted to look like gold. If worn by the actor portraying Richard II in Shakespeare's play, that simple object acquires its first layer of significance as the symbol of Richard's kingship. In the scene when it is taken from him it gains a further layer of significance as his whole kingdom. The text, the plot, the action, of course indicate the circumstances, but the single action of the crown being removed from Richard's head sums up and concentrates that whole complex cluster of ideas and facts into one dense, emotionally charged focal point. It becomes the sign, the true dramatic symbol, for a complex emotional and intellectual situation. It embodies and incarnates that situation in a uniquely effective and expressive way. But, of course, there is a further layer of significance which that crown, in that moment of the play, may well carry. The king, by the very fact that he appears on a stage which transforms the individual into a representative, an archetype, will, at least to those spectators who identify with him and his fate, become a representative of all mankind. The action of his divesting himself of his crown will be emblematic, symbolic, an image of the loss of sovereignty that all of us must sooner or later suffer; the farewell to the crown will become symbolic of man's farewell to his life.

We thus have here a whole hierarchy of significations in that one humble object of paper and paint. On the first level it is merely itself, paper and paint. On the second level, as soon as it is put onto a stage it becomes the symbol of royalty: the object is raised to the status of a sign, an object inside a fiction. On the third level, it becomes, by metonymy or synecdoche, the embodiment of the whole of the kingdom. On the fourth and highest level, it concentrates upon itself the image of human existence and mortality on the most general metaphorical level, the level of the lyrical image. It will be seen that there is a curious dialectic in this hierarchy. On the lowest level the object itself is anonymous, not individualised. As it is raised to the level of a sign and symbol it becomes, first, individualised, as King Richard's crown, King Richard's kingdom, while at the highest level it is then again generalised from the individual to the universal. This particular example concerns an object which already carries a built-in symbolic meaning. The crown is conventionally recognised as a symbol of kingship. In this case Shakespeare is using a conventionally accepted symbolic object as the starting point from which all the higher and wider significances derive.

A second, even more complex type of such symbolism involves an object which is not in itself pregnant with conventionally established meaning, so that the playwright has to *confer* symbolic overtones on it, either implicitly, simply by putting it on the stage, or explicitly, by having that significance talked about, pointed to. Chekhov's use of the map of Africa in *Uncle Vanya*, which is barely referred to in the text, is an example of an object which is simply there and which gradually makes its point to those members of the audience who notice it and ponder its significance. The seagull in Chekhov's play and the wild duck in Ibsen belong to the category of the explicitly introduced symbol. Nina identifies herself with the seagull, and Gregers Werle draws Hedvig's attention to the parallel between her own position and that of the crippled duck in her grandfather's loft. In these two cases the function of the symbol is to parallel and duplicate the character's predicament and to establish a rich context of correspondences and contrasts between itself and the character. The casualness with which Trigorin has used the seagull and then forgotten the whole episode brings home to Nina – and to the audience – the casualness with which the successful writer seduces and discards his mistresses; the forlorn exile of the wild duck in the grotesque caricature of the open countryside represented by Old Ekdahl's loft becomes an image of the false situation of Hedvig in a household where her putative father has had her foisted upon him by deceit.

In these two cases the symbolism is fairly laboriously established. It is the method of much of the Symbolist movement in drama and poetry. And it seems to me that it is somewhat over-explicit. Far more subtle is the symbolic overtone which arises without elaborate stressing and underlining. In Chekhov's oeuvre, for example, the cherry orchard organically grows into a powerful and highly charged symbol without anyone drawing explicit parallels between it and the family's fate. In *Three Sisters* it is Moscow, of which the three women dream and which recedes from their grasp, which serves an analogous function and is equally powerful and suggestive. In the later Ibsen, Hedda Gabler's pistols, Solness's tower, and Borkmann's attic represent a similarly less explicit and more powerfully suggestive use of symbolism. These symbols, moreover, introduce another dimension of the symbolic function in drama, opening up another use of the term: for they are not only dramatic symbols, they are also powerful symbolic archetypes from the vocabulary of dreams and the subconscious. Whether Ibsen was himself aware of it or not, these are symbolic archetypes.

Since Freud, playwrights and the public at large have become increasingly aware of this type of symbolism. And it is questionable whether such an awareness is to the advantage or to the detriment of the power of *dramatic* symbolism. It might be argued that this awareness has merely added a new set of conventionalised symbols to the list of emblematic images like the king's crown. The awareness has reduced rather than increased the power of the surprising and truly original symbolism which playwrights have at their command. On the other hand, the opening up of the stage to the world of dreams, of the interior landscape of the soul, by Strindberg, the Expressionists and the movements which followed them, has greatly enriched the expressive potential of the stage. For it has made it possible to use the stage in the freest possible manner as an arena for the symbolic representation of the subconscious where the real and the fantastic can mingle, co-exist, or coalesce. When Pirandello, deliberately making use of the situation which Max Frisch describes in that passage from his diary, lets his audience witness the casual goings on at a rehearsal of a play by Pirandello and then suddenly brings on his six characters who have sprung, incomplete, from their author's brain, he is expressing a complicated psychological situation in his own mind: the conflict between the external reality of his daily existence as a playwright and the inner reality of his imagination from which the external reality was nourished. The play in question brilliantly illustrates one of the ultimate paradoxes of the theatre: however realistic a dramatic action may be, ultimately it is the product of the fantasy-life of its author, his imagination. The frame the stage provides, which is a window into another reality, is also a window into a world of fantasy and dream. Even the most realistic play can thus be seen as a piece of fantasy.

Pirandello, Ionesco, Beckett and other authors who clearly use dream imagery may have highlighted this phenomenon, but it is as old as the theatre. The Australian aborigines speak of the world of their myths and stories as the 'dream time': mankind's great archetypal myths are humanity's collective dreams. The gods and heroes of the Greek tragic universe are dream images of overwhelming power and universal significance, but so also are the comic archetypes of the ancient comedy, Aristophanic as well as that of Menander, Plautus and Terence, which developed into the comic types of the *commedia dell'arte* and its successors.

Similarly, the religious drama of the Middle Ages fused the 'realistic' representation of scriptural events (which were clearly regarded as hard facts by their producers and performers) with a higher symbolic function, on the pattern Dante adhered to in his *Divina Commedia*. There were four levels of meaning: literal, allegorical, tropological (symbolic of a gradual increase in insight) and anagogical (the level of deepening spiritual illumination through grace). In passing we may note the correspondence to the ascending levels of dramatic symbolic meaning we arrived at in our example of the crown. Allegorical dramas, such as the morality plays of which *Everyman* and *The Castle of Perseverance* are the best-known examples, or the Spanish *autos sacramentales* such as Calderon's *El Gran Teatro del Mundo*, use the most explicit symbolism in the whole history of drama. They are dream plays long before Strindberg and Beckett. But even the most realistic plays of the nineteenth century – not to speak of melodrama or farce with their heightened fantasy-images, sentimental reversals of fate and nightmarish complications in the pursuit of amorous adventure – are also the products of the fantasy-life of their authors; and this is merely another way of saying that the stage transmutes everything that is put upon it into a dramatic symbol.

And yet, to come back to where we started from, everything that is on the stage is also essentially *real*, in the sense that we are dealing with real people, the actors, with real objects, the properties. It is merely that the stage, by its very nature, turns these realities into images of themselves, into signs of themselves and of a hierarchy of significances. Lear naked and raging against the storm on his heath, Vladimir and Estragon waiting by their leafless tree, which in the second act mysteriously has sprouted a few leaves, Béranger refusing to turn into a rhinoceros, Hedda Gabler burning Løvborg's manuscript, Eliza Doolittle rebelling against Henry Higgins, the clergyman in the Aldwych farce who has lost his trousers, Sherlock Holmes solving a murder mystery – they are all themselves but they are also archetypal images of the human condition, incarnations of universally experienced situations and emotions and as such symbolic of whole complexes and clusters of human experience, concentrated concretisations of innumerable individual situations, experiences and feelings. The stage becomes a metaphor – which is to say a system of symbolic representations – of the world itself. Shakespeare speaks of the world as a stage, and Schiller's famous phrase 'die Bretter die die Welt bedeuten' characterises the stage as the boards that *signify* the world. And, indeed, if the stage can represent the world, the world must in some sense *be* a stage. Reality itself, even the most mundane, everyday reality, has its own symbolic component. The postman who brings me the telegram which announces the death of a friend is also, in a sense, a messenger of death, an Angel of Death. Whether he is perceived in that symbolic sense is merely a matter of my own way of looking at him, my own awareness, my own mood. An old beggar who is asking me for alms outside an Italian cathedral may be perceived as no more than that: but he may also be perceived by me as a symbol of poverty, misery, old age, sickness, as an embodiment of my own fears and anxieties. Reality itself thus has the four levels of Dante's poem – literal, allegorical, tropological and anagogical – for the old beggar's image might also increase my thinking by a sudden illumination or insight, or give me a spiritual experience by triggering a flash of mystical illumination. Thus reality itself, of necessity, contains all the symbolic levels. 'Alles Vergängliche / Ist nur ein Gleichnis': the whole evanescent world is merely a metaphor, as the mystical chorus sings at the end of Goethe's *Faust*. What the stage does – as a symbol-producing space – is to sharpen our awareness by concentrating our eyes on events which, by being on a stage, are proclaimed to be worthy of such a concentrated contemplation. What the stage gives us is an *enhanced* reality that itself becomes a sign, a metaphor, an image, a dramatic symbol. This is why all the attempts to create a truly realistic theatre, that would be no more than a photographically exact copy of external reality, ultimately merged into symbolism, dream plays, landscapes of the soul, allegory, surrealism, or the Pirandellian oscillation between illusion and reality discovered to be no more than an illusion.

The explicit symbolism of the turn of the last century can, in this light, be seen to be something of a tautology. There is no need specially to stress the symbolism of the theatre, since the stage itself produces symbols simply by drawing attention to the inherent symbolism of reality itself. And how could it be otherwise? We merely have to remember that the stage provides us with the most complex interaction of the maximum number of semiotic systems: a concurrence of all possible codes of meaning; the ideogrammatic representation of human beings by human beings; the system of index signs represented by gesture and facial expression, movement and stillness; a multitude of symptomatic signs; the whole complicated semiotic code of costume; the sign system of painting (representational as well as abstract, in the shape of light and colour coding); the rich semiotic system of musical sound as well as natural sound effects; the consciously or unconsciously perceived symbolic system of mythical and dream symbolism; and, to crown it all, the full impact of the most highly developed semiotic system of all, that of language in its fullest and most complex form, richer than merely read or printed texts by the addition of the full panoply of voice timbre, pitch, rhythm and expressive nuance; and language, to boot, not only of a factual discursive type, but also charged with all the emotional overtones of poetic form, rhythm, imagery and expressive force.

Moreover, these rich interacting combinations of semiotic and symbolic systems operate not only simultaneously but in a structured time-scheme, so that they can intensify and modulate their interaction in an infinite number of significant variations. If Lear raging naked on the heath is a powerful single image, the full force of the symbolic representation of the human condition which he embodies unfolds in time: if he is now naked, we have also seen him fully clothed in purple and ermine and the full panoply of kingship, if he is now mad and deranged, we have seen him in the full force of his intellectual superiority; it is only along this temporal axis that the full impact and meaning of the complex symbolic image that is Lear, the metaphor of the human condition that he incarnates, can be fully perceived.

This is where the stage has an advantage over mundane reality which also operates on a temporal axis: the old beggar we saw at the church door perhaps also went through all the phases of Lear's decline, but over a long period and in fits and starts. The stage can concentrate the movement along the temporal axis even more efficiently than it can concentrate the action into a compressed space. Here, then, we have the main elements that make the stage into a symbol-producing instrument. It is first of all a frame for reality which insists on the spectator concentrating on it as a venue for significant sights and events; and it can concentrate reality in space and time; and in doing so, it converts the real into a signifier for itself and beyond itself, pointing into areas of meaning transcending itself. It is the tension between these basic significations and the multiple layers of transcending, derivative, secondary and tertiary meta-significations that creates the power, the emotional impact and the magic of the dramatic symbol.

NOTES

1. *As You Like It*, II, vii; 'An die Freunde'; *Faust*, part II, act V, lines 12, 104–5.
2. C. K. Ogden and I. A. Richards, *The Meaning of Meaning: A Study of the Influence of Language upon Thought and the Science of Symbolism*, with Supplementary Essays by B. Malinovski and F. G. Crookshank (London: Routledge & Kegan Paul, tenth edn, 1952).
3. Max Frisch, *Tagebuch 1946–1949* (Frankfurt am Main: Suhrkamp Verlag, 1950), pp. 63–5.

Heute wieder einmal an einer Probe, und da ich eine Stunde zu früh war, verzog ich mich in eine Loge, wo es dunkel ist wie in einer Beichtnische. Die Bühne war offen, zum Glück, und ohne Kulissen, und das Stück, das geprobt werden sollte, kannte ich nicht. Nichts ist so anregend wie das Nichts, wenigstens zeitweise. Nur gelegentlich ging ein Arbeiter über die Bühne, ein junger Mann im braunen Overall; er schüttelt den Kopf, bleibt stehen und schimpft gegen einen andern, den ich nicht sehen kann, und es ist eine ganz alltägliche Sprache, was auf der Bühne ertönt, alles andere als Dichtung – kurz darauf erscheint eine Schauspielerin, die gerade einen Apfel isst, während sie in Mantel und Hut über die leere Bühne geht; sie sagt dem Arbeiter guten Morgen, nichts weiter, und dann wieder die Stille, die leere Bühne, manchmal ein Poltern, wenn draussen eine Strassenbahn vorüberfährt. Die kleine Szene, die sich draussen auf der Strasse tausendfach ergibt, warum wirkte sie hier so anders, so viel stärker? Die beiden Leute, wie sie eben über die Bühne gingen, hatten ein Dasein, eine Gegenwart, ein Schicksal, das ich natürlich nicht kenne, dennoch war es da, wenn auch als Geheimnis, es hatte ein Vorhandensein, das den ganzen grossen Raum erfüllte. Ich muss noch bemerken, dass es ein gewöhnliches Arbeitslicht war, ein Licht wie Asche, ohne jeden Zauber, ohne sogenannte Stimmung, und die ganze Wirkung kam offenbar daher, dass es ein anderes als diese kleine Szene überhaupt nicht gab; alles andere ringsum war Nacht; ein paar Atemzüge lang gab es nur eins: einen Bühnenarbeiter, der schimpft, und eine junge Schauspielerin, die gähnt und in die Garderobe geht, zwei Menschen, die sich im Raume treffen, die gehen können und stehen, aufrecht, die eine tönende Stimme haben, und dann wieder ist alles vorbei, unbegreiflich, wie wenn ein Mensch verstorben ist, unbegreiflich, dass er gewesen ist, dass er vor unseren Augen gestanden hat, gesprochen hat, alltäglich und belanglos, dennoch erregend –

Etwas an dem kleinen Erlebnis scheint mir wesentlich, erinnert auch an die Erfahrung, wenn wir einen leeren Rahmen nehmen, und wir hängen ihn versuchsweise an eine blosse Wand, und vielleicht ist es ein Zimmer, das wir schon jahrelang bewohnen: jetzt aber, zum erstenmal, bemerken wir, wie eigentlich die Wand verputzt ist. Es ist der leere Rahmen, der uns zum Sehen zwingt. Zwar sagt uns der Verstand, dass der Putz, den ich umrahme, nicht anders erscheinen kann als auf der ganzen Wand; er ist ja nicht anders, in der Tat, nicht um ein Korn; aber er erscheint, er ist da, er spricht. Warum werden Bilder denn gerahmt? Warum wirken sie anders, wenn wir sie aus dem Rahmen lösen? Sie heben sich nicht mehr von den Zufällen der Umgebung ab; sie sind, einmal ohne Rahmen, plötzlich nicht mehr sicher; sie beruhen nicht mehr auf sich allein; man hat die Empfindung, sie fallen auseinander, und man ist etwas enttäuscht: sie scheinen schlechter, plötzlich, nämlich schlechter als sie sind. Der Rahmen, wenn er da ist, löst sie aus der Natur; er ist ein Fenster nach einem ganz anderen Raum, ein Fenster nach dem Geist, wo die Blume, die gemalte, nicht mehr eine Blume ist, welche welkt, sondern Deutung aller Blumen. Der Rahmen stellt sie ausserhalb der Zeit. Insofern ist ein ungeheurer Unterschied zwischen der Fläche, die innerhalb eines Rahmens liegt, und der Fläche überhaupt, die endlos ist. Gewiss wären es üble Maler, die darauf vertrauen, dass sie es mit dem Rahmen retten können; gemeint ist nicht, dass alles, nur weil es innerhalb eines Rahmens stattfindet, die Bedeutung eines Sinnbildes bekomme; aber es bekommt, ob es will oder nicht, den Anspruch auf solche Bedeutung. Was sagt denn ein Rahmen zu uns? Er sagt: Schaue hieher; hier findest du, was anzusehen sich lohnt, was ausserhalb der Zufälle und Vergängnisse seht; hier findest du den Sinn, der dauert, nicht die Blumen, die verwelken, sondern das Bild der Blumen, oder wie schon gesagt: das Sinn-Bild.

4. Umberto Eco, *A Theory of Semiotics* (Bloomington: Indiana University Press 1976). But see his 'Semiotics of Theatrical Performance' in *The Drama Review* 21 (1963), 107–17.

Reprinted from *Themes in Drama; 4: Drama & Symbolism*

Symbolic functions in dramatic performance

JOHN FLETCHER

In drama production – *mise en scène*, as the French more accurately put it – even more than in the play text, symbolic functions are omnipresent. What we see on the stage affects us far more rapidly and directly than what we read on the page. The scenic space is a totality in which décor and props, costume and gesture impress us as an almost simultaneous object. Nearly everything making up that totality – that simultaneity – is symbolic in one way or another; this can be demonstrated of almost any text and almost any production. One that proves it as well as any is Jean Genet's play *The Maids*, as Michel Vaïs has argued:

> A study of the dramatic function of accessories in this play shows that for every 'naturalistic' object, such as the telephone, there are several symbolic ones, however realistic in appearance, such as mirrors, windows, the key to the writing-desk, the cup of 'tillol', the alarm-clock, and above all the flowers. Madame's dresses, in particular the red one (a scenic 'talisman'), are objects of veneration by virtue of the magic power which is ascribed to them. As a result they underline the relationships of domination existing between the characters, and enable the maids to overturn them by manipulating these 'sacred' objects.[1]

Vaïs goes on to point out that in *The Maids* mirrors favour the 'connivance of illusion' which underlies the whole play by assisting the sisters in their disguises, and so do the flowers (which Genet insists should be real ones). Such features were brought out very clearly in various productions by Victor Garcia; these are documented in the monumental series of studies published by the French national research institute (CNRS) under the general title *Les voies de la création théâtrale*.[2] Using these magnificent volumes, and production records of my own, I want to consider a number of recent productions, from the point of view, in particular, of their use of symbolism. Before that, however, a word about the CNRS studies, which are edited by Jean Jacquot and/or Denis Bablet. The first volume appeared in 1970, and was introduced by Jean Jacquot in the following terms.

The collection grew, he said, out of his research group's investigations into the relationship between dramatic writing and production (*mise en scène*); he and his colleagues avoided dissociating these, although this is so often done, either by giving the text a greater importance than its *mise en scène*, or worse, by reducing theatre studies to the study of a purely literary genre.

They started from the prevailing situation of a play being first written and then produced, and thus became interested in what seemed to be exceptions to the rule since they indicated that other modes of creation could exist. Nevertheless it is fair to say that productions illustrating the more traditional procedure represent the majority of those featured in the first six volumes, especially so because (as we shall see) volume VI is largely devoted to the classics. Instances of the author's involvement are touched upon, especially in the cases of Arthur Miller and Aimé Césaire. Another development of the 1960s and 1970s which is given attention is 'collective creation' by a theatre group in which verbal and other forms of expression are elaborated together, and gradually, through discussion and improvisation, attain their final shape; most of the first volume is given over to this, and part of volume V is devoted to an important study of *créations collectives* by the Théâtre du Soleil, *1973* and *L'âge d'or*. Yet, however 'collective' the work, a leading mind, functioning as a producer of a sort, remains indispensable. Moreover, in spite of this evolution, and of the increasingly frequent use of montages or adaptations of non-dramatic texts, the problem of the written play and its handling by successive producers remains central. It requires a study of socio-cultural contexts, and it may lead to a more precise definition of aesthetic criteria for the criticism of plays in performance.

As one would expect with a publication sequence extending over more than a decade, Professor Jacquot and his team progressed pragmatically from volume to volume. They were, as I say, frequently interested in productions in which the author became involved, with the result that 'a collaboration developed between the director and the playwright', who considerably changed the text during rehearsals, or shortly afterwards once public reaction became known. Sometimes a producer has, like Planchon, become his own author; sometimes a writer such as Gatti has directed his own plays.

Professor Jacquot is of course quite right that such 'role-fusions' are of considerable interest to the student of contemporary theatre. In the second part of this essay I shall be looking at two particularly relevant figures in contemporary European drama, one a director first and foremost, Ingmar Bergman, the other primarily a writer, Samuel Beckett. But before that I should like to take up a topic examined at some length in one of the most recent of the CNRS volumes, that of the revival of the classics. In both cases, however, I shall be looking especially for symbolic functions, figurations and configurations underlying valid *mise en scène*.

I Phaedra's breast and Alceste's tie

Writing in volume VI of *Les voies de la création théâtrale*, Anne Ubersfeld asked 'what is happening to the classics?' There is no dearth of productions of the standard repertoire, she pointed out; if anything, they are on the increase. This is understandable, since they are the cornerstone of the general public's theatrical culture (statistics show that the vast majority of theatregoers have been educated at least to A-level standard, or its equivalent abroad, and so have studied the classics as 'set books'). Miss Ubersfeld noted that Jean Vilar was both correct and shrewd to launch the Théâtre National Populaire in Paris with a new production of that French classic of classics, *Le Cid* by Pierre Corneille.[3]

Nevertheless (she went on) there has been, especially for French audiences, a questioning (*mise en question*) of the official, 'school' version of the classics. First of all, there is the obvious fact that the language and the preoccupations of today's audiences are very different from those of past audiences. In the first place, French is not even pronounced the way it was in Racine's time. In the second place, we are much more sensitive to the political overtones in Racine than were nineteenth- and even early twentieth-century audiences. But nor, of course, can we read *Phaedra*, politically, precisely as Louis XIV's courtiers did: as exploring the problem of legitimacy, of usurpation, and of dynastic change. On the other hand, the social sciences and in particular a wider understanding of historical materialism can illuminate in our day the socio-political conflicts underlying the plays, so that, 'in large measure, the readings appear convergent' (p. 183). What is more difficult to bridge, Miss Ubersfeld says, is the *cultural* gap: we have no notion, for example, of how, in any given milieu, people conducted love relationships in the seventeenth and eighteenth centuries.

Fortunately we can avoid some of the grosser errors of the nineteenth-century schoolroom, such as that which asserted confidently that in creating Alceste, in his greatest play *The Misanthrope*, Molière was appointing a spokesman for himself. The argument, although now happily discredited, is an interesting one, and runs something like this: Molière was unhappily married, in failing health and tormented by professional worries when he embarked upon his masterpiece; so he poured into the creation of Alceste all his accumulated bitterness and disappointment. The truth – or something closer to it, at least – is that in this play, as in all his mature comedies, Molière sets up a debate between, on the one hand, a monomaniac – who, as in all good debates, is allowed to make some telling points and unleash barbs which strike home at the conceit, frivolity and self-satisfaction of his hearers – and, on the other, a more rational figure who argues, not always very convincingly, that all excess is reprehensible, however worthy the motive. Contrary to the old-fashioned view, therefore, it would no more have occurred to Molière to air personal grudges in public than to have worn his night-cap at an audience with the king. Both actions would have seemed to Molière – and *a fortiori* to his contemporaries – not merely gross lapses of taste and decorum, but far worse, the actions of a man who had temporarily taken leave of his senses. Neo-classical writers, like Molière and Racine, had a view of their calling which we have entirely lost today, at least in the west; it survives perhaps in the Soviet Union (in the doctrine of socialist realism) and in parts of the third world. They conceived their duty, following Horace whose *Ars poetica* was their aesthetic credo, as being simultaneously to instruct and divert their spectators; the *dulce*, they felt, should not outweigh the *utile*, nor vice versa.

But in avoiding this error of the classroom we should not, Anne Ubersfeld believes, fall into another, that of excessively or improperly updating the classics, a fault she finds in 'those productions of *The Misanthrope* in which the cast wear long dresses and tuxedos and which confuse the high society of the seventeenth century with that of our own day' (p. 187). Even here, though, she thinks that 'it is not impossible that violent modernisation can lead to a truly dialectical function which highlights the objective relationship be-tween two historical periods'. Everything in the theatre, she argues, can be dialectical (hovering between 'mimesis and symbolism', p. 186), but there are three dangers to be avoided. The first is that of making Racine (or Molière, or Shakespeare) into our contemporary; the second is the old-fashioned interpretation mentioned earlier, which rests upon inadequate historical knowledge; and the third is something which she calls 'pedantic archeology', a misguided attempt to see Molière as he 'really was'. To counter these errors we should, firstly, seek what, for the author and for his audience, represented the fundamental issue, the heart of the matter, which the play seeks to resolve 'fantasmically'; secondly, we should examine the history of dramatic forms and of contemporary attitudes towards moral issues, in order to understand through what layers of meaning the text comes to us; and thirdly, we should investigate our own contemporary history to ascertain, or construct, the meaning which will bring the text alive for us (p. 187).

As dangerous an illusion as that of modern dress is that of so-called 'contemporary' costume, or worse, lack of costume altogether. 'To imagine that we are in the timeless, in the a-historical, because naked bodies writhe on the stage', is, she says, an illusion no less than that of directors of the early decades of this century who, like the great Antoine, believed that their décors were historically authentic (p. 188). As Antoine Vitez put it, when speaking of his own productions of *Andromaque* and *Phaedra*, the works of the past are broken pieces of architecture, sunken galleons, and we try to being them to light piecemeal; we can never rebuild them exactly as they were because certain habits of craftsmanship are lost, but we can at least use the fragments to construct something different; we should seek, he says, not to restore, but to reveal the ravages of time (p. 195).

Anne Ubersfeld stresses that while the permanence of a classic play cannot be justified any longer in traditional nineteenth-century psychological terms (such as the eternal quality of passion, the unchanging features of human nature, and so on), modern psychoanalysis *can* help (p. 188). Vitez's production of *Phaedra*, superbly documented in the same sixth volume of the CNRS series, provides a good example of this. Eroticism lies at the heart of the Racinian vision, as Robert Lowell well understood when he translated Phaedra's fevered words 'je languis, je brûle pour Thésée' by the subtly expressive 'I hunger for Theseus',[4] and as Vitez rendered brilliantly in his production, by having Phaedra (at line 702, 'the wife of Theseus loves Hippolytus!') sit, her legs wide apart and raised horizontal, and deliver the monologue, which follows this line, in a kind of 'erotic daydream' (p. 235). But perhaps Vitez's most stunning effect – one of those of whose genuineness Anne Ubersfeld would entirely approve – is the moment in act IV, scene vi, when Phaedra utters these lines:

> Yet I live on! I live, looked down upon
> By my progenitor, the sacred sun . . .

At this point she loosens at the neck the long white shift she is wearing, and bares her left breast (see plate 1). This, Vitez explains, is the breast – the nipple indeed – gazing, like an eye of the body, upon the sun (p. 237). By the same token, the sun, symbol of purity, is forced to sustain the sight of this exposed body, this 'forever culpable' flesh.

The act of denuding Phaedra's breast as she exposes herself to the light (in a guilty yet defiant gesture of lascivious incestuousness, since the sun after all was her mother's father) shows how far she has come – or rather, how low she has sunk – since she first crept into the open in act I, scene iii:

> *Phaedra.*   My emotions shake my breast,
>   the sunlight throws black bars across my eyes . . .
> *Oenone.*   It's no use, you decide
>   that sunlight kills you, and only want to hide.
> *Phaedra.* I feel the heavens' royal radiance cool
>   and fail, as if it feared my terrible
>   shame has destroyed its right to shine on men.
>   I'll never look upon the sun again.
> *Oenone.* Renunciation on renunciation!
>   Now you slander the source of your creation.
>   Why do you run to death and tear your hair?
> *Phaedra.* Oh God, take me to some sunless forest lair . . .

As Vitez perceived, the whole play grows out of these lines, rich in symbolic utterance. The function of the *mise en scène* is to bring out the full symbolic significance of initial statements like these.

Symbolic functions can however be extremely unobtrusive and yet still remain effective. In BBC television's 1980 production of *The Misanthrope*, there was of course nothing as stirring or as disconcerting as Phaedra's bared breast, but there was a telling touch: Alceste's pale blue tie exactly matched the shade of Célimène's cocktail dress, thus hinting how completely wrapped up in her he is, to the extent of unconsciously adopting her colours. This

1   Antoine Vitez's production of *Phaedra* (IV, vi). From *Les voies
de la création théâtrale*, vol. VI

production was set in the 'jazz age', and might well have deserved Anne
Ubersfeld's strictures on improper updating. More likely, though, this and
the better known British National Theatre production, which set the play in
de Gaulle's Paris exactly 300 years after the first performance of the play in
1666, both give rise, to use her terminology, to a dialectical function which
highlights the objective relationship between two historical periods. To me,
the hollowness and the frivolity of the 1920s, so poignantly anatomised in
The Waste Land, are an appropriate correlative of the first decade of the Sun
King's absolute rule. Mervyn Jones, reviewing the BBC production in *The
Listener* (31 January 1980), did not agree, however. 'Proust was evoked by

the sets', he wrote, 'but one is tempted to think of this period in terms rather of Fitzgerald – of a lack of intellectual seriousness. What was lost, specifically, was the heavy shadow of the autocratic Court, closely related to the time-serving and hypocrisy that concerned Molière . . . If it was necessary, as I'll grant, to get away from the periwigs, I suggest that the Second Empire would have provided the right atmosphere' (p. 151). I'm not so sure about that: the Second Empire would, for most viewers, have been as remote and 'costumey' as the *grand siècle*: and some fine effects were achieved by exploiting the particular bronze filters that go so well with art déco, particularly in the crucial opening scenes, which were set at Célimène's reception, with Alceste haranguing Philinte on the balcony as the camera looked in through the open french windows at the other guests sipping their martinis and noisily murdering reputations.

It is a pity the CNRS collection did not take account of one of the most remarkable re-creations of Molière in recent years, John Dexter's *Misanthrope* at the National Theatre, London. (Instead space is devoted to Planchon's equally remarkable *Tartuffe*.) The National commissioned the poet Tony Harrison to prepare a new translation for the tercentenary of Molière's death in 1973. Harrison's most daring liberty – apart from his verse, which I shall come to in a moment – was the transposition of the play to de Gaulle's Paris. This was prompted by Moisan's famous cartoons in *Le Canard Enchaîné* of de Gaulle decked out like Louis XIV. The result of this bold renovation and modernisation was a play full of vigour and invention. Harrison chose contemporary idioms and syntax, and although he, like Molière, chose to write in verse, he used a loose form of the rhyming couplet with frequent enjambment which linked lines to make a single phrase, as in this characteristic fragment from the first scene which I referred to earlier:

> *Philinte.* 'Bile' 's no more philosophical than 'phlegm'.
> In social intercourse the golden rule
> 's not curse, like you, but, like me 'keep one's cool'.
> *Alceste.* So, whatever vast disaster or mishap
> you're philosophical and never flap?[5]

Although this looks awkward on the printed page – especially the enjambment of *'s* – it speaks very smoothly. In the best poetic drama, the spectator is conscious that the language is stylised in relation to everyday speech, but is not continually aware of being addressed in verse. Of course, Tony Harrison did not invent enjambment. Even a traditional production of Molière seeks to loosen up the lines, as with this famous couplet from *Les femmes savantes* (I, i):

> Mariez-vous, ma soeur, à la philosophie
> Qui nous monte au-dessus de tout le genre humain.

Jean Meyer's costume production for the Comédie Francaise, since filmed, betrays its ideological slant in every detail of casting (Henriette is a touching ingénue and not the hard-headed girl of sound common sense which the text

suggests) and gesture (the movements and 180° turns are straight out of
Hollywood), but still breaks the couplet interestingly: 'Mariez-vous, ma
soeur / à la philosophie qui nous monte au-dessus . . .'

W. Stephen Gilbert praised Tony Harrison for a 'jaunty translation, in
one-two-ouch punchy couplets larded with nudges, wisecracks and verbal
raspberries'.[6] The sort of wisecrack he had in mind was probably one like this
'switchback' rhyme, an act of homage to George Formby's *Mr Wu*:

> Prim and proper is she. Oh that's rich.
> She's stupid, rude . . . in fact a perfect . . . Dar-
> [*Enter Arsinoé*]
> -ling!   (p. 30)

Not all the critics were equally impressed. J. W. Lambert praised the
'splendidly deft and mobile and witty' writing, but felt 'rather patronized'
over the heavily underlined parallels between Louis XIV and General de
Gaulle.[7] Mr Harrison's 'natty topical references' were likely 'to date more
quickly than the original', he argued, thereby making a point which links up
with Anne Ubersfeld's warning we noted earlier. John Elsom did not agree;
he felt that the decision to set the play in 1966 'provides a wealth of audacious
parallels . . . the references to powers behind the scenes acquire', he said, 'a
telling edge';[8] so he would, presumably, concur with Mervyn Jones who, as
we saw, criticised the BBC director Michael Simpson's 1920s version for not
giving due weight to the autocratic political atmosphere with which Molière
surrounds the action.

The critics were equally divided over Alec McCowen's portrayal of
Alceste. Gilbert said he was 'believably both a captive of Célimène's set and a
prickly idealist'; Elsom agreed, seeing him as 'a short, grim-jawed man,
always about to explode in righteous anger . . . when the outbursts come, his
control disintegrates into a clamour of cockatoo squawks'. Indeed Elsom
thought McCowen acted 'against the obvious interpretation of the part by
compelling us to admire Alceste's restraint'. Elsom here implies that
McCowen went fruitfully beyond the standard view of Alceste to give a
performance that was quite unique in its originality, a claim incidentally
made by Mervyn Jones also for Ian Holm in the television version, although
the two interpretations of the role were quite different. Lambert, however,
was more critical of McCowen's reading of the part: his Alceste was 'simply a
spoiled child, an absolute geyser of petulance' with hardly 'any disappointed
idealism in his outbursts of scorn and contempt'. This, Lambert felt, was to
diminish the character.

The set, by Tanya Moiseiwitsch, was described by Gilbert as 'half period,
half Heals', the perfect décor for a 'beautiful, smart, witty drawing-room
comedy in verse', a 'great comedy of feelings'. The setting was indeed exactly
right for the play; the music, appropriately by Lully, which is playing on the
hi-fi as Alceste sits sulking apart from Célimène's party disco in full swing

downstairs, was just right, too, and the costumes, particularly Diana Rigg's swirling low-cut dresses so apt for the flirtatious Célimène, the more severe long dress and jacket worn by Eliante, and Alceste's deliberately rakish open-necked shirt and loose neckerchief, all symbolised the characters' personalities to perfection.

The end of the play, in Dexter's production, was to my mind just right as well. Molière has Célimène exit some two dozen lines before the final curtain. Harrison places her alone on stage at the last. Molière leaves it ambiguous whether she departs defeated or unbowed, but I think he intended the latter. She should not, I feel, be shown as having been brought face to face with any 'truth' about herself; she should leave with a defiant flourish, as if – like Mlle Mars in the role in the early nineteenth century – she were dismissing Alceste, rather than he her. After all, the action takes place in her salon, and her departure is a signal to the others to begin to take their leave. Even though she stayed behind in the John Dexter production, perhaps obeying a later social convention, she triumphed in the end, because she uttered a rebellious little giggle for the audience alone. This sublime touch – after all, Célimène is very young, and a kind of gurgled titter is exactly how she would react to such a terrible ticking-off – was perfect. Neither Lambert, who thought that the production 'softened' Molière's ending, nor Elsom, who said that she and Alceste 'retreat into different forms of loneliness', quite appreciated how faithful Dexter and Harrison were to the spirit of the original, even if they betrayed the letter in not sending Célimène off after Alceste has hurled his last curses at her. As a result, Elsom believed that the play gives 'supreme expression' to the truism 'that human relationships survive through reasonableness and tolerance', whereas to my mind Molière is saying something rather less in the spirit of a *Guardian* leader: what he conveys is that Alceste is a fool and a boor, and has all the basic egoism of the self-righteous. He is as self-centred as Célimène, in fact, although she at least has the excuse of her youth, which she turns to good effect in refusing his ultimatum to retire with him to his estates: 'I'm only twenty! I'd be terrified! Just you and me, and all that countryside!' she smirks (p. 61). Hence, no doubt, their curious attraction for each other.

In the re-creation of the classics, then, symbolic functions can be all-important. A whole production can be articulated around a particular symbol – like Phaedra's breast or Alceste's tie – and where this occurs the effect is rather like the concentric ripples a pebble makes in a pond: everything is expressed in one way or another in function of that epicentre. Or, to change the metaphor, the note struck by such a complex symbol reverberates through the whole production, lending it a unique tone. This is because classic plays, especially those in the French tradition, tend to be unified structures. What happens in the case of contemporary drama is another, albeit related, question to which I now turn.

2   Victor Garcia's production of *The Maids*. From *Les voies
de la création théâtrale*, vol. IV

II *Bergman's 'nothing' and Beckett's 'perhaps'*

What Anne Ubersfeld referred to as the 'improper updating of the classics'
and John Elsom as treacherous 'Cliffs of Cultural Equivalents' – that is, our
incorrigible tendency to treat a dead author as if he were our contemporary,
a tendency sanctified by Jan Kott and condemned by Denis Donoghue[9] – is
not, of course, a pitfall in dealing with works written in our own time. But
there are others, equally to be avoided. *Mise en scène* in such circumstances
can almost overdo the symbolic function, and make the whole play a massive
arcane symbol. Some of the productions exhaustively described and analy-
sed in *Les voies de la création théâtrale* succumb, perhaps, to this temptation.

One which does not is Victor Garcia's realisation of Genet's masterpiece
The Maids, to which a large part of the fourth volume of *Les voies de la création
théâtrale* is devoted. According to two recent critics of Genet, there are 'two
primary, inseparable sources of form' present in all his theatre work: sexuality and language.[10] His early directors – Roger Blin in particular, who
'realised' Genet's texts in the fullest sense of that often trivialised term –
stressed the language in all its baroque, magnificent richness. Garcia empha-
sises the paradoxes of illusion, appearance and reality with which Genet's
greatest play engages and which undoubtedly arise from the ambiguities
inherent in the playwright's own sexuality. Production photographs (see, for
example, plate 2) make clear how powerful were Garcia's erotic effects on a
set which was stark in the extreme (not at all the décor which Genet himself
calls for). As Odette Aslan put it: 'Claire-Madame's dressing and undres-

sing, the beatings, the bitch-and-cat games and the church prayers all constituted a scenic rhetoric which transcended and intensified the verbal content of the speeches' (p. 299). This volume of *Les voies de la création théâtrale* would be worth having for the photographic and diagrammatic illustrations of Garcia's production alone.

A less sensational but equally potent force in contemporary theatre is Ingmar Bergman. Although better known perhaps as a film and television director, he is at the same time a theatre man through and through, and one of a unique kind. He comes from a long apprenticeship in the writing and producing of stage plays. He does not always direct Ibsen and Strindberg, by any means; he brought a highly-acclaimed *Urfaust* to London in 1959, and more recently he did *Twelfth Night* which, he said puckishly, he found 'a wonderful change'. But there is no doubt that it is in the works of his fellow Scandinavians that he finds the greatest inspiration for his theatrical talents. His productions of Ibsen, especially his *Hedda Gabler* and his *Wild Duck*, have – like his productions of Strindberg – made history. They have been unorthodox and controversial, but they have undoubtedly permitted a fresh view of the plays even if it has been an idiosyncratic one.

The Wild Duck, seen at the World Theatre Season in London in 1973, featured Max von Sydow as a fidgety, lanky, eternally smiling, emotional Gregers, one of the well-intentioned but dangerously clumsy incompetents who wreak such havoc in other people's lives; a rather different, and to my mind more convincing interpretation than the usual one which presents him as a moral fanatic. But it was not a particularly faithful version, at least as far as the letter of Ibsen's text was concerned; certain details were added, such as the portrait of Gregers's dead mother (whom Gregers is obscurely seeking to avenge for his father's infidelity with little Hedvig's mother, the former servant Gina), a picture which was hung obtrusively in Werle's drawing-room. And, not unexpectedly since Bergman has many times said what little interest he has in ideology and even in ideas, the debate between tolerance and idealism, which was certainly an important element in the play as far as Ibsen was concerned, is subordinated to the clash between the volatile personality of Gregers and that of the rock-like Gina, portrayed as the exact opposite – earthy, efficient, motherly, gruff, brisk and cool – a clash of temperaments such as Bergman explores uniquely well. Technically, too, the production was innovatory: the wild duck's attic was actually shown on the forestage, the rafters being represented by a kind of back-projection, so that the presence of the frail creature so closely identified with the vulnerable Hedvig was made physically palpable in a way not possible in a faithful adherence to Ibsen's intentions.

The key-word in Bergman's world – especially his cinema, which is not my concern here – is *ingenting* ('nothing'). In Samuel Beckett's it is *peut-être* ('perhaps'). His plays eschew the positive and the definite like the plague.

3   Samuel Beckett directing *Warten auf Godot* at the Schiller Theater, Berlin, 1975

On the other hand, seldom has language been used more effectively in the theatre. As a director of his own plays, Beckett maintains an emphasis on the symmetries of speech and on action punctuated by stylised gesture; tempo and manner alike make few concessions to verisimilitude. In his 1979 London production of *Happy Days* with Billie Whitelaw at the Royal Court Theatre, for instance, he safeguarded, over Willie's intentions at the end of the play, the carefully structured ambiguities of the text; is Willie wearily struggling uphill to touch Winnie, or the revolver, and if the weapon, for what, one wondered: to keep it from Winnie, or to use it on her? Or on himself? The curtain fell on Willie reaching out still.

For the 1975 Berlin Schiller Theater production of the German translation (by Elmar Tophoven) of *Waiting for Godot* (*Warten auf Godot*), the text was amended and corrected by Beckett himself (often extensively, since his German is excellent), with greater stress on fidelity to the French original and on the network of motif-words. Beckett has a long and intimate connection with the Schiller: *Endgame, Krapp's Last Tape, Happy Days, Play, That Time* and *Footfalls* have all been directed by him there. In the Schiller *Warten auf Godot* (see plates 3, 4 and 5) the major symbolic function was the costuming of Vladimir and Estragon. They each wore half of the other's suit, that is to say Estragon wore a blue-grey jacket with black trousers in act I and the opposite (black jacket and blue-grey trousers) in act II, while Vladimir's costume was identical but exactly the inverse of Estragon's in both acts, as if to underline, Irving Wardle said, that they were inseparable. The result, for Wardle, was 'one of the most superbly balanced double acts I have seen': Estragon was a 'frisky troll' and Vladimir a 'knock-kneed, shambling and blank-faced' clown (Wardle noted too Estragon's 'nautical roll' and Vladimir's 'splay-footed shuffle').[11] Clearly Beckett intended to emphasise that if Estragon's physical resources are greater than his companion's, Vladimir's linguistic reserves are more remarkable. As Hilary Spurling commented in *The Observer* (25 April 1976), 'Beckett's exhilaratingly precise orchestration brings out the play's plastic and above all musical qualities to a miraculous degree.' Beckett himself refers to this characteristic as 'ballet-like'.[12] Verbal repetitions are reflected in similar repetitions of physical movements. For example, when Pozzo in act I lights his pipe, takes a puff and says 'Ah! Jetzt geht's mir besser' ('Ah! That's better'), he is echoed a few minutes later by Estragon, having gnawed the discarded chicken bones, burping heavily (the burp is not indicated in the printed text), and saying 'Ah! Jetzt geht's mir besser'.[13] This is all the more pointedly comic in that Estragon, unlike Pozzo, has not had the benefit of a full meal. 'In Beckett's ambiguous "tragicomedy" the clown is a figure who embodies [the] inscrutability of existence. He creates laughter out of failure, irresolution and frustration; his is not a comedy of affirmation, but the bitter half-laugh of a "perhaps" ', writes Elizabeth Winkler.[14]

Beckett's manuscript production notebooks, now in the Samuel Beckett Archive at Reading University (MS 1396/4/ 3 and 4), show extremely detailed annotations of stage movements in relation to the German text, with diagrams by Beckett himself, and offer a thorough and minute design of the play. They reveal a strong interest in pattern, shape and the return of motifs (doubts, sleepiness, recollection, the sky, and so on), as well as in lighting and in the principal prop (the tree). Throughout, Estragon and Vladimir's close relationship is stressed, for instance by their whispering in unison 'Wollen Sie ihn loswerden?' ('You want to get rid of him?' – again not in the published text, pp. 61, 388) from their shared position left, or by their superbly choreographed saunter down imaginary boulevards as they exchange thoughts about Godot's need to consult his agents, his correspondents, his books and his bank account before taking a decision (p. 375); this is deftly paralleled in act II after Vladimir says 'Let us not waste our time in idle

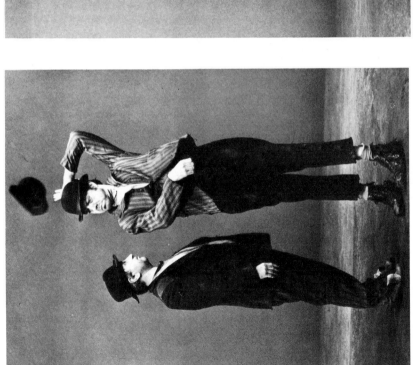

5   Stefan Wigger and Horst Bollmann

4   Horst Bollmann as Estragon and
Stefan Wigger as Vladimir

discourse!' and, taking Estragon's arm, walks him round the stage (p. 436). Symbolism as expressive, and yet as muted as this, is encountered in only the greatest productions, like those examined here, by Vitez, Dexter, Garcia, Bergman and Beckett; and as such it serves, perhaps, to reassert magnificently the symbolic nature of all art.

NOTES

1. Michel Vaïs, *L'écrivain scénique* (Montreal: Presses de l'Université du Québec, 1978), p. 135. Unless otherwise stated, translations, here and elsewhere, are my own.

2. Eight large, copiously illustrated volumes have appeared so far, published in Paris by Editions du Centre National de la Recherche Scientifique. Volume I is devoted to Grotowski, Odin Teatret, the Living Theatre, the Open Theatre and Victor Garcia's production of Arrabal's *Le cimetière des voitures*; vol. II deals with productions of Brecht, Frisch, Weiss, Césaire among others; vol. III, Genet, Brecht, Schwarz, etc.; vol. IV, Arthur Miller, O'Neill, Genet, Pinter (*The Homecoming*), etc.; vol. V, Shakespeare (*Timon of Athens*), Arden, Beckett (*Endgame*); and vol. VI, theatre and music, and the productions of classics (Racine, Molière, Marlowe (*The Jew of Malta*) and Shakespeare (*King Lear*); this last volume was published in 1978, and is most closely examined here. Vol. VII features productions of the 1920s and 1930s (Meyerkhold, Taïrov, Pitoëff, Piscator, etc., and vol. VIII is devoted to theatre and history, a study of social and cultural patterns. See *Themes in Drama 2* (Cambridge University Press, 1980), p. 170, for Richard Proudfoot's reference to vol. V in his discussion of Peter Brook's production of *Timon of Athens*.

3. *Les voies*, VI, 181; page numbers of this volume are hereinafter given in parentheses.

4. Robert Lowell, *Phaedra* (London: Faber & Faber, 1971), p. 42; other quotations from the play are taken from this translation.

5. Tony Harrison, *The Misanthrope* (London: Rex Collings, 1973), p. 6; other quotations from the play are taken from this translation. For the formulation of some of the sentences in the paragraph preceding this quotation I am grateful to my colleague Elfrieda Dubois. Later sentences bear the stamp of colleagues Tony Gash, Stan Gontarski and Rosemarie Remshagen. A more generalised debt is owed to students taking part in my seminar on 'Contemporary Drama' at the University of East Anglia.

6. *Plays and Players*, XX, 7 (April 1973), 39–41 (p. 40).

7. *Drama*, 109 (Summer 1973), 29–32.

8. *The Listener* (1 March 1973), pp. 288, 290.

9. Jan Kott, *Shakespeare Our Contemporary* (London: Methuen, 1964); Denis Donoghue, *Jonathan Swift. A Critical Introduction* (Cambridge University Press, 1969), p. vii. See also my essay 'Does It Help To Read Swift As If He Were Samuel Beckett?' in *Hungarian Studies in English*, XII (1979), 49–59.

10. Peter Brooks and Joseph Halpern (eds), *Genet: A Collection of Critical Essays*

(Englewood Cliffs: Prentice-Hall, 1979), p. 3. The next page reference is to *Les voies de la création théâtrale*, vol. IV (1975).

11. *The Times*, 26 April 1976. Actually, Vladimir's toes turned in and Estragon's pointed out.

12. See *Theatre Quarterly*, v, 19 (Sept.–Nov. 1975), 26.

13. Samuel Beckett, *Dramatische Dichtungen in drei Sprachen* (Frankfurt am Main: Suhrkamp Verlag, 1963), I, 51, 55, 383, 385. Other page references are to this volume.

14. *The Clown in Modern Anglo-Irish Drama*, by Elizabeth Hale Winkler (Frankfurt am Main: Peter Lang; Bern: Herbert Lang, 1977), p. 252; see also pp. 240–4 for an excellent detailed discussion of this production.

Symbolic action in modern drama: Maurice Maeterlinck*

LINN B. KONRAD

Une vérité cachée est ce qui nous fait vivre.
(Maurice Maeterlinck in 'Novalis')

L'action est le principe même de la vie.
(Antonin Artaud in 'Maurice Maeterlinck')

It has become almost commonplace to refer to Maurice Maeterlinck's early series of plays, from 1889 to 1894, as 'static theatre'. This term is misleading because it tells only half the truth about Maeterlinck's tragedies.[1] Used to characterize his most original work, it becomes in fact a contradiction in terms because theatre is by definition action. I shall argue that minimal realistic action on Maeterlinck's stage functions as a necessary condition for bringing out the essential action, which can only be conveyed symbolically since it is determined by unknown forces. Physical immobility does not preclude significant action in Maeterlinck's view; on the contrary it permits the dramatic experience of a symbolic action not perceivable by the senses. We must therefore look at action in this theatre as constituting a radical break with the traditional concept of dramatic action, which was conceived as a 'realistic' representation.

In order to appreciate this important change it is necessary to discuss action in theatre diachronically, and attempt to define the meaning of a symbol in the context of drama. Before talking about symbolic action, we must ask what we mean by an action pure and simple. Without going into a philosophical analysis of the concept, we may simply state that action generally implies an agent having a certain intention, that is, the subject intends to achieve something through a specifically chosen way of acting. In theatre the agents are, of course, the main characters, the hero or heroine representing the focal point around which the plot revolves. The characters, however, are of secondary importance in the Aristotelian hierarchy of elements necessary for tragedy as set forth in the *Poetics*. The action itself is clearly the most important element, and for Aristotle dramatic action is

* A draft of this paper was read at the *Themes in Drama* International Conference on 'Drama and Symbolism' held at the University of California, Riverside, in May 1980.

mimesis. But what exactly is meant by mimesis or representation? The philosopher emphasizes the meaning of the word 'poet': he is a maker of plots, and the dramatic action is therefore his creation and cannot be a faithful imitation of reality as observed in life or in other texts. The Aristotelian action is 'real' insofar as the artistic expression corresponds to the creator's mental idea. This is effected by metaphorical use of language which Aristotle maintains is the true mark of genius. Good metaphors, he claims, reveal hidden resemblances and so bring one closer to truth. It is not surprising that such a definition of creative mimesis has caused much discussion throughout the centuries, and we are much aware of its actual significance since it calls attention not only to the idea of representation of specific acts but also to the function of poetic language.

It was of course Aristotle's ideas about tragedy, based on actual Greek theatre and Sophocles's plays in particular, that reached France through the Renaissance and came to represent perfection of creative form, the purpose of which was to convey universal truths. Although imitation of the Greeks constituted the highest poetic ideal within this period, it is obvious that the individual poet contributed elements both social and personal. The important requirements of *bienséance* (propriety) and *vraisemblance* reveal a concern with truth that is problematic because the former implicitly recognizes the limits of the audience's assumed tolerance of truth and serves as protection of social values, and the latter assumes that art is *convincing*, even if it does not exactly imitate observed behavior. In other words, French seventeenth-century dramatic theory recognizes poetic creativity as a particular kind of action that is nevertheless based on a rational structure of language understood as meaningful gestures. Maeterlinck says about Racine's characters that '[ils] ne se comprennent que par ce qu'ils expriment; et pas un mot ne perce les digues de la mer' ([they] understand one another only by what they express; and not a word penetrates the sea-walls), and concludes by stating that 'ils n'ont pas de *principe invisible*' (they have no *invisible principle*).[2] What could not be clearly apprehended in thought, it was believed, was not apt to appear in art; there must be direct correspondence between conception and expression according to this ideal. Consequently, aesthetic perception on the part of the audience must be unobstructed by such elements as shock, deviation or ambiguity.

With the Romantics there appeared a manifest need to break with the classical ideal of purity. The theatrical revolution – initiated by Hugo and stated in terms of the juxtaposition of high and low styles and a disregard for unity of action – opened possibilities for exploring the unknown through different channels. Now it was felt that classical tragedy, however powerful in its dramatic appeal, did not fully represent human beings in their complex reality and variety of experience. Action was no longer limited to considerations of universally acclaimed values; its purpose was to reflect individual aspirations and conflicts and so to become closer to everyday reality. The earlier demands for *bienséance* and *vraisemblance* were modified in order to satisfy a claim for reduction of distance between the audience and the heroic action represented on stage. Attempts to diminish theatrical distance with regard to speech as well as to plots continued until the beginning of the Symbolist movement when poetry reappeared on the stage, but with a new claim.

Poetic theatre in its most ambitious mode is nothing less than a quest for the absolute. Villiers de l'Isle-Adam set the example with *Axël*, more important as a text than as a performable play. Although very personal in its tragic aspects, this work introduces mysticism and idealism to the stage and defines earthly existence as a prison from which only death constitutes a true liberation. At the moment of apotheosis, when he has discovered his love and incredible wealth, Axël rejects physical as well as materialistic enjoyment. 'Vivre!' he exclaims, 'les serviteurs feront cela pour nous' (Live! The servants will do that for us), and he convinces Sara that the only action worthy of their status and aspirations in this hour of happiness is to commit suicide together, which they proceed to do. This aristocratic, idealist vision proved to be strong medicine for aspiring artists who were sick of vulgarity and concerned about genuine experience. It should be noted that a double quest motivates the action in this drama: for knowledge and also for a hidden treasure of precious stones. The two aspects of the quest converge in the discovery of the stones in a sudden experience of love which ends in death. It seems that the brilliant, blinding, gems represent the illusion of both knowledge and love and so point to a Platonic conception of reality that Villiers himself termed 'illusionisme'.

In Plato's view, creative mimesis had a negative value because it puts further distance between reality and our perception of it. The *real* world is for him the world of *eidos* of which the physical world is but an imperfect representation. So mimesis of the physical objects commonly called 'real' becomes a representation of a representation, making perception of reality yet another step more distant from ultimate reality. In contrast to Plato, Aristotle conceived of individual existence as fundamentally real because it contains form, that is, *eidos*. The epistemological problem for Aristotle is recognition of the *eidos* imbedded in particular existences, and the purpose of artistic expression is to exhibit this form. Dramatic action, including poetic language, is genuinely significant in the Aristotelian conception of theatre; it plays a positive epistemological role, whereas the opposite is true for Plato. Although Plato condemned theatre along with other artistic manifestations, it is clear that his view of the perception of reality gradually comes to replace the traditional Aristotelian view within the movement termed Symbolism. Already in Villiers's work, which constitutes a bridge between Romanticism and Symbolism, we see that a dramatic image is no longer the direct expression of an inner reality. Action does not here pretend to be realistic; it is becoming symbolic.

What then is a symbol? Toward the end of the so-called Symbolist revolution an inquiry pertaining to this subject was conducted by Jules Huret and was published in 1891 under the title *Enquête sur l'évolution littéraire*. The result shows an astonishing variety of definitions. There are still discussions and disagreement among critics about precisely what we mean by a symbol as well as to what Symbolism means as a literary movement. The problem lies in the fact that there are inherent ambiguities in both terms. To put it simply, we can say that a symbol is by definition dual: an ineffable element presented through a concrete image. A symbol cannot therefore be reduced to a single cognitive idea. And since Symbolism was a poetic adventure into the unknown through symbolic means, it becomes clear that any revelation that might result from a series of symbolic steps – symbolic action – can only be expressed through the same form, so that clear intellectual analysis of such phenomena is impossible.

A symbol then can best be defined as an experience, not only from the perceptive point of view but also the creative; for the poets do not have some secret knowledge that they find impossible to impart due to limitations of language alone. Symbolic images invite the spectator to participate in a particular adventure that will not explain, but rather suggest or evoke new perspectives in human experience. In fact, many Symbolist poets do not create as much as *receive* means of communication; at least this is Maeterlinck's view as he confesses to J. Huret:

> Une image peut faire dévier ma pensée; si cette image est exacte et douée d'une vie organique, elle obéit aux lois de l'Univers bien plus strictement que ma pensée; et c'est pourquoi je suis convaincu qu'elle aura presque toujours raison contre ma pensée abstraite; si je l'écoute, c'est l'Univers et l'ordre éternel des choses qui pensent à ma place, et j'irai sans fatigue au-delà de moi-même; si je lui résiste, on peut dire que je me débats contre Dieu ...[3]
> (An image may cause my thought to deviate; if this image is exact and has organic life, it obeys the laws of the Universe more strictly than does my thought; and that is why I am convinced that it is always right against my abstract thought; if I listen to it, it is the Universe and the eternal order of things which think for me, and I will move beyond myself without fatigue; if I resist it, one might say that I am fighting against God ...)

When Claudel offers his recipe for a symbolic poem: 'on prend un trou et on met quelque chose autour' (one takes a hole and puts something around it), it is certainly not meant as a joke. One must understand that it is the particular 'trou' that will determine the concrete image in the poet's mind and not vice versa: for a symbol is not arbitrary. It does require, however, keen sensitivity in the audience in order to be effective, if not as a total revelation, at least as an opening or as a step toward it. Symbolic expression is therefore a process of approximation, and its epistemological status cannot be understood in terms of rational truth, since that would depend on cognitive understanding. The symbolic experience is more like an intuitively convincing experience. The Symbolist aim is to discover and convey truth. Nevertheless, the process itself, the symbolic action, is more important than projected end results. It is evident that this kind of dramatic action has its basis in Platonic epistemology but, ironically, it can be realized only insofar as it complies with the Aristotelian requirement for action on the level of *re-action* since, although secondary, this is directly perceivable action. Maeterlinck's early plays demonstrate this combination, and that is why his work has remained unique. Most Symbolist playwrights failed either because the basic demand of the theatre, for at least a minimum degree of representation, was neglected or because the unknown realm was portrayed in excessively elaborate hermetic symbolism, which paralyzed the very force that was to carry the drama.

A particular force can only reveal its characteristics through the effects it has on its environment. It cannot be directly observed as an object because once stopped it is no longer a force but a phenomenon. Normally the idea of death is approached through the phenomenon of death, but Maeterlinck the playwright attempts to focus dramatic attention on the force itself and creates 'le personnage sublime' (the sublime character). He postulates a destructive force as an agent with no other intention than to destroy life: not indiscriminately, however, for Death – *la Mort* – is an extremely jealous and cruel character who is increasingly disturbed and incited to action by movements displaying creativity and love among the living. There is then a latent conflict between the forces of life and death, and the Maeterlinckian drama is characterized by the movement toward an inevitable encounter between the two, the fatal force being victorious without exception.

The question is how does Maeterlinck create action on a symbolic level carried out by a silent and invisible agent? And the answer must be given in two steps. First of all the fatal action as such is perceived through the *reaction* among the characters that we see and hear, and secondly they react to symbols manifesting Death's progressive action. It is only through the apparent passivity of 'real' characters on stage that we perceive the essential action. But this superficial immobility should not prevent us from seeing another kind of action which in its nature corresponds to the already established metaphysical action: all of Maeterlinck's important characters are suffering and striving desperately to understand what is happening. This effort must also be termed action and is eminently brought out through a juxtaposition with normally active, rational and eloquent characters who serve as comparisons and pitiful examples of how totally inadequate the human mind is in dealing with the unknown. Death, as its most striking manifestation, turns out to govern life symbolically in all its aspects. Reason protects one from a realization which might lead to insight about the nature of Death but which also creates fear. Thus symbolic action overcomes a limitation of cognitive understanding.

There are two ways to overcome a state of anguish: by escape or by an attempt to understand its source. In Maeterlinck's dramatic world the first alternative is demonstrated by young men incorporating traditional physical and intellectual values; whereas the other is sought by characters who are normally perceived as handicapped: old people, blind people, women and children. Thus the 'weak' conquer. This ethical reversal alone should direct one's attention toward the 'real' action although it is by no means obvious to senses conditioned by unambiguous expression. Maeterlinck's drama is extremely demanding in that it is asking us to take simple and naive, even senile, and sometimes mad characters seriously in their painful effort to understand the Self in a state of fear, since an unknown inner force – the curious life-force – has to meet with and try to grasp the meaning of an intruding exterior force that threatens the individual's very existence. This is metaphysical theatre on the level of primary action and it is drama of apprehension on the reactional level since the attempts to understand – *apprehendere* – are determined and accompanied by anguish.

As opposed to realistic action on stage Maeterlinck claims that:

> Il s'agirait plutôt de faire voir ce qu'il y a d'étonnant dans le fait seul de vivre. Il s'agirait plutôt de faire voir l'existence d'une âme en elle-même, au milieu d'une immensité qui n'est jamais inactive. Il s'agirait plutôt de faire entendre, par-dessus les dialogues ordinaires de la raison et des sentiments, le dialogue plus solennel et ininterrompu de l'être et de sa destinée.[4]
> (It would rather be a question of making visible that which is amazing in the very fact of being alive. It would rather be a question of making visible the soul's existence in itself, in the middle of an immensity that is never inactive. It would rather be a question of making audible, over and above the ordinary dialogues of reason and feelings, the more solemn and uninterrupted dialogue of the being and its destiny.)

The verb 'faire' here reveals the difficulties encountered by the playwright who is after all forced to *realize* this spiritually active search. In his theatre the quest becomes apparent because it is undertaken and continually intensified as a result of reaction to the march of Death. As the encounter between the approaching force of Death and the characters' clear perception of imminent danger becomes increasingly possible, a full understanding of their suffering becomes a solution that can be hoped for. The drama seems to move toward a revelation that would be a sudden and total release from unbearable tension and simultaneously constitute an explanation of death sufficient to throw some light on the value and meaning of life. When Death has achieved its goal and leaves a dead body, relief is experienced by those characters who never felt its active presence but escaped through physical and linguistic action, whereas the central Maeterlinckian characters are left in such a state of anguish that we must see the essential tragedy as being in the impossibility of grasping the meaning of Death's active presence in life, rather than the arrival of Death itself.

All efforts to perceive this silent, invisible presence are vain, but its impact on sensitive beings increases to the extent that suffering proves to be the most paradoxical kind of vital experience. There is hardly any consciousness of time or place in these extreme moments, and there is no thought of making any move that might alleviate this state of anguish. The characters can only make an imaginary jump outside in the form of a wish; they are physically and mentally paralyzed. And yet there is an intensely strong vibration in their experience, expressed by their looks, abortive movements, questions and exclamations, which indicates a spiritual action intended intuitively to reach a level of unity between interior and exterior forces, but which is constantly frustrated – contradicted – by the unknown, the force of the completely Other. This kind of suffering is an abyss, since it suggests a sense of being fully present and at the same time totally absent in a given situation: the impossible which must nevertheless be endured. Maurice Blanchot discusses such a dramatic experience in the following terms:

> La souffrance est souffrance, lorsqu'on ne peut plus la souffrir et, à cause de cela, en ce non-pouvoir, on ne peut cesser de la souffrir. Situation singulière. Le temps est comme à l'arrêt, confondu avec son intervalle. Le présent y est sans fin, séparé de tout autre présent par un infini inépuisable et vide, l'infini même de la souffrance, et ainsi destitué de tout avenir: présent sans fin et cependant impossible comme présent; le présent de la souffrance est l'abîme du présent, indéfiniment creusé et, en ce creusement, indéfiniment gonflé, extérieur radicalement à la possibilité qu'on y soit présent par la maîtrise de la présence.[5]
> (Suffering is suffering when it can no longer be suffered (tolerated), and because of this, within this non-capacity, one cannot put an end to suffering it. A strange situation. Time seems to be at a halt, confused with its interval. The present is here without end, separated from any other present by an inexhaustible and empty infinite, the very infinite of suffering, and thus stripped of any future; a present without end and yet impossible as present; the present of suffering is the abyss of the present, indefinitely hollow, and in this hollow space, indefinitely inflated, radically exterior to the possibility of one's being present in it through mastery of presence.)

It seems that symbolic action has reached its limits because there is no solution, no way out of the most intense moment of life – apparently so close to some understanding and yet so far that one can only wish for death as an escape from such an active life. In all of Maeterlinck's plays where Death is the protagonist we sense that the survivors who have been profoundly affected by its power are worse off than the dead.

The protagonist's female characteristics put her in a direct relationship to the other central characters so that the fatal conflict and battle take place in beings of presumably identical nature. This dramatic technique does not so

much confirm the myth of particular creative and destructive tendencies in
women as it demonstrates human ignorance with regard to their own destiny
and points to spiritual blindness as its cause. Physical blindness invites
another vision in this world suffused by the unknown, and women play
important parts because their function of giving birth keeps them in closer
contact with the fundamental mysteries of life and death. In every one of
Maeterlinck's early plays there is a child involved whose mother has to face
death in one way or another. The case of Tintagiles is a particular one which
culminates the relationship between two women of totally opposite intentions. Here it is not the giver of life but the protector who is emphasized in
the character of Ygraine, Tintagiles's sister, and it is not the woman but the
child – a child old enough to become conscious of what is in store for him –
who is the victim of Death, the all-powerful Queen. The power of the Queen
is symbolically expressed by the high, solid tower in which she resides next to
the castle which ironically is situated in a valley and seems to be sinking into
a shaky, muddy foundation and so indicates a literal *de-pression* of vital forces
due to unclear origins. In addition to this topographical symbolism Death's
arrogant reign is reinforced by the fact that she does not even have to move in
order to claim her victims: she has invisible servants to do the job and her
pleasure is to perform the final stroke. The road to death for Tintagiles is an
ascent, and the tragic, desperate battle that Ygraine delivers at the iron door
is highly dramatic not only because Tintagiles is behind and can convey his
fear in sensing the Queen's approach, but because here we experience the
most direct encounter between the two women who in Maeterlinck's theatre
represent life and death respectively. It is a solitary battle; for 'le personnage
sublime' on stage is never really threatened, and the final impression is that
Death is actually the Queen of life. It is significant, however, that she
strangles the child; she takes his breath away so that he is unable to
communicate the final moment. The Queen cannot let him reveal her secret!
Death will always remain the ultimate unknown. Nothing is more certain
than the effect of her action: the phenomenon of death. Yet nothing is more
intolerably mysterious than her power. That is the conclusion we read in this
most desperate attempt at reaching the force itself. The iron door is a symbol
that seems to close any further investigation on the part of the poet. After this
play the terrifying invisible character disappears from Maeterlinck's work
and he turns to a theatrical form that relies more heavily on language as
dramatic action. It seems to be a complete reversal from the early plays
where silence is more eloquent than words, but in fact it is a continuing
questioning into the nature of the unknown, at once accepting the necessity
of language and exploring its symbolic, ambiguous, active potential.

Language not only distorts, it establishes its own reality in Maeterlinck's
view. In *Le trésor des humbles* we find this description of the process of
exteriorizing an inner, genuine experience:

Dès que nous exprimons quelque chose, nous le diminuons étrangement. Nous croyons avoir plongé jusqu'au fond des abîmes et quand nous remontons à la surface, la goutte d'eau qui scintille au bout de nos doigts pâles ne ressemble plus à la mer d'où elle sort.

(p. 61)

(As soon as we express something, we diminish it in a strange way. We believe we have plunged to the bottom of abysses and when we return to the surface, the drop of water glittering at the tip of our pale fingers, does not resemble any more the sea from which it comes.)

Communication through words, while giving the illusion of meaning and understanding, does in fact remove one from intimate contact with both self and others, according to the author. Worse, language may prevent one from even attempting the more direct approach that Maeterlinck seeks to achieve in his theatre. But since dramatic action is primarily constituted by dialogue and Maeterlinck finds the physical presence of actors as much of an obstacle in his quest as the concreteness of rational language, he obviously meets with a tremendous challenge. He manages to deal with it through the very means that he seeks to overcome. By stripping the dialogue of direct significance he uses words not as conveyors of meaning but as conductors to another level of communication. Whereas traditionally moments of silence serve to emphasize significant statements, in Maeterlinck's dialogues it is usually the reverse. Silence, of course, cannot be dramatically expressive in and by itself, but surrounded by words that evoke a certain quality, a suggestion of something ineffable, it can be extremely effective in creating an entire atmosphere in which indefinable forces operate. It is in fact a necessity to avoid clarity and completion; for as Antonin Artaud puts it:

Tout sentiment puissant provoque en nous l'idée du vide. Et le langage clair qui empêche ce vide, empêche aussi la poésie d'apparaître dans la pensée. C'est pourquoi une image, une allégorie, une figure qui masque ce qu'elle voudrait révéler ont plus de signification pour l'esprit que les clartés apportées par les analyses de la parole.[6]

(Any strong emotion provokes in us the idea of emptiness. And clear language which prevents this emptiness, also prevents the appearance of poetry in thought. That is why an image, an allegory, a figure, which mask that which they would like to reveal have more significance for the mind than the clarities provided by analyses in words.)

Maeterlinck's plays may be deceptive at first glance. They are not as simple as one might think from an intellectual point of view; on the contrary, they demand a sensitive attitude that will allow one to follow the direction indicated – by simple statements, repetitions, rhythms, interjections – into what the author himself has termed the second dialogue, which is, of course, the essential one. This dialogue corresponds to the most significant action which is also silent and invisible. So what we see and hear on stage is only the perceivable part of a vast symbol; the entire play draws attention to the mystery of the unknown which is in continual movement and conflict through a proliferation of manifestations, all related to the female characters who represent the forces of life and death.

Woman assumes yet another power in this dramatic world: that of passionate love, and she thus establishes a link between birth and death. Again she is rather silent but not inexpressive. Maleine's eyes fascinate Hjalmar, Mélisande's hair tells us more about her feelings than her words, and Alladine's pet lamb reveals her desire to everyone including herself, and even predicts her fate as it bounces toward Palomides on the bridge, slips and falls into the water. The fact that these young women do not understand what is happening to them and consequently do not burst into beautiful expressions of love must not blind us to the total character of their experience. They feel fear; they are in fact almost paralyzed with fear, due to the force that inhabits them, and such a state does not lead to coherent eloquent expressions in Maeterlinck's theatre. His heroines simply do not have the command of language that full participation in the rationally active world requires; nor are they strongly influenced by the formative power of language. They must therefore experience existence in silence and try to communicate by silence. Their suffering is convincing because the dilemma is real: each one loves a person who within the social context is taboo. But their desire is irresistible and so they can neither give in to nor escape from the grip of love. Like death, love operates as a tyrannical force, but the desire for union and happiness becomes overshadowed by the fear of destruction. Love in its fullest sense is called into being in an impossible situation here and grants the highest moment of pleasure in the face of death; for it is only when the lovers see their own end that they fully realize their emotions. Maeterlinck gives a dramatic demonstration of Freud's speculation that 'the pleasure principle seems actually to serve the death instincts'.[7]

The answer to the question of what love is thus becomes buried in the mystery of death, but the solution to this enigma cannot be found in the phenomenon of a dead body. Both forces act symbolically in Maeterlinck's drama; they retain their essential secret in their perceivable manifestations and give only partial relief since death always leaves its own impenetrable realm behind, sensed through an intense state of apprehension. This kind of revelation, however, imposes a silence that finally threatens with madness and calls back the question of language – with regard to function rather than meaning. And it is this question that was subsequently explored by Maeterlinck and increasingly by twentieth-century playwrights.

Clearly Maeterlinck offers no catharsis of the emotion elicited by the tragic action of love and death. Aristotle's purge of emotions, or Hegel's elevated ethical resolution, or even Nietzsche's 'metaphysical comfort' experienced by the fullest display of life even in pain and suffering, can only serve to illuminate the difficulties inherent in Maeterlinck's dramatic adventure. The ambition to see more clearly as it is implicitly posed in the opening of *L'intruse*, becomes at once thwarted and more acute as the questions and anguish deepen throughout the first series of plays. Finally, the fatal force but also the creative force seem to mock the human inquiry by the very symbolic forms through which they reveal nothing but the fact that they hide. The grotto scene in *Alladine et Palomides* and the tower scene in *La mort de Tintagiles*, two of the last plays in this group, are the most forceful examples of a recognition that symbolic action can never reach its conclusion.

NOTES

1. It is true that Maeterlinck uses the term himself in the essay 'Le tragique quotidien' – *Le trésor des humbles* (Paris: Mercure de France, 1907), p. 169 – when he discusses a new form of drama, but it must be noted that he also characterizes the best of classical theatre as 'static' where he sees the essential action as a spiritual experience rather than as direct perception.
2. *Le trésor des humbles*, p. 33.
3. Quoted by Guy Michaud in *La doctrine symboliste: documents* (Paris: Nizet, 1947), p. 52.
4. *Le trésor des humbles*, p. 162.
5. In *L'entretien infini* (Paris: Gallimard, 1969), p. 63.
6. In *Le théâtre et son double* (Paris: Gallimard, 1964), p. 108.
7. In *Beyond the Pleasure Principle*, trans. James Strachey (New York: W. W. Norton & Co., 1961), p. 57.

Kabuki: signs, symbols and the hieroglyphic actor*

LEONARD C. PRONKO

Signs and symbols

When we speak of symbols in theatrical production, we are most often referring to what Jung called signs. In his *Symbols of Transformation* he made the classic distinction between the two:

> A symbol is an indefinite expression with many meanings, pointing to something not easily defined and therefore not fully known. But the sign always has a fixed meaning, because it is a conventional abbreviation for, or a commonly accepted indication of, something known.[1]

In addition to the things signed or symbolized, signs and symbols have, of course, a fundamental reality, whether this be a word in a poem, the paint in a painting, a person or an object on the stage. Realism tends to prefer this fundamental reality, presenting it as an end in itself. In a naturalistic drama a trash can is offered simply as a trash can, a tree as a tree, each adding something to our understanding of a milieu, but meant to represent little beyond itself. Characters, too, are of interest in themselves, as particular cases, and not as representatives of humanity in general. The actor's own reality is, ideally, hidden behind that of the character, the actor as sign disappearing.

Non-realistic drama, by contrast, deals largely in signs. The great theatres of the past – and even the mediocre ones – presented actors as actors disguised as characters in a presentational, non-illusionist manner. The actor as sign, and his stylized performance of conventionalized scenes which also acted as signs (monologues, soliloquies, narratives, murder scenes, duels, spying etc.) evolved within a staging made up of signs: fixed décors masquerading as forests, battlefields, palaces, costumes with conventional colors to indicate character, race, function.

Although the texts of non-realistic theatre may use symbols, most western theatre before the end of the nineteenth century did not use symbols in its

---

* This paper incorporates material from Professor Pronko's lecture/demonstration on symbolism in *kabuki* at the *Themes in Drama* International Conference on 'Drama and Symbolism' held at the University of California, Riverside, in May 1980.

production techniques. Those techniques we call symbolic, like the mansions of the medieval stage, were actually conventions which were commonly understood and possessed none of the vagueness or suggestiveness of symbols. Shakespeare's rich suggestivness lies in his texts, not in the performances of his day – for the so-called symbolic areas were in fact signs of 'a balcony', 'a battlefield', and the entire audience understood this.

Most theatre, then, uses signs. Realism prefers the solid reality (or rather, its illusion, mistaking the sign for the fundamental reality). The Symbolist theatre of Villiers de l'Isle-Adam, Maeterlinck and others, and more recent drama which inherited Symbolism's aesthetic (or parts of it), uses theatrical symbols with great frequency. The great dramatists who stand at the beginning of modern drama all present symbolic elements in their plays, and the resulting ambiguity is one mark of their modernity. The doors in *Hedda Gabler*, real in their solidity, suggest something more than a mere entrance. The tree in *Godot*, a bona fide symbol, is as mysterious as any swan or reed pipe in Mallarmé's poetry.

The oriental theatre, like traditional non-realistic theatre in the west, is rich in signs, never masking them beneath an illusion, but instead allowing us the double experience of actor *and* character which has been the theatrical experience since the beginning. Realism, in this regard, is an upstart heresy of recent manufacture. The *kabuki* theatre, like other Asian forms, uses signs on every level of the performance, and occasionally turns to symbols.

Just which elements are signs and which symbols must be determined by the attitudes of the Japanese audience, because signs, at least, are the result of a common consent, a general acceptance. What are clear signs for the *kabuki* connoisseur may appear as symbols to the uninitiated outsider, for, when crossing cultures, signs and symbols slip about. What is conventional for one culture may seem fresh and poetic in another. In Japan the view of cherry blossoms (or the word alone) suffices to set off automatic associations. For centuries, in poetry, prose and painting, cherry blossoms have been used to evoke a sense of ephemerality, of the evanescence of human life. For a westerner, however, such an association is not immediate, and the blossoms may appear to be somewhat symbolic, since we are free to interpret them in a number of ways.

Some objects have different conventions depending upon the culture. For the westerner, peonies and butterflies suggest something light, lovely, perhaps even feminine. In Japan they are invariably associated with the strong *shishi*, a mythical beast usually called a lion in English, but combining attributes of dragon, dog, and other animals. A Japanese therefore does not automatically think 'feminine' at the mention of butterflies. Instead he may think 'masculine' or 'heroic'.

An outsider is often tempted to read more into foreign signs and symbols than the average enlightened native might. The analytical western tradition delights in explanations and equations, ever seeking to 'understand'. The Japanese, aided by the very nature of his language, is often content to live an experience in a more integrated way without constant recourse to intellect and analysis. When he views, for example, the dedicatory dance, *Sambasō*, he accepts it simply as that and does not wonder *why* the dancer uses a tree-shaped bell-prop and a fan, sometimes hitting them together. The bell-tree, or *suzu*, he will grant, is shaken in such a way as to represent the sowing of seeds to the four corners, but there the Japanese association with fertility will probably stop. The westerner, bred on Freud, does not take long to see the bell and fan as signs of male and female sexuality. There is every indication that this is indeed their function in the *Sambasō* dances, but for the Japanese spectator they are more symbols than signs, suggesting perhaps a variety of meanings, but not tied down specifically to the sexual dimension which is so striking for the westerner.

Kabuki's rich use of signs and symbols is to be expected in a traditional non-realistic form of theatre. The highly ritualized Japanese way of life encouraged it as well, as did the earlier performing arts which contributed to *kabuki*'s rich heritage, and most notably the aristocratic *nō* theatre, highly symbolic and ritualized both in text and performance. That signs are more numerous than symbols in *kabuki* is not surprising either, for *kabuki* is a popular form, and the popular audience demands an instant understanding. It is the elite audience of *nō*, of Maeterlinck and Beckett, that thrives on ambiguity.

Astonishingly, this popular theatre – so popular that for almost three hundred years in Japan the word for 'play' (*oshibai*) simply meant *kabuki* – lies close to the ideals of the elitist Symbolist theatre. Like the Wagnerian music drama, so admired by the French Symbolists, *kabuki* uses a synthesis of the arts in a non-realistic form based largely on legend, myth or folktale. In Wagner, however, music is the major focus and one rarely sees a performance in which movement and acting match the calibre of the voices. *Kabuki*, however, offers a true synthesis. The visual impression which appears most important to the foreigner is a result of the ease with which he can appreciate and understand the visual force of the performance, whereas he finds the words difficult or incomprehensible and the music perhaps totally foreign. But even without understanding the words, the westerner should be able to appreciate the immense impact of the sounds, music and vocal intonations, including shouts, whines, grunts, occlusive vocalizations. Indeed, attending *kabuki*, one is often reminded of Artaud's admonitions regarding the non-intellectual use of words and sounds in his idealized concept of total theatre.

In fact, intellectualization is as rare in *kabuki* as it is in Symbolist drama and literature. Eschewing direct expression, both use suggestion, connotation, association. 'To name an object', Mallarmé wrote, 'is to destroy three quarters of the enjoyment of the poem' (*Réponse à une enquête*, 1891). Earle

Ernst, in his superlative study of *kabuki*, sounds curiously Mallarmean when he writes that it is 'characteristic of Kabuki to present to the audience not the thing itself, but the designed impression of the thing'.[2]

Stylized, often larger than life, *kabuki* rarely delivers a precise message. Instead, by indirect means, it suggests perceptions. Like the forest of symbols described by Baudelaire, a *kabuki* performance seems to be speaking a forgotten language of the senses. The supreme satisfaction experienced by anyone who gives himself totally to this experience derives perhaps from some intuition of what David Gascoyne has called the poetic landscape of Eden. In the sensual *kabuki* world we recapture as adults something of the paradise of childhood: 'Instinct has not yet been completely outlawed by reason. Sensation is still vivid and feeling unrestrained.'[3] In the total theatre of *kabuki* we find again the past moment in which we once operated as a unity.

No wonder a Japanese critic once described *kabuki* as the nearest possible approach to a paradise on earth.[4] Without the *conscious* idealism of western Symbolism, without the planned program of the Wagnerian and Artaudian total theatre, *kabuki* offers us something like the realization of the Symbolist ideal.

It is in the *kabuki* actor, the absolute focus of a *kabuki* performance, that we best see this ideal realized. In all aspects of *kabuki* signs abound: in décor, music, sound effects, costume, wig, make-up, props. It would require dozens of pages to set forth the impressive usage found in any single performance. The *kabuki* actor, however, midst all these signs, occupies a very special place: he is reality (actor), sign (character) and symbol (visual and aural resonances) all at once. E. T. Kirby, following the lead of such illustrious predecessors as Sergei Eisenstein and Antonin Artaud, calls him a hieroglyph. Kirby goes on to describe a hieroglyph as the 'intersection of more than one mode of knowing or more than one medium of communication'.[5]

Words written phonetically (as in letters of the alphabet) can only with difficulty, if at all, suggest something other than what they denote. Their appeal is largely to the intellect. This is one of the major problems of Symbolist poetry, and explains why Mallarmé constantly reduced the words in his poems and would finally have ended with a blank page. It also explains why the Symbolists wanted to find the musical values of words and 'take back poetry's own from music'. Hieroglyphs, unlike phonetically written words, offer a physical presence which, at the same time that it indicates a precise conventional meaning, speaks directly to our visual sense and suggests much beyond what it actually signifies. A circle with a dot in it, the sun for the ancient Egyptians, and a square with a line through its center, the sun for the modern Japanese, also carry a secondary meaning of 'day'. They *can* be used phonetically, but the sign of the eye-like sun, looking up at us from the page, carries overtones impossible with a phonetic writing system. The hieroglyph

– physical reality, convention, symbol all in one – exemplifies synesthesia as phonetic writing cannot.

If the Symbolists had been able to write with hieroglyphs many of their problems would have been solved. As a matter of fact, they did what they could to make hieroglyphs of phonetic signs by disposing the words suggestively on the page as Mallarmé did in *Un coup de dés.* And one of Symbolism's immediate heirs, Apollinaire, wrote a number of poems (calligrams, he called them) in the shapes of objects.

In the theatre, the realistic actor in his everyday clothing corresponds to the phonetically written word. He has for us the literalness of such writing and little of the suggestivness of the hieroglyph. Nor can he extend himself gesturally in graphically suggestive ways. It is difficult to take symbolically a man in a business suit, particularly if he is only doing the things we normally do in coat and tie and handling such unsuggestive objects as cocktails, cigarettes and money. This is one of the stumbling blocks of modern poetic drama, over which Ibsen triumphed magnificently in his last plays, but one which has stymied most would-be creators of poetic contemporary drama in the twentieth century.

The actor in period costume can be suggestive. He is even more so if he is clad in leotard or some neutral garb allowing maximum freedom of movement and possessing a minimum of specific denotation. The actor can then assume almost any posture, take on the suggestiveness of pictograms, eschewing the literalness of dry words.

People and objects used in works of art necessarily take on the value of signs. Realism militates against this fundamental vitality of art, attempting to deny the sign-value and convince us that the thing we see is the thing itself. Realistic drama is most successful if we forget the actor and recognize only the character. Hollywood and television seem most often to take just the opposite tack: we are conscious instead of the actor who forever plays the same role. Great traditional theatre has always dealt with the double identity of the actor as actor and as sign. In modern western theatre, because of its realistic bias, its phonetic limitations so to speak, the actor can rarely go beyond his role as sign to become a symbol. Dancers easily achieve symbolic status because they are not tied to words and are rarely limited to specific characters or situations. Moreover they may use their bodies pictorially. Since the 1960s we have seen liberating experiments, but by and large the dominant form of acting today is illusionistic and not much bigger than real life. Indeed, in film and television it is sometimes even smaller.

The hieroglyphic actor

The *kabuki* performer, dancer–singer–actor, in violent contrast to his western counterpart, is permitted to use all his bodily and vocal resources, disciplined according to traditional patterns. Clad in non-realistic costumes, often highly fanciful, with generous padding, platform shoes, immense wigs, colorful make-up, the actor moves in carefully designed, dynamic patterns in order to suggest the essence of a character. Speaking in a deep voice, or in falsetto, or on the break between the two, rising to a high pitch, falling to a low, interspersing words with grunts, muffled sounds, the actor creates the aural *impression* of his character rather than an imitation. 'Intersection of more than one mode of knowing or more than one medium of communication', he is indeed a hieroglyph. Blending voice, shape, color, pattern, movement and precise gestures, he appeals to the spectator through eyes and ears at both conscious and unconscious levels. As a certain character in a certain play, he is a sign. As a famous actor portraying that character, he is his fundamental reality – in *kabuki* almost always apparent through pounds of costume, wigs and make-up. But, like a true hieroglyph, his extravagant visual or aural impact causes the spectator to feel there is more, something mysterious, vague perhaps, but meaningful, beyond what is apparent and signaled by the conventions of the role. Perhaps this theatre of essences suggests somehow a fleeting glimpse of the Absolute – the experience yearned for by the Symbolist poets, and summed up in Mallarmé's mad cry, 'L'azur! L'azur! L'azur! L'azur!'

The 'archetype of hieroglyphic expression',[6] in Kirby's words, is the *mie*, that dynamic pose which, summing up the emotions of a peak moment, gathers all the energies of the actor at one focal point, then lets them explode in a carefully balanced display of controled tensions. Like the great Buddhist guardian deities which may have inspired the *mie* (although their origin is ultimately unknown), the actor performing (or *cutting*, as the Japanese has it) a *mie* may dispose his limbs in a number of ways, but he always expresses immense controled energy. Although one or more limbs may move away from the body, the final feeling is that of returning to center, as the actor ends the pose by sinking low, pelvis perfectly centered, head moving in an arc, then settling with chin pulled in.

The synesthetic–kinesthetic experience of the *mie* is accentuated by the sharp sound of wooden clappers accompanying it in a stylized rhythm. The piercing whack attacks us through the senses, drawing the attention of all our senses to this supremely expressive moment. Standing there like 'some huge insects full of lines and segments drawn to connect them with an unknown natural perspective', as Artaud might have said,[7] *kabuki* actors at this moment represent the hieroglyphic actor at his zenith: actor, sign and symbol. As actor, his art is vocally appreciated by the spectators who now shout their approbation, often using his clan name (*yago*). Clearly in evidence, then, is his fundamental reality as an actor whose skill is being judged and enjoyed. As sign, he stands for the character he is portraying, decked out in costume, wig and make-up which contain yet other signs.

6   Onoe Shōroku in *Kumagai's Battle Camp*

In the central *mie* from Kumagai's narrative in *Kumagai Jinya* (Kumagai's Battle Camp) as performed by Onoe Shōroku (see plate 6), we observe the easily recognized features of one of contemporary *kabuki*'s most impressive performers. Disguised by the contours of a wig, strong make-up and a massive costume, *kabuki*'s major actor of heroic roles is still easily distinguished. The richness of the costume, its bold pattern, and the breadth of the wing-like upper garment indicate his rank and strength as a warrior. The

strong but elegant line of his wig again signals his rank, as does his shaved
head. Some actors of this role wear a wig with a mixture of human hair and
bear's hair, the addition of the latter thought to give more body and strength
to the wig. Around the top inner edges of the wig there is a small amount of
curly hair, also a sign of strength. The make-up again stresses the heroic
power of Kumagai, eyebrows and lips stronger than for ordinary mortals,
eyes and forehead stressed with heavy brown lines, nostrils similarly reinforced. The pose, with the entire body firmly centered and the right fist
held before the chest, suggests solidity, strength, self-assurance.

All these may be considered signs; but Kumagai's pose possesses symbolic
elements also. What, for example, is meant by the inverted fan held in the left
hand? Why precisely is his right hand clenched at his chest? Although this
clenched fist is used in many *mie*, its meaning may differ somewhat, determined by the context of the pose. Kumagai is recounting his fight with a
young warrior whom he killed. The warrior's mother, to whom he is deeply
indebted, is listening. What Kumagai does not tell her is that, in reality, he
substituted his own son, in order to repay his debt of gratitude to the mother.
The spectator is free to view this fist as an indication of frustration and anger,
or as an effort on the part of Kumagai to restrain his own emotions. The
inverted fan is usually interpreted as representing the mountain referred to
in the accompanying narrative text. At this point in his tale, Kumagai has
urged the young warrior to flee, but the boy refuses, insisting he should die
honorably. Kumagai, unable to draw his sword, hesitates when he hears the
voice of a fellow warrior urging him to strike. 'Then I heard!' chants the
Narrator, temporarily speaking for Kumagai, 'From the mountaintop behind me, routed Hirayama cried out!!'[8] The actor opens his fan and assumes
the pose in the photograph (plate 6). We may feel the fan is purely decorative, or we may prefer to think of it as standing for a mountain. The
narrative movements are not precise enough to require a single meaning
here; but combined with the rich accoutrements, and the rapt concen-
tration of the crossed eyes, they are deeply suggestive. The icon-like pose
even intimates that Kumagai, because of his sublime sacrifice (incomprehensible and grisly perhaps in western terms, but a standard device in
kabuki), attains a divinity-like stature.

Some *mie* are more patently iconographic. In *Narukami* (Thundergod),
when the seduced priest discovers he has been betrayed, he transforms
himself into a demon to pursue his seductress. Stopped by his acolytes, he
fights against them, striking a series of *mie*, many of which have names
and specific connotations, although they too, like most movement, are
suggestive. Tearing the sacred sutras in two, he tosses the ends to two
acolytes, and holds two ends to his chest, thus creating diagonal lines
resembling a mountain, with himself at the peak. The pose is known as the
Fuji *mie*. Later he leaps onto the backs of his acolytes, his feet forward, his

hands clasped before him, in what is known as the Riding the Clouds *mie*. Mounting a hillock he grasps a rope in one hand, and a sacred object in the other, holds them before him, one to each side, in a pose reminiscent of the god Fudō in Buddhist iconography and hence called the Fudō *mie*.

Although the figure of Kumagai may not strike the western observer as realistic in any way, it represents a *comparatively* realistic style in *kabuki*. The role of Tadanobu in *Yoshitsune Sembonzakura* (Yoshitsune's Thousand Cherry Trees) is an example of high stylization in which the fanciful dominates (see plate 7). Shōroku here plays the role of a fox that has taken on human shape in order to accompany Princess Shizuka who has in her possession a keepsake drum made with the skins of the fox's parents. In the photograph, Tadanobu has just vanquished a number of warriors, and places his foot victoriously on the back of one. Holding the precious drum in his extended hand, he brings his right hand in front of his mouth. The photograph was taken before the *mie* had reached its climax: slowly bringing his hand up and out to the right, Tadanobu utters a dry, snarling sound representing his fury. Finally, the hand comes to his chest in a fist much like Kumagai's, he moves his head in an arc, draws in the chin, and crosses his eyes as the clappers deliver a loud whack.

Tadanobu's signs are many and complex. He is both fox and samurai, and his make-up indicates this double nature. The shaved head of the samurai, the strong black lip line, and red circular lines over the temples are often used for strong warriors in the *aragoto* (rough house) tradition. The eyebrows, however, with their broken lines, are distinct indications of an animal nature and are meant to suggest the flickering flames of supernatural foxfires. The arm and leg decorations (formerly painted, now worn on a cotton garment), like the temple lines, are indications of heroic strength, emphasizing the bulging blood vessels of an irate warrior. The braided rope around the shoulders is another indication of *aragoto* style strength, as is the dark, plain colored *obi* (sash) which ties at the back in a huge stuffed rope-like bow known, because of its shape, as a dragonfly *obi*. The wig is particularly strong with its light blue forepart of metal to represent the shaved area of the pate. Made of lacquered, slightly curly hair, it gives an impression of force, and is used for supermen characters in several plays. Tadanobu's two swords indicate that he is a samurai, since commoners were allowed only one. His fringed garment indicates his squire's rank, and the wheel-like crest on his costume might well be interpreted as representing the crest of his master, Yoshitsune, who belongs to the Genji clan. The Genji wheel, however, was also the crest of the puppet theatre narrator who first chanted this play, and it is for this reason that the design is used here.

Tadanobu, cutting across the boundaries between the human and the supernatural, is a particularly rich hieroglyph. His signs point both toward the world of everyday reality and that of magic and animals. His visible

7   Onoe Shōroku in *Yoshitsune's Thousand Cherry Trees*

manifestation suggests a world of hidden possibilities. When he snarls, as in the photograph, he is both human and animal, as he is when he makes his dazzling exit *roppō*, a magnificent stylized flying dance. Accompanied by the strong rhythms of drums and flutes, and the sharp percussion of the clappers, casting his limbs in all directions in varied patterns, he presents the spectacle of a moving hieroglyph, mysterious, suggestive, yet meaningful and dramatic within the specific context.

Dance as Symbolist poetry

Tadanobu's *roppō* also reminds us that the *kabuki* actor is a dancer. In a later act of the same play he will perform an entire scene in dance, speaking only a few lines of dialogue. It is in such moments, when the *kabuki* actor is most clearly performing as a dancer, that his acting becomes most symbolic. Within the framework of any play, usually the more highly stylized period plays (*jidaimono*), an actor may revert to dance to express his emotions, as Kumagai does when he performs his battle narrative. Like the more poetic moments of western drama, these moments of visual poetry – of what Cocteau might have called 'poetry of the theatre' (see his preface to *Les mariés de la Tour Eiffel*, 1921) – normally occur at emotional climaxes within *kabuki* plays which are not specifically dance plays. Other pieces, known as *shosagoto* (posture pieces) or *buyō geki* (dance plays) use dance throughout to portray emotion, character and actions, sometimes with no dialogue, sometimes with a good deal. It is in these pieces, and particularly those with little speech, that *kabuki* most clearly achieves the ambiguity of Symbolism. Choreographed, according to old traditions, by living dance teachers, rather than being passed on within the *kabuki* families, these dances are invariably accompanied by a song, which the movements are meant to illustrate to some degree. One might say that they stand in the same relationship to a long *kabuki jidaimono* that a poem of Mallarmé stands to a play of Shakespeare. Concentrated, pared to essentials, often performed by a single dancer, they present, like most verbal poetry, a fundamental meaning, secondary resonances, and a wide margin of ambiguity. Like poetry, they use rhythm, music, decorations, allusions, and of course synesthesia. But the synesthesia available to the *kabuki* dancer is necessarily more complex than that of verbal poetry, since he blends the words of a poem with music and the visual appeal of movement, color, design.

To the visual and aural elements in Tadanobu's poses and exit we must add a rich network of gestures tied, now closely, now only tenuously, now not at all, to the words of the accompanying song. One Japanese choreographer, sounding very much like a modern poet, claimed 'We make a dance, but we don't explain it.' As in Symbolist poetry, and its posterity, part of the pleasure arises from this area of ambiguity which allows us our own interpre-

tation beyond the specific meanings either given by tradition or made clear
by gestures which work as signs rather than symbols.

In Japanese dance the vocabulary of gesture and movement may be seen
as falling into two fundamental categories, not always mutually exclusive:
concrete or mimetic gestures which carry a specific meaning; and abstract
gestures which are used decoratively, or for accent, or as 'pure' dance. Since
the dance is always performed to words, an understanding of the text will
give meaning to gestures which otherwise might appear to be quite abstract,
or will at least suggest a way of interpreting otherwise 'decorative' gestures.

Among the gestures with specific meanings, there are imitative, evocative,
and grammatical expressions. Imitative gestures are stylizations of real-life
movement, like laughing, weeping, drinking, gazing with eyes shaded by one
hand etc. With such gestures there is usually no difficulty of interpretation.

Evocative gestures are usually just as comprehensible: they include
movement which is not strictly imitative, but suggests objects or natural
phenomena, often using a fan or a towel as a hand prop. The fan held open
vertically and gently fluttered may represent falling snow, rain, or blossoms,
depending upon the style of movement (and the words of the song). Large
waves, ripples, swords, halberds, pipes, umbrellas etc., may all be suggested
by various uses of the fan.

Grammatical gestures may derive from natural gestures, as when one says
'I' and points to oneself (one's nose, in Japan), or indicates a negative by
waving the hand back and forth at about waist level, a normal everyday
Japanese gesture simply stylized in the dance. Other grammatical gestures
may be signs requiring some acquaintance with conventions of dance: a
small vertical slice of the hand, moving from left to right, is an indication of
time, 'once', 'some day', 'forever'. A male character holding the hand to the
chest with elbow protruding, glances down at his elbow where presumably
his crest would be, as an indication of 'I/me', 'myself', 'my identity' etc.

An example of these and other mimetic gestures: in *Gojōbashi* (Benkei at the
Bridge), Benkei does the following:

Text	*Movement*
As for me, he thinks aloud,	*Right hand to chest, looks at crest.*
	Left hand to chest, looks at crest.
None can match	*Waves hand in sign of negation, shakes*
My peerless strength.	*head. Strokes beard with hand.*
I would like to have at hand,	*Stamps right foot and thrusts right*
Ah! a worthy foe.	*hand forward. Laughs.*

Non-mimetic gestures are often used to create an atmosphere or suggest an
emotion. Often they are decorative, and whether they bear a precise meaning will depend upon the context in the dance, words, music, surrounding
movement. The gesture known as 'tying the *obi*', for example, could be used
to indicate that the character is really adjusting his or her sash, and in this

case would be considered mimetic. Often, however, it gives the feeling of girding the loins for action, getting ready for whatever one must accomplish. The hands rise close to the face, palms in, then turn palms out and circle in a wide arc around to the back of the dancer's waist – the style is, of course, different for male and female characters, as in all phases of *kabuki* dance.

Stamping plays a large part in all *kabuki* dance, but the stamps are rhythmic devices, normally decorating the performance rather than adding meaning. Here, too, however, a character who is angry might well stamp rhythmically to indicate his fury, in which case we are once again witnessing mimetic movement. By and large, however, the so-called *hyōshi* or stamping and clapping rhythms are pure dance and used most often in the flamboyant finale section known as the *odoriji*, which usually has less meaning than other sections of a dance.

The *mie* is used to accentuate the dances of strong male characters, but it could also indicate that one is looking, or glaring, at one's enemy. Similarly, the gentle three-part head movement used in women's dances (*mitsuburi*) could show a woman glancing coyly at her lover, but often it simply serves as a way to give a feeling of finality to a phrase or a section of a dance.

Whether concrete or abstract, dance movement may be allusive as well. Like the allusions of verbal poetry, these moments, usually poses, refer us to other works in which similar characters or emotions were exhibited. Or they might suggest some occasion, some season which is connected with the performance at hand. Many allusions are recondite and understood only by the most learned connoisseurs of the dance, just as the allusions of, say, *The Wasteland* or 'La chanson du mal aimé', will be understood by a small number of readers. For those sensitive to them, however, they add layer upon layer to the meaning of the poem or the dance.

In *Ame no Gorō* (Gorō in the Rain), for example, the young hero who frequents the pleasure quarters, but also must remember it is time to avenge his father's murder of some eighteen years ago, strikes a number of poses which are taken from earlier *kabuki* plays based on the same theme. In one pose, he extends his left hand at an angle before his body, the hand upright, and places his right hand at his right chest, elbow extended and hand upright – this pose reminds us of a fiery old *aragoto* piece in which the young hero goes on New Year's Day to the home of his enemy and tells him officially that he intends to seek revenge. During the course of *Kotobuki Soga no taimen* (The Sogo Brothers Confront their Enemy) young Gorō strikes the pose at least eight or ten times, so it is intimately identified with this particular play (although it occurs in many other plays as well).

Another incarnation of Gorō occurs in the celebrated play, *Sukeroku*. Here we see the dandified behavior of the young man as he struts among the courtesans of the pleasure quarter. In Sukeroku's famous entrance dance, he poses holding his umbrella overhead and looks off at the mountains. *Ame no*

Gorō alludes to this aspect of Gorō's character, and adds the multiple associations of the heroic dandy, Sukeroku, by including several of his poses in its choreography.

The early play, *Kotobuki Soga no taimen*, itself contains a famous allusive pose of a different nature. Since it is usually performed in January (when the events of the play took place), it is fitting that the final pose be of an auspicious nature. Accordingly at the finale we see the following tableau: at stage left on a platform stands the powerful villain, Kudō. He holds his sword in his left hand extended straight out left, and in his right hand a fan held against the chest with the fan pointing at the audience. With his 'beak' and 'wing' he is understood to represent a crane, a sign of longevity. At stage right, near center, are grouped Gorō, his brother Jūrō, and their friend Asahina. Gorō stands in the middle of the group, his hands extended in the manner described above, suggesting his anger toward Kudō. Kneeling to his left his brother holds up his right hand to restrain the fiery Gorō. To the right, Asahina, his knees bent, crouches low, extending his hands also, wrists broken in comic effect. This group is meant to represent Mount Fuji. The entire tableau, a crane flying over the sacred mountain, is auspicious indeed.

Whether this or the other allusive poses are signs or symbols will depend upon the understanding of the spectator. For the cognoscenti they are signs with precise characteristics; for the uninitiated, however, they possess the ambiguity of the true symbol. Even for the initiate, they add layers to the meaning of the dance and, like true symbols, possess a power of endless expansion. Like the allusion to Andromaque, for example, in Baudelaire's 'Le cygne', these visual reminders do not make us stop at the association between exiled swan and exiled queen, between young Gorō as Gorō-at-his-enemy's-mansion, or Gorō as Sukeroku-in-the-gay-quarters. Instead they add to our aesthetic enjoyment of poem and dance the multiple associations of the Trojan War and of Greek culture, on the one hand, and the rich world of eighteenth-century pleasure quarters and of twelfth-century Kamakura, on the other.

If anything, the symbolic possibilities of the dance are richer than those of poetry, because they are not impeded by the rational function of the word which, despite associative values, equates word with concept, because that is the function of words. In order to escape this limitation Mallarmé kept paring down, attempted to avoid the precise word in order not to limit the possibilities of meaning. Defeat in such a struggle was, of course, inevitable. In dance, however, the true Symbolist poem can be realized. Associated with words because he performs to a text, yet endlessly suggestive and multivalent because his vocabulary is that of movement, color, pattern, sound, the *kabuki* actor escapes the limitations of the word. A living hieroglyph, constantly moving, changing, he is, at precious moments, actor, sign and symbol.

NOTES

1. Carl G. Jung, *Symbols of Transformation*, trans. R. F. C. Hull (Princeton University Press, 1956), p. 124.
2. Earle Ernst, *The Kabuki Theatre* (Honolulu: University Press of Hawaii, 1974), p. 178. All of Ernst's book can be consulted with great benefit. He treats at length many of the questions which can only be hinted at here.
3. Robin Skelton, *The Poetic Pattern* (Berkeley and Los Angeles: University of California Press, 1956), p. 172.
4. Hamamura Yonezo *et al.*, *Kabuki* (Tokyo: Kenkyusha, 1956), p. 45.
5. E. T. Kirby, *Total Theatre, A Critical Anthology* (New York: E. P. Dutton & Co., 1969), p. xxix.
6. *Ibid.*, p. xxx.
7. Antonin Artaud, *The Theatre and its Double*, trans. Mary Caroline Richards (New York: Grove Press Inc., 1958), p. 64. Much of what Artaud says of the Balinese dancers might well apply to *kabuki*, and one can only lament the fact that Artaud never witnessed a *kabuki* performance. He, too, alludes to the dancers as 'living hieroglyphs', p. 61.
8. James R. Brandon, *Kabuki, Five Classic Plays*, (Cambridge, Mass.: Harvard University Press, 1975), p. 195.

Hedda Gabler and the sources of symbolism*

A. R. BRAUNMULLER

The Victorian attacks on Ibsen's symbolism actually sought to defend both a certain style of drama and a specific view of how plays work. The second goal remains interesting long after other forms have superseded Ibsen's strategies. Here are three representative complaints:

> Allegory, mysticism, and symbolism are all very well in their place, but I submit that they are not in their right place on the stage.[1]

> I don't take much stock in symbolic lobworms, Norwegian or otherwise. The difficulty is that you can't fix them with their symbols.... The dramatist who wishes to be heard, and who thinks he has a mission to fulfil, should say what he means and mean what he says.[2]

> ... this sort of thing will not do for the theatre, where the materialized idea is the only thing that counts; or, to put it plainly, where seeing is believing.[3]

These critical notices – of *The Master Builder, When We Dead Awaken,* and *The Wild Duck,* respectively – are the cries of an audience which feels cheated. In effect, they resist accepting that the realistic drama has as many conventions as any other; consequently, the appearance of a 'symbol' seems both incongruous and distracting.

A modern audience, accustomed to wilder and faster variation in artistic styles, believes – as the Victorians did not – that 'Representation in art, however realistic, is always an imagery.'[4] Conventions of representation – single point perspective or the fourth wall or the *kabuki* stagehand's kimono of invisibility – are grammars and vocabularies of symbols and metaphors. Every play forces us to make a series of symbolic interpretations, and these critics groan at having their unconscious and unself-conscious confidence challenged. Ibsen at long last exploded the Victorians' alliance with the dominant playwrights of the nineteenth century. That alliance was a conspiracy of silence. Audiences tacitly agreed not to notice outrageous contrivance so long as it appeared suitably disguised in contemporary costume and practicable doors and windows.

* A draft of this paper was read at the *Themes in Drama* International Conference on 'Drama and Symbolism' held at the University of California, Riverside, in May 1980.

We need a more refined and narrowly limited definition of 'symbol' if we are to disentangle Ibsen's curious and powerful and sometimes clumsy symbolic procedures in *Hedda Gabler*. If we are not to wonder at the two possible extremes – everything in a play or other literary representation is symbolic, or (Edmund Gosse's view) 'there is ... no species of symbol' in *Hedda* – we must also understand how a play encourages us to view certain signs (word, prop, action) as symbolic.[5] That is, how does a play enhance the value of one sign over another? How does it invite us to consider a white shawl more than a garment or a fish pond more than plain water? Finally, once we have settled on a working definition of symbol and uncovered some of the ways Ibsen announces their presence, we may investigate the dramatic sources of those symbols. This last project is particularly important because, whatever their initial attitudes toward symbols and however different their methods of interpretation, many readers and spectators ignore or obscure the fact that their evidence has varied sources.

Most modern treatments of literary symbolism fall into variations of Coleridge's famous and confused antinomy between allegory and symbol (a formulation which emphasizes referentiality) and of more recent structural or semiotic theories which examine the relation of signs with one another rather than with what they signify.[6] For literature and especially for drama and above all for realistic drama, the issue will always return to the relation between representation and what is represented. Since the Romantic period, symbols have been thought to overleap subject–object divisions, to fuse the two, while 'allegory' (or some other term set in contradistinction to 'symbol') painfully announces its analogical function.[7] A young and rather romantic Ibsen claimed that dramatic symbolism should remain hidden 'like a vein of silver ore in a mountain', that is, exist as both silver and mountain at once. The audience, he believed, does not recognize any sharp distinction between ore and mountain, but at the same time does understand the difference between symbol and symbolized when the play's 'human conflicts' manifest the conflict of ideas.[8]

In *Freud and Philosophy*, Paul Ricoeur deliberately seeks a rapprochement between these alternative views of 'symbol'. I would like to borrow his definition and modify it slightly to fit a theatrical piece and my own enterprise: 'A symbol is a double-meaning linguistic expression that requires an interpretation' and 'symbols call for interpretation because of their peculiar signifying structure in which meaning inherently refers beyond itself'.[9] If we extend 'linguistic expression' to include, potentially, any 'sign' in the play – words, of course, but also props, actions, character groupings and the like – these remarks will give our project a manageable scope and direction. Ricoeur also reminds us that a symbol 'presupposes signs that already have a primary, literal, manifest meaning',[10] or, as Ezra Pound more vividly wrote, 'if a man uses "symbols" he must so use them that their symbolic function does not obtrude; so that *a* sense, and the poetic quality of the passage, is not lost to those who do not understand the symbol as such, to whom, for instance, a hawk is a hawk'.[11]

Pound's insistence on unobtrusiveness cannot really be satisfied. The artist may rightfully claim to have succeeded if the hawk remains sufficiently hawk-like while at the same time and for some audiences containing a further signification. Deciphering this further signification may only begin through some 'obtrusion'. Otherwise we will ignore the bird. The symbol must solicit interpretation. The audience must be encouraged or invited to regard an event, a phrase, a word, or an object as a symbol requiring decipherment. Even the barest stage set – Samuel Beckett's, for choice – confronts us with so many signs that we cannot possibly attend to each with the same intensity. We cast about for clues and hints. What should we pay attention to? Incongruity is a common hint: thus, Krapp's banana looks promising, but it comes to naught. It merely assists our view of Krapp as vaudeville comedian: Krapp the constipated man. The sounds of the words on his tapes, however, do become important. Krapp's repetitions and re-enunciations thrust his dead voice on our attention as something worthy of decipherment and emotional response. The words are important not only for their designation, but for the sounds required to produce them ('Sp-o-o-l', for example, or 'veduity'). Likewise, in *Hedda Gabler*, we might be tempted, especially if we had just read or seen *Rosmersholm*, to regard Berte's lamp (act IV: opening stage direction) as a sign worthy of decipherment, but it is not. In this same category of potential symbols which prove uninteresting, trivial, or peripheral, might fall the 'vill dansemelodi' Hedda plays just before her suicide. We smile at the sly allusion to Nora's tarantella, but that is all.

How does Ibsen initiate a fruitful process of decipherment? His most obvious and least loved method is repetition. Certain words, props, or events beg interpretation as something other than their literal signification because we hear or see them over and over again. The 'white horses' of *Rosmersholm* would be an obvious example, or the dark forest of *The Wild Duck*. Other repetitions involve visual association: white horses and white shawl, for example, or the echoing scenes of Hedda and Lovborg looking at the photograph album and the earlier conversations behind an illustrated magazine while General Gabler remained blissfully ignorant. No audience will long remain unaware that these horses eat no terrestrial oats or believe that the shawl is merely for warmth or that the forests produce only lumber. We have accepted the invitation to perceive symbolic values. Moreover, even these few examples illustrate the overlapping quality of both invitation and interpretation. Ibsen promotes a second-order reading of his symbols in more than one fashion, and the same symbol may obtrude in more than one way.

Since this catalogue should be indicative rather than exhaustive, I will mention only a few other ways Ibsen encourages us to view certain signs as having a latent as well as a manifest signification. Several people responded to the original Scandinavian and English productions of *Hedda Gabler* by suggesting that the play ought to have been presented as a novel.[12] This response is in fact a sublimated desire to have the symbols pre-digested by a narrator. If only Ibsen had singled out which of the signs deserved our fullest attention! If only he had relieved his audience of the need to make an initial arrangement of the play's data! Such reactions call for the play to speak to the audience over the characters' heads, or behind their backs, and it seems to me an extremely important demand not only because it seeks precisely what drama cannot ever fully provide (a mediating consciousness), but also because Ibsen himself could not always resist trying to provide such mediation. A common realistic resort at this point would be some form of raisonneur, a Chekhovian doctor, for example, who could guide our reactions, even if we then felt obliged to press beyond those interpretations. When the dramatist forgoes this device, as Ibsen sometimes does in his later plays, it is still possible to have one or more characters make overt invitations to a symbolic reading. Thus, we have Hedvig's much-mocked comment on Gregers Werle:

> ... all the time it was just as though he meant something different from what he was saying.[13]

The other version of this emphatic over-emphasis is an equally emphatic suppression of emphasis, as when Kroll responds to Rosmer's confidence that Rebecca will keep him from becoming lonely: 'Ah ...! Even that too! Beata's very words!' The stage direction helpfully adds, '*A suspicion seems to cross his mind*', but Kroll '*dismissing the thought*', continues, 'No, no ... that wasn't nice.... Forgive me' (VI, 316–17).

This survey of the way actions and speeches invite symbolic interpretation introduces a final distinction concerning the varieties of symbolic procedure in *Hedda Gabler*. On occasion, the characters recognize and prompt the audience to recognize symbolic forces, but on other occasions the play communicates directly with the audience without any of the characters being conscious of a symbolic dimension. I believe the former type of symbolism often proves the more effective in realistic drama, but I should like to begin with the latter, which frequently appears in places critics have found puzzling, or inept, or unsatisfying.

Jens Arup, a very sensitive reader of the play, comments at length about Tesman's dullness:

> ... are we really to believe in a character as dumb as he is shown to be? He misses the most obvious hints at Hedda's pregnancy. One would imagine him to be totally unaware of the facts of life.[14]

Arup goes on to defend the play's 'fantastically unrealistic quality'[15] and rightly claims that 'In some respects Ibsen evidently did not feel fidelity to reality to be of the first importance.'[16] Arup ends this section of his study with appropriate comments on the relativity of character portrayal. The realistic convention denies us those occasions (like soliloquies) when a character can establish his absolute nature without the need for comparison or contrast with another character.

In seeking to explain Tesman's ignorance about his wife's pregnancy, however, Arup shifts our attention from the immediate dramatic fact toward an abstract consideration of the social implications of Hedda's marriage. A brief elaboration of Arup's general statements will not, I hope, violate his argument. To have Tesman's child means once and for all lying in the bed Hedda has made for herself. It means entering the middle-class, the tedious, academic, family- and money-obsessed bourgeoisie. (Her conversations with Brack substantiate the horror this future holds for her.) Moreover, her romantic fantasies about her heritage tell her that she need not have accepted this existence. Death, then, is the only response to her new life and the new life she carries. To escape the 'strange and hostile power' which Ibsen said the Tesman ménage represented, Hedda must die.[17] Even the lesser capitulation of becoming Brack's mistress – in fact or emotional reality – would disappear if she had a child. In Ibsen's final draft, Brack specifically describes children as 'intruders'; a child 'completely monopolizes the lady of the house' (VII, 332).

All this may be so. Indeed, no one would deny the overwhelming importance of social status and inherited values (good and bad) in the play, but this explanation takes us a long way from Tesman's stupidity and just how it comes to be. Again, we may attribute Tesman's nature to Ibsen's sardonicism: one of his notes on Tesman threatens to make him a complete buffoon.[18] This latter resort really would not have worked. The character relations are so thoroughly intertwined that to unbalance one character in this way seriously distorts or threatens to distort our judgment of all the other characters: not just the woman who accepted Tesman, but the man-about-town who indulges him and the supposed genius who regards him as a worthy competitor. My own view is that while we may have adequately deciphered the symbolism of Hedda's pregnancy, Ibsen presents it very awkwardly because he is trying to create a symbol for his audience and also trying to disguise that fact. This attempt – symbolizing and concealment – not only makes Tesman disastrously stupid, it often causes almost literal fits for the actress: one recalls all those Heddas bent double with morning sickness as they try to communicate what Tesman is too dull to understand and the dialogue too subtle or too clever to state.

My analysis complements Arup's reading because it tries to identify Ibsen's immediate reasons for ruffling the play's realistic surface. Having

avoided certain substitutes for the author's mediating consciousness – the
soliloquy, the chorus, the raisonneur, and so forth – Ibsen still seeks to offer
the audience a symbol. Before speculating on the consequences of this choice
and some of the reasons for it, I would like to examine an example of the
other kind of symbol, a symbol which the characters themselves create.

Ibsen lingers over Løvborg's attitude toward his lost manuscript in a way
which characterizes both Thea and Løvborg very effectively. Løvborg is too
ashamed to admit that he has lost his precious manuscript during his sordid
revels. Instead, he claims, 'I've torn the manuscript into a thousand pieces'
and goes on to make the act symbolic: 'I've torn my own life to pieces. So I
might as well tear up my life's work as well' (VII, 247). The lie, he discovers,
has a pleasing symmetry; life and life's work may each be shredded, scat-
tered, and eventually each will sink into the fjord. Thea accepts the invitation to treat this sign as a 'double-meaning expression' and provides her
own decipherment:

> I want you to know, Løvborg, what you've done to the book. . . . For the rest of
> my life it'll be for me as though you'd killed a little child.   (VII, 247)

The Norwegian text is a little more formal, and Thea's language emphasizes
the mental act: 'Vil det stå for meg some du hadde drept et lite barn.' In his
turn, Løvborg accepts this new symbolism, 'It was like killing a child' (VII,
248), and Thea completes the new interpretation by claiming her part: 'The
child was mine, it was also mine.' The dialogue has clearly entered a new
level of implication, so we readily accept Thea's powerful exit line: 'Oh, I
don't know myself what I'll do. There's nothing but darkness ahead of me.'
The echo of Brendel's departure from Rosmersholm adds to the moment.

In this episode Ibsen offers a diagram of characters making symbols, and
the symbols may of course be shared with other characters. Played correctly,
these exchanges prepare for and guarantee Hedda's otherwise melodramatic
closing lines as she throws the manuscript on the fire: 'Now I'm burning your
child, Thea . . . Your child and Ejlert Løvborg's. I'm burning . . . your child'
(VII, 250). One of the principal drawbacks to this kind of symbolism is that it
exhausts the symbol's potential for the audience. Once the characters launch
their own symbolic interpretation – and we even hear a false start (life-
work/life becomes life-work/child) – the audience's only recourse is to accept
the symbol as having its declared meaning. We may, if we wish, attach this
episode to others: Hedda's cruel insistence upon Thea's childlessness in the
non-symbolic sense (VII, 186), for instance, or the subsequent 'marriage' of
Thea and Tesman as they resurrect the lost child from Løvborg's original
notes, but our own active engagement with the 'double-meaning' can go no
further.

What about a symbol which does speak to the audience and does offer us a
chance to draw together threads of response and interpretation without at

the same time arising from the characters' own symbol-making *or* requiring them to be preternaturally imperceptive? I suggest that we look at one of the play's most melodramatic figures: the singer–dancer–courtesan we never see, but who is present at Løvborg's death. This entire layer of the play – the attempt to characterize Løvborg's wild, uncontrolled, socially unacceptable behavior – smacks of a creator with little experience of such things and little interest in them beyond the necessary generalized indications of debauchery. As it proves, Ibsen turns his own limitations to good account, since neither Tesman nor most of the audience can really envisage this low-life very clearly. Brack responds with appropriate sophistication, but even he is uncomfortable at having to use his police contacts to find out what occurred.

What do we learn about this woman? Thea thinks she is the person who casts an ominous shadow between her and Løvborg (VII, 194–5) and also mentions the woman's threat to shoot Løvborg. Ibsen has made in important change here. His earlier draft explicitly identifies this threatening figure as Hedda herself and omits any mention of the other woman (VII, 287). According to Thea, the 'red-haired singer' is 'in town again' (VII, 195). Like Løvborg, she has been away; perhaps, like him, driven away. She is a singer and dancer. Brack says that she is a singer 'among other things' (VII, 242). Brack repeats that she has red hair and gives her name: '*frøken* Diana' (VII, 241). He first invites us to think about the woman in more than mechanical terms when he describes her as 'a mighty huntress of men'. The joke is a fair one: *frøken* Diana is actually the reverse of the chaste goddess. It is possible Ibsen borrowed the joke from Strindberg, who was usually quick to detect what he considered 'thefts': Miss Julie's promiscuous dog is also called 'Diana'.[19]

Frøken Diana has three significant attributes: name, hair-color, and occupation. Brack has made the first step: Diana, 'huntress of men', but he goes no further than an obvious and negligent irony. We, however, are free to compare Diana with the other two women in Løvborg's life, Thea and Hedda, who are also hunting him. Each woman has a different set of motives and different goals, though sexual attraction presumably underlies each of these differences. However varied the motives and purposes, each woman wants Løvborg as a captive. For Thea and Hedda, Løvborg is more useful stripped of the very qualities which initially make him attractive: Thea would turn him into a tame, academic house pet, Hedda into either a surrogate debauchee or a dead, Dionysian hero. That is, 'control over a human destiny' (Arup's persuasive formula for the play's central theme) necessarily implies the corruption or destruction of what made the 'victim' originally attractive. So, too, with Diana. Løvborg over-steps the decorum of the brothel (or café or night-club) and dies as a result. Social code and scandal prevail even there. The three women attract him; they want him to be a certain way. When he fails their designs, each makes what she can of the result: a murder–suicide; a lost author to be memorialized; a romantic, vine-leaf-laden renegade.

Of Diana's red hair, the audience may make a rapid, but very effective, symbolic interpretation. Ibsen has ensured that hair will strike us as important: Hedda envies Thea's hair and imagines that Løvborg's will be wreathed. Hedda associates hair with potency and excess in their blunt sexual meanings and, more abstractly, with intellectual fertility and emotional excess. Diana's hair, however, is red, and ancient European, as well as English, folk-tradition associates red hair with lustfulness, betrayal, the unorthodox, and the threatening. Diana betrays her name and her lover; her hair signals danger, anger, impulsiveness. These traditional associations allow the symbolic attribute to speak to the audience without at the same time impugning the characters' intelligence or arising from their own antecedent symbolizing. The audience may be expected to come to the theatre with certain preconceptions about red hair. Likewise, the characters may be assumed to share such preconceptions without convicting themselves of Tesman-like dullness when they do not explicitly state them. Moreover, Brack's off-hand phrase, 'huntress of men', satisfies our sense of verisimilitude, but does not pre-empt our further symbolic interpretation.

I have tried to discriminate among three classes of symbols: a class which the author attempts to communicate while keeping his characters ignorant of their symbol-laden environment; a class which the characters explicitly denominate as symbolic; a class which enhances formal verisimilitude by allowing the characters to begin a symbolic interpretation but at the same time leaves the audience scope for further interpretation. While the first group of symbols, represented in my discussion by Hedda's pregnancy, is fairly easy to identify, the other two groups often overlap, and they have certainly caused the most critical difficulty. These two categories raise many issues, but one stands out: the dramatic character's expressed self-awareness.

Every dramatist faces the problem of how to adjust the degree to which his characters can interpret themselves and their surroundings. Of course, such interpretation and its expression first reach the audience as elements of characterization: Mrs Helseth is a less able interpreter than Rebecca West, and that quality helps distinguish their dramatic characters. Symbols and symbolizing can also be included as characterizing elements, and they are manifestly part of the character's power to interpret self and environment. When the dramatist misadjusts the level of self-awareness, a symbol becomes over-obtrusive: the analogical machine can creak just as loudly as the plot of a *pièce bien faite*. Misadjustment in the opposite direction buries a potential symbol so deeply within a character's dramatized self-consciousness that we feel forbidden to develop our own separate interpretation while at the same time continuing to accept the play's announced degree of verisimilitude.

(This last qualification concerning the way in which interpretation may threaten a play's asserted 'realism' will require further discussion.)

Once something has become a symbol for one of the characters, we are restricted in our re-making or modifying of that symbol. The act of symbolizing serves the individual element in the play's rhetorical strategy, and we risk damaging that element – the 'character' – if we wrest the symbol from his or her meaning and give it a different meaning. The act of symbolizing tends to displace the symbol itself. We read the act of symbolizing symbolically: it remains itself, but if the author has done his job properly we can also fit this event into a coherent but unstated pattern – the character's 'character'. We infer, generalize, abstract, and hypothesize, but we focus these often unconscious interpretative acts on the supposed source and not the effect. As we move forward through the play's action, the earlier act of symbol-making controls our expectation and directs our attention. Will the character handle later opportunities for symbolic interpretation in the same way? Thus, Thea thinks tearing the manuscript is 'like' infanticide. We cannot make the manuscript anything other or more than a 'child' because Thea has restricted its symbolic potential, though she may not have filled in all the details of that interpretation. We can infer, and do, why she might regard the manuscript as a child, and why Løvborg eventually agrees. Further, we see that this symbolizing can be communicated from character to character. Hedda accepts the idea that Thea's influence over Løvborg is represented by the product of their collaboration. Her words as she burns the manuscript are symbolic only in the sense that she accepts a symbol another character has created.

In describing the different categories of symbol, I have also tried to examine their dramatic advantages and disadvantages, but no playwright can control his audience's preconceptions. Ibsen is especially vulnerable to preconceptions about technique and subject matter. Many apparently unrelated factors contribute to this vulnerability: for example, his steady biannual production; the patterns in his plays which critics and audiences detected very early; the careful accumulation of detail evident in Ibsen's extensive notes and drafts as well as, less demonstrably, in the final stage texts themselves. Attitudes based on these qualities exacerbate our failure to discriminate among the symbols' sources. This double liability infects the traditional view of General Gabler's pistols, my final example of a symbol and its interpretation.

Hedda Gabler, we may agree, comes at an odd moment in Ibsen's career. Sandwiched between *The Lady from the Sea* and *The Master Builder*, it seems to share little of their experimental technique and few of their 'issues'. Instead, one turns back to *Ghosts* or *A Doll's House* to find similar characters and similar situations, or so it appears. General Gabler's pistols, especially, have

raised much critical hilarity at Ibsen's expense. They seem to have a ponderous 'symbolism' like the orphanage of *Ghosts*, or Engstrand's limp, or the joke
when Nora is called a 'spillefugl'. Here I believe we may use the distinction
between symbols Ibsen directs at his audience and those symbols which arise
within the created character's psychology. Hedda, not Ibsen, may be the
source of the pistols' obviousness, of their obtrusive symbolism. We may meet
conscious design, not imaginative or technical failure.

Ibsen attempts to make complicated distinctions between his own artistry
and Hedda's 'aestheticism', and one signal of this attempt appears when he
re-uses his own earlier symbolic techniques. In *Hedda Gabler*, however, Ibsen
does not always use the devices to present *his* material. They are not
transparent conventions, but part of a character's imagined nature. Perhaps
an obvious example from another writer will clarify this point. Pirandello's
six wandering characters clearly want to be in an Ibsen-like play, as Ibsen's
plays were and are popularly conceived. It is no new observation that
Pirandello analogizes the artist's creative process with the methods ordinary
mortals employ to constitute their identities. His six characters, like the rest
of us, are embryonic artists of the self, and their chosen form is one of Ibsen's
realistic social dramas. They seek refuge from one dramatized universe in
another, and Pirandello makes the conflict between the philosophical assumptions and dramatic techniques of each competing universe central to
his play. Pirandello simplifies his problem because the competing styles are
so evidently discordant: we rarely have trouble distinguishing the characters' demands from the demands of the theatre or the world as Pirandello
conceived it.

Ibsen's attempt is riskier. He has not reformed all his techniques so that
the earlier, clumsier one (now assigned to the character) stands out from its
surroundings. The dramatist himself can be faulted for an episode or a line or
a symbolic prop which, properly construed, criticizes the character. In fact,
Ibsen wants to have it both ways. Sometimes he wishes to use a convention
(here, the symbolic quality of the pistols) as a device of characterization or as
itself a subject of study; at other times, he wishes to retain the device as a
purely conventional means for presenting his material. Pirandello had so
sharply changed his style that there could be little doubt how the six
characters' demands would be received. Ibsen, on the contrary, had not
broken so radically with his earlier practice and does indeed confuse us by
trying to make certain conventions work in two conflicting ways.

A strain of pseudo-romantic aestheticism dominates Hedda's view of the
world. The play is littered with examples. She refuses to join Tesman at Aunt
Rina's bedside: 'I don't want to look at sickness and death. I must be free of
everything that's ugly' (VII, 239). She imposes her own conception of the
beautiful on her surroundings: Tesman's old hand-embroidered slippers are
no more satisfactory than her own old piano which 'doesn't go with the rest

of the things' (VII, 184). The most prominent example of this strain in her character is her unrelenting effort to make something beautiful of Løvborg's death. Seeking to make Løvborg commit suicide, rather than fulfilling her earlier threat to shoot him herself, she is of course also seeking to avoid scandal, but her truest pleasure lies in the aesthetic perfection of the act. Believing that he has executed himself in the requisite manner, she can exult in 'an act of spontaneous courage... An act that has something of unconditional beauty' (VII, 262) while at the same time savoring her own control. But Løvborg has failed this demand as he had failed Thea's and Diana's. Hedda's only recourse is to commit a beautiful, perfect suicide herself, thus establishing the primacy of her aesthetic convictions. One critic has argued that 'to regard her act as "courageous" in any real sense or her death as "beautiful" would be to accept the same demented set of values Hedda has lived by'.[20] Those values are demented because the moral and social have been subordinated to the aesthetic: her fear of scandal and publicity is always couched in terms of beauty and ugliness rather than right or wrong.

In all of this, the general's pistols are merely instruments. They are just pistols in precisely the sense that Hedda means when she objects to regarding Løvborg's manuscript as a 'child': 'when all's said and done ... this was only a book ...' (VII, 249). A fair reading or viewing of the play must admit that Hedda does not truly over-value her social heritage. She objects to the scrimping and barrenness of life with Tesman, but the same is true – with different objections – of life with father. Her personal demands of existence cannot be satisfied in his household, or Tesman's, or in Lady Frick's old villa. The drive to shape destinies in what she considers beautiful patterns overrides any given social station. Thus, the pistols have for her a specific symbolism: they permit at least the fantasied destruction of all she finds ugly; they represent freedom from ugliness, not freedom from Tesman or Brack or Løvborg or Norway or the past.

We may imagine, if we wish, that Ibsen cast about for some plausible explanation of why Hedda has the pistols in the first place and that he hit upon the idea that she inherited them (along with the piano and the portrait). This decision in turn permitted him, or so he hoped, to talk past Hedda and invite us to decipher the symbol as a sign both of the past's destructive influence and of Hedda's hatred of her father. But I submit that this decision makes for a fatal confusion between the melodramatic, 'demented', and aesthetic use Hedda makes of the pistols – a value which works only if we accept her symbolism – and the symbolic value Ibsen would have us find in those pistols considered quite apart from Hedda's view of them. In the terms I outlined above, Ibsen is crossing symbolic categories. He tries to have the pistols retain a conventional transparency and a practical, textual solidity. If P. F. D. Tennant correctly derives the pistols from the older 'romantic fate-tragedy' and its ready-made symbols, we may observe that Ibsen is attempting both to scrutinize the assumptions of that dramatic form and also to exploit its conventional advantages.[21]

I should like to return very briefly to the larger questions I mentioned at the outset. Those questions are closely linked with our natural interest in preserving the play's own announced 'realism'. Certain critical theories would not acknowledge that it is important to discriminate among various symbols' sources. A typical essay on 'Thematic Symbols in *Hedda Gabler*', for example, takes its evidence from the spoken text, the stage directions, and even Ibsen's letters, drafts, and notes without any sense that these sources should also control our methods of interpretation.[22] If we wish to analyze Ibsen's own consciousness, then all these forms of evidence have roughly equal status, and the critic does not really care what literary form the artist's work takes. My argument has assumed that Ibsen – indeed any dramatist – makes at least a conscious distinction between his personality and those dramatized personalities we call characters. The more he attempts to present a superficially unmediated representation of the world, the more he will insist, as Ibsen frequently did, on this distinction. That is, the mimetic rather than the rhetorical predominates.[23] We recognized at the start that 'realism' is no less conventional and no less an 'imagery' than any other artistic formula, but the requirements of the drama and especially the historical form of realistic drama combine to hide those facts. Moreover, the realistic dramatist carefully distinguishes his characters from himself and from each other in order to promote the effects he believes realistic drama can achieve. If we have no particular interest in preserving the play's announced degree of verisimilitude, we may dissolve it in order to lay bare the mythic patterns, or structural logic, or psychological contours which probably precede and underlie its creation. Many dramatic effects do depend upon just such foundations.

I have the unhappy suspicion that Ibsen himself might well agree with these and other objections to my treatment of *Hedda Gabler*: after all, Archer claims the master once dismissed complaints about his dramatic symbolism by saying that life is one tissue of symbols.[24] And many years earlier, Ibsen had praised Andreas Munch because that forgotten dramatist 'allowed the symbolic to stand there without commentary like a runic inscription, leaving it to each member of the audience to interpret it according to his or her individual needs'.[25] This observation and the one to Archer may (deliberately?) rebuke critical exuberance, but they also show Ibsen at his most elusive. The same review of Munch's play claimed 'every notable human being is symbolic, both in his career and in his relationship to history'. Despite Ibsen's seeming endorsement (and some fairly evident coat-trailing), these meanings of 'symbol' truly obscure Ibsen's success. Like many of Ibsen's critics, Paul Ricoeur investigates symbols through Freud's view of the symbolic process, but Ricoeur amplifies what he calls the 'archeological', or regressive, Freudian conception into a double interpretation which moves both backward into the past and projects or innovates meaning (a 'teleological' movement in his terms). This innovative or revelatory power appears most fully in cultural objects, works of art, because they 'are not mere projections of the artist's conflicts, but also a sketch of their solution'.[26] In distinguishing the dramatic sources of Ibsen's symbolism, I have tried to locate this power and also to suggest where it may fail.

NOTES

1. Anonymous, *Black and White*, 25 Feb. 1893, p. 224, repr. in Michael Egan (ed.), *Ibsen: The Critical Heritage* (London: Routledge & Kegan Paul, 1972), pp. 281–2.
2. Anonymous, *Referee*, 1 Feb. 1903, p. 2, repr. in Egan, *Ibsen*, p. 400.
3. 'Mordred', *Referee*, 22 Oct. 1905, p. 3, repr. in Egan, *Ibsen*, p. 430.
4. Ronald Peacock, *The Art of Drama* (1957), repr. in J. W. McFarlane (ed.), *Henrik Ibsen*, Penguin Critical Anthologies (Harmondsworth: Penguin, 1970), p. 209; see also E. H. Gombrich, *Art and Illusion*, second edn (Princeton University Press, 1969), ch. 9, esp. pp. 313 and 321.
5. Northrop Frye offers a deliberately capacious example of the first view: 'the word "symbol" ... means any unit of any literary structure that can be isolated for critical attention' (*Anatomy of Criticism*, 1957; New York: Atheneum, 1967, p. 71). Ernst Cassirer defines 'symbol' even more broadly in *The Philosophy of Symbolic Forms* (1923–29) and *An Essay on Man* (1944). For Gosse's remark, see his *Henrik Ibsen* (New York: C. Scribner's Sons, 1908), p. 176.
6. The latter view derives largely from linguistics; for a survey, see, e.g. Karl D. Uitti, *Linguistics and Literary Theory* (New York: Norton, 1969) and for a characteristically personal study, Kenneth Burke's 'What Are the Signs of What? A Theory of Entitlement' in *Language as Symbolic Action* (Berkeley and Los Angeles: University of California Press, 1966), pp. 359–79. Before Coleridge, Goethe had begun the denigration of 'allegory' in favor of 'symbol'.
7. See Paul De Man, 'The Rhetoric of Temporality' in Charles S. Singleton (ed.), *Interpretation: Theory and Practice* (Baltimore: Johns Hopkins University Press, 1969), pp. 173–209.
8. From Ibsen's review (1857) of Andreas Munch's *Lord William Russell*, quoted by Michael Meyer, *Ibsen: A Biography* (Garden City, New York: Doubleday, 1971), p. 148.
9. Paul Ricoeur, *Freud and Philosophy: An Essay on Interpretation*, trans. Denis Savage (New Haven: Yale University Press, 1970), pp. 9 and 495.
10. *Ibid.*, p. 13
11. Ezra Pound, 'Credo' (1918) quoted in Christopher Ricks, 'The Tragedies of Webster, Tourneur and Middleton: Symbols, Imagery and Conventions' in Ricks (ed.), *English Drama to 1710*, Sphere History of Literature in the English Language, III (London: Sphere Press, 1971), 306–53.

12. For example, Gerhard Gran's response, quoted in J. W. McFarlane (ed.), *Ibsen*, VII (Oxford University Press, 1966), 506; Gran's comments are quoted at greater length in Jens Arup, 'On *Hedda Gabler*', *Orbis Litterarum*, 12 (1957), 16.

13. Quoted from J. W. McFarlane (ed.), *Ibsen*, VI (Oxford University Press, 1960), 172. All subsequent citations of Ibsen in English translation are from this edition; references appear parenthetically by volume and page number.

14. Arup, 'On *Hedda Gabler*', p. 14.

15. *Ibid.*, p. 16.

16. *Ibid.*, p. 17.

17. See Ibsen's letter to Kristina Steen, 14 January 1891, repr. in Evert Sprinchorn (ed. and trans.), Ibsen, *Letters and Speeches* (New York: Hill & Wang, 1964), p. 299. The entire passage reads: 'Jørgen Tesman, his old aunts, and the faithful servant Berte together form a picture of complete unity. They think alike, they share the same memories and have the same outlook on life. To Hedda they appear like a strange and hostile power, aimed at her very being.'

18. Ibsen's note is translated in McFarlane, *Ibsen*, VII, 485: 'Tesman is short-sighted. Wears spectacles. Oh, what a lovely rose! Then he puts his nose into a cactus. Since then − !'

19. See Strindberg's letter to Birger Mörner, 10 March 1891, referring specifically to *Hedda Gabler*, but omitting this example; repr. in McFarlane, *Henrik Ibsen*, p. 127. In another contemporary letter, Strindberg claimed that Løvborg was based on his own biography; see Meyer, *Ibsen*, pp. 648–9.

20. James Hurt, *Catiline's Dream: An Essay on Ibsen's Plays* (Urbana: University of Illinois Press, 1972), p. 153.

21. P. F. D. Tennant, *Ibsen's Dramatic Technique* (1949; New York: Humanities Press, 1965), p. 115.

22. Caroline W. Mayerson, 'Thematic Symbols in *Hedda Gabler*' (1950), repr. in Rolfe Fjelde (ed.), *Ibsen: A Collection of Critical Essays* (Englewood Cliffs: Prentice-Hall, 1965), pp. 131–8. Compare the thoroughly biographical and psychoanalytic method in Arne Duve, *Symbolikken i Henrik Ibsens skuespill* (Oslo: Nasjonalforlaget, 1945).

23. For an example of this distinction in Elizabethan drama, see E. T. Schell, 'Who Said that − Hamlet or *Hamlet*?' *Shakespeare Quarterly*, 24 (1973), 135–46.

24. William Archer, 'Ibsen and English Criticism', *Fortnightly Review*, 1 July 1889, repr. in Egan, *Ibsen*, p. 117.

25. Quoted in Meyer, *Ibsen*, p. 148.

26. Ricoeur, *Freud and Philosophy*, p. 521. Kenneth Burke had earlier raised the possibility of seeing condensation and displacement in all symbol-systems and not just the Freudian (*Language as Symbolic Action*, pp. 7–8); Burke also regards Freudian nomenclature as partial to 'archaizing' (*ibid.*, pp. 67–8).

Monuments and ruins as symbols in *The Duchess of Malfi*

MICHAEL NEILL

A Monument is a thing erected, made, or written, for a memoriall of some remarkable action fit to bee transferred to future posterities. And thus generally taken, all religious Foundations, all sumptuous and magnificent Structures, Cities, Townes, Towers, Castles, Pillars, Pyramides, Crosses, Obeliskes, Amphitheaters, and the like, as well as Tombes and Sepulchres are called Monuments. Now above all remembrances (by which men have endevoured, even in despight of death to give unto their Fames eternitie) for worthinesse and continuance, bookes or writings, have ever had preheminence. ... Bookes ... and the Muses workes are of all monuments the most permanent; for of all things else there is a vicissitude, a change both of cities and nations. ... every man desires a perpetuity, after death, by these monuments.   (John Weever, *Ancient Funerall Monuments*)[1]

In Henslowe's famous inventory of stage properties, amongst rocks, steeples cages, hell-mouths and cities, one structure has particular prominence:

> *Item*, i rocke, i cage, i tombe, i Hell mought.
> *Item*, i tome of Guido, i tome of Dido, i bedsteade.[2]

Three tombs! Yet no one seems to have asked why so thrifty an entrepeneur should have felt it necessary to triplicate his investment in a large property of this kind. In fact the investment is probably proportionate to the importance of tombs and monuments in the iconography of English Renaissance drama. Like many other pageant properties and mansions used on this stage, the tomb was a survival from the mystery cycles, where it had featured in such plays as *The Raising of Lazarus* and *The Resurrection*; and it had an obvious and continuing appeal as a melodramatic accoutrement of the tragedy of blood. The extravagant popularity of the device is revealed in a whole succession of plays from Greene's *James IV* (*c.* 1590) to Ford's *Love's Sacrifice* (*c.* 1630): prominent examples include *Titus Andronicus* (1589–94), *Romeo and Juliet* (*c.* 1595), *Antonio's Revenge* (1599–1601), *The Widow's Tears* (1603–9), *Antony and Cleopatra* (*c.* 1606–8), *The Atheist's Tragedy* (1607–11), *The Second Maiden's Tragedy* (1611), and the play which is the principal subject of this paper, Webster's *Duchess of Malfi* (*c.* 1613). In the old religious theatre the tomb had been a sign of transcendence, the Christian victory over death; in the new secular theatre it quickly developed an extended range of emblematic meanings,[3] connected in part with the classical idea of the monument. A parallel development can be detected in the architecture of the tomb itself, whose function as a sepulchre for those awaiting resurrection was increasingly usurped by monumental ostentation – the celebration of worldly achievement which Bosola satirizes:

> princes' images on their tombs do not lie, as they were wont, seeming to pray
> up to heaven . . . but as their minds were wholly bent upon the world.
>
> (IV, ii, 156–61)[4]

In *Titus Andronicus*, a consciously 'classical' play, the tomb or monument of the Andronici, which dominates act I, stands as the physical statement of a great family's idea of honour. Addressed by Titus as 'sacred receptacle of my joys, / Sweet cell of virtue and nobility' (I, i, 92–3), it is the focus of a kind of religious awe whose barbaric power depends, at least in part, on the recollection of a very different kind of tomb-opening. Ironically enough, its role as a place of human sacrifice tends to equate it with the 'blood stained hole' of act II, whose 'swallowing womb' (II, iii, 239) marks it as a secular equivalent of the medieval hell-mouth. Hell-mouth and tomb, the typological opposites of the old drama, are here conflated in a pit which to the terrified imagination of Martius and Quintus itself recalls a 'monument' or 'grave' (ll. 228, 240). The splendid monument of the Andronici, as befits a tragedy of revenge, comes to stand for nothing more than the dead hand of memory, the murderous tyranny of the past upon the present. The tomb of Andrugio in Marston's *Antonio's Revenge* has a similar function: from it issues the Ghost which saddles Antonio with the fearful commandment to remember and revenge (III, i, 32–51, 174); and it becomes the altar on which Antonio performs the sacrifice of the hapless Julio in monstrous parody of the requiem mass:

> Ghost of my poison'd sire, suck this fume;
> To sweet revenge, perfume thy circling air
> With smoke of blood. I sprinkle round his gore
> And dew thy hearse with these fresh-reeking drops.
>
> (III, i, 207–10)

In other plays, such as *James IV* or *The Atheist's Tragedy*, the tombs (like *Hamlet*'s graves) are simple emblems of mutability and the vanity of human pride. Elsewhere, however, the monumental function of the tomb is emphasised to create a secular equivalent of the motif of resurrection – a meaning closely bound up with the humanist aspiration of the dramatists themselves.

The tomb in which the action of *Romeo and Juliet* concludes mediates between all three types: insofar as it is the family vault of the Capulets, it is, like the tomb of the Andronici, a visible sign of the tyrannous past to which the lovers have fallen victim; as Romeo's 'detestable maw [and] womb of death' (v, iii, 45) it is an emblem of mortality and death's inevitable triumph; but it proves to be a 'triumphant grave' in a double sense (l. 83), for as we look at the figures of the young lovers stretched out upon the bed of death, the tomb begins to assume its role of monument, anticipating the 'statue in pure gold' which the old men promise to raise to the memory of their children. In this sense the arrival of the Prince and the others at the monument can be seen to foreshadow the supreme moment in Paulina's chapel at the end of *The Winter's Tale*, where a monumental statue comes to life in what Glynne Wickham has seen as a reworking of the old *Visitatio Sepulchri*, the drama of resurrection.[5] And in the *Romeo* scene, too, we may already find a hint of that conceit, fully developed through the magnificent artifice of Cleopatra's death, 'marble-constant' in her monument, by which the play itself becomes a kind of monument to its triumphant dead, outliving 'marble [and] the gilded monuments / Of princes'. So too in *Antonio's Revenge* the hero's concluding oration is made to present the play as a memorial to 'immortal fame of virgin faith' whose enactment religiously preserves the tragic Mellida. Webster's *Duchess of Malfi* continues this tradition of resurrection by artifice. Here the dramatist has his murdered heroine literally speak from her grave in a climactic scene which emblematises the Triumph of Fame through Fame's agent, Poetry. At the end of *The White Devil*, Death had been in unchallenged possession of the stage, as even the brilliant Flamineo sank into the 'mist': 'I recover like a spent taper, for a flash / And instantly go out' (v, i, 263–4); but in *The Duchess of Malfi*, which forms a kind of diptych with the earlier tragedy, the reign of Death is challenged by Fame. In a sense Webster reverses Marlowe's procedure in the two parts of *Tamburlaine: The Duchess of Malfi* is a Triumph of Fame as surely as the second part of *Tamburlaine* was a Triumph of Death. And in place of *The White Devil*'s despairing emblems of mortality – 'A dead man's skull beneath the roots of flowers' (v, iv, 136) – it erects a monument of eternal artifice.

  Much recent criticism of *The Duchess of Malfi* has tended to polarise between those critics, such as John Russell Brown and Robert Ornstein, who see it as a characteristic expression of Jacobean scepticism, and those, like David Gunby and Dominic Baker-Smith,[6] who interpret the play in the light of Calvinist doctrine, typing it 'essentially a work of theodicy'.[7] *The Duchess of Malfi* is, I believe, in the broad sense a religious play, but not one which espouses any secure doctrine. The teaching of Calvin, like the sceptical reservation of Montaigne, should merely be numbered among the more striking intellectual influences which contribute to Webster's heteronymous vision of the world – a heteronymy which only the integrity of art can bring to order.[8] The key to the play's meaning is, I shall argue, to be found in act v, scene iii, the echo scene which, because traditionally regarded as one of the gothic extravagances of a 'Tussaud laureate', has been the object of embarrassed critical evasiveness. It is a scene which, like the Duchess's torture scene (iv, ii), so brilliantly anatomised by Inga-Stina Ekeblad,[9] will yield its full meaning only when it is 'read' visually; for it relies on that favourite Websterian device, the 'figure-in-action', to create a powerful iconographic effect.[10]

The stage in this scene is meant to be dominated by the last in a succession of splendid pageant properties around which the action of the play's central section is developed. The first of these is the altar at the Shrine of our Lady of Loreto which is the setting for the Cardinal's rites of martial initiation and his formal banishment of the Duchess and her family (iii, iv); the second is the display of waxwork figures, representing the dead bodies of Antonio and his children, in act iv, scene i; and the last is the Duchess's own tomb at Milan. Visually speaking, the two earlier properties are probably designed to prefigure the tomb, since there is often a close morphological resemblance between Renaissance tombs and altars; while the 'sad spectacle' of the waxworks will have recalled the waxwork figures displayed on hearses at great men's funerals – themselves resembling painted marble tomb sculpture. For the tomb itself, John Russell Brown has plausibly suggested that the King's Men will have employed the same property designed for *The Second Maiden's Tragedy* two years before – which in the fourth act *'flies open, and a great light appears in the midst of the tomb; his lady, as went out, standing before him'*.[11] Here we have a clear analogy for the spectacle Antonio seems to describe in his sudden vision of 'a clear light [and] a face folded in sorrow' (v, iii, 44–5). A full realisation of the effect intended by this spectacle might also have required some realisation of the ruined abbey in which the tomb is placed and on which Antonio's imagination lingers (ll. 9–19) – but this need have presented no great problems on a stage whose stock properties could include such spectacular architectural effects as 'ii stepells ... and the sittie of Rome'.[12]

Graves, monuments and decaying ruins are recognisable staples of Webster's imagery, familiarly dismissed as the trappings of a morbid imagination. Their real importance for an understanding of *The Duchess of Malfi* is, however, suggested in Webster's dedication and in the encomiastic verses contributed by his fellow dramatists, Thomas Middleton, William Rowley and John Ford. As is frequently the way in such occasional pieces,[13] all four spin conceits around the governing ideas and images of the play; and in each case the conceit draws on the ancient trope of poetry as monument. Ford, most simply, declares that Webster 'to memory hath lent / A lasting fame, to raise his monument' (ll. 37–8). Middleton extends the metaphor:

> Thy monument is rais'd in thy life-time;
> And 'tis most just; for every worthy man
> Is his own marble; and his merit can
> Cut him to any figure and express
> More art than Death's cathedral palaces,
> Where royal ashes keep their court ...

Thy epitaph only the title be –
Write, 'Duchess', that will fetch a tear for thee.
(ll. 8–16)[14]

And the Latin couplet with which he concludes recalls the symbolic chiaroscuro of that moment in act v, scene iii when the light of the Duchess's memory triumphs over the ruin about her grave:

Ut lux ex tenebris ictu percussa Tonantis,
Illa, ruina malis, claris fit vita poetis.
(ll. 20–1)
(As light springs from darkness at the stroke of the Thunderer, / So [Tragedy], while bringing ruin to the wicked, brings life to illustrious poets.)[15]

Rowley's rather clumsy verses invite us more directly to see the play as a monument to the Duchess herself, a device which (like the echo scene's own monument) enables her to speak beyond death: 'my opinion is, she might speak more, / But never, in her life, so well before' (ll. 29–30). Webster's own dedication, predictably enough, extends the monumental conceit to his hoped-for patron, Lord Berkeley: 'by such *poems* as this, *poets* have kissed the hands of *great princes* and drawn their gentle eyes to look upon their sheets of paper when the *poets* themselves were bound up in their winding sheets. The like courtesy from your *Lordship* shall make you live in your grave and *laurel* spring out of it, when the ignorant scorners of the *Muses* ... shall wither, neglected and forgotten' (ll. 18–25). The dedication also (like Middleton's verses) links the monumental function of poetry to the closely related theme of reputation and true greatness: 'I do not altogether look up to your *title*, the ancientest *nobility* being but a *relic* of time past, and the truest *honour* being indeed for a man to confer *honour* on himself.' This too is to be a theme of the play, where the Duchess becomes a figure cut (as Middleton expresses it) with her own merit from enduring marble, while the mighty edifice of her brothers' pride is reduced to a 'great ruin', an empty relic of time past:

I do glory
That thou, which stood'st like a huge pyramid
Begun upon a large and ample base,
Shalt end in a little point, a kind of nothing.
(v, v, 76–9)

These wretched eminent things
Leave no more fame behind 'em than should one
Fall in a frost, and leave his print in snow;
As soon as the sun shines, it ever melts,
Both form and matter.   (v, v, 113–17)

If act v, scene iii celebrates the Duchess's monumental triumph over time, then scene v is a sequence of melancholy epitaphs for those whom time destroys. Bosola speaks his own: 'We are only like dead walls, or vaulted graves, / That ruin'd yields no echo' (v, v, 97–8); and his similitude recalls the echo of the Duchess's voice, sounding defiantly over the Ruins of Time. Against the 'shadow, or deep pit of darkness' to which Bosola's despair reduces human life, we are to set the potent image of her mysteriously illuminated tomb. The power of this image is drawn, at least in part, from an elaborate pattern of figurative prolepsis through which the revelation of her tomb is made to seem a natural and inevitable climax. This pattern includes the pageant properties of acts III and IV, but it begins much earlier, in the first scene of the play. When Antonio concludes his introductory eulogy of the Duchess with 'She stains the time past, lights the time to come' (l. 209), he not only initiates the motif of symbolic chiaroscuro associated with the Duchess, but provides a kind of proleptic motto for the echo scene; indeed the line provides compelling evidence that Webster's imagination was already firmly fixed upon the spectacular climax of act V, scene iii when he began the play. It is repeated in *A Monumental Columne*, the memorial poem for Prince Henry which Webster is known to have composed at about the same time as his second tragedy. Since this elegy was registered in late December 1612, and published in 1613, it was almost certainly in print by the time of *The Duchess of Malfi*'s first performance,[16] and it is even possible that Webster expected discerning members of his audience to pick up the echo. Certainly the two works are very much companion pieces. Like the play, the poem is a meditation on the mutable frailty of worldly pride and a celebration of Fame, which poetry renders immortal:

> O Greatnesse! what shall we compare thee to?
> To Giants, beasts, or Towers fram'd out of Snow,
> Or like wax-guilded Tapers, more for show
> Then durance? Thy foundation doth betray
> Thy frailty, being builded on such clay.
> This shewes the al-controuling power of Fate,
> That all our Scepters and our Chaires of State
> Are but glasse-mettall, that we are full of spots, ...
>
> And though he died so late, hee's no more neere
> To us, then they that died three thousand yeare
> Before him; onely memory doth keepe
> Their *Fame* as fresh as his from death or sleepe.
>
> (ll. 109–23)[17]

Not only do the two share important themes and images; Henry's death, which the dramatist still recalled with painful nostalgia twelve years later in his civic pageant, *Monuments of Honour*, may be felt to supply the emotional impulse for this most elegiac of Jacobean tragedies.[18] In *A Monumental Columne* Webster invoked the Prince of Wales as

> Yong, grave *Mecænas* of the noble Arts,
> Whose beames shall breake forth from thy hollow Tombe,
> Staine the time past, and light the time to come!
>
> (ll. 276–8)

The context makes the connection between Antonio's admiring metaphor and the illuminated tomb of act v, scene iii as explicit as one could wish: it is almost as though he were being made to quote prophetically from a poem whose elegiac vision he will help to fulfil. The link with Prince Henry may be closer still: Glynne Wickham has proposed that *The Winter's Tale* should be read as an entertainment for the investiture of the Prince, and that Hermione's statue alludes to the monument to Mary, Queen of Scots, which James installed in Westminster Abbey to complete his emblematic celebration of the Union. Alternatively, David Bergeron has argued that the resurrection of Hermione was added in the course of revision in 1613 and was meant as a response to the public grief surrounding Henry's death.[19] In *The Duchess of Malfi* the monument of a murdered princess is once again mysteriously animated, but this time in a setting more fitted to funeral than triumph.

In elegy and tragedy alike, the tomb becomes a kind of Horatian cipher for the monumental poem itself:

> And by these signes of love let great men know,
> That sweete and generous favour they bestow
> Upon the *Muses*, never can be lost:
> For they shall live by them, when all the cost
> Of guilded Monuments shall fall to dust.
> (*A Monumental Columne* ll. 317–21)

And just as the Duchess's tomb is set against a prospect of ruins, so Henry's burial, in the poet's fancy, reduces the architecture of worldly pride to ruinous collapse:

> Time was when Churches in the land were thought
> Rich Jewel-houses, and this Age hath brought
> That time againe – think not I faine – go view
> *Henry* the sevenths Chappell, and you'le find it true,
> The dust of a rich Diamond's there inshrin'd
> To buy which thence, would begger the *West-Inde*.
> What a darke night-peece of tempestious weather,
> Have the inraged clouds summon'd together,
> As if our loftiest Pallaces should grow
> To ruine, since such Highnesse fell so low!
> (ll. 289–98)

Henry shares with the Duchess the emblem of the flashing diamond;[20] but the imagery of the poem also links him with Antonio: the melancholy ambiguity of the Duchess's betrothal kiss ('Being now my steward, here upon your lips / I sign your *Quietus est*', I, i, 463–4) would have had a deeper and more ominous resonance for those who remembered Webster's picture of a dying Prince who

in such joy did all his sences steepe
As great Accountants (troubled much in mind)
When they heare newes of their *Quietus* sign'd.[21]
(*A Monumental Columne*, ll. 218–20)

If Antonio's *quietus* anticipates the 'perfect peace' signed for the Duchess in
Bosola's dirge (IV, ii, 185), that is appropriate to spousals whose language
and ritual are closer to those of funeral than holy matrimony. The Duchess
presents herself to Antonio first as making her 'will'; and when he attempts to
redirect her conceit by urging her to 'provide for a good husband' by giving
herself in marriage (I, i, 385–8), she turns the jest back on him with 'In a
winding sheet?' (l. 389). It is an ingenious and unwittingly sinister elaboration of the familiar imagery of erotic death – wedding sheets become grave
clothes, the Duchess 'shrouds' her blushes in Antonio's bosom (l. 502).
Fittingly the emotional climax of the scene comes in a speech which directly
evokes the tomb icon of act V, scene iii:

Make not your heart so dead a piece of flesh
To fear, more than to love me: sir, be confident –
What is't distracts you? This is flesh and blood, sir;
'Tis not the figure cut in alabaster
Kneels at my husbands tomb. Awake, awake, man!
(I, i, 451–5)

These lines constitute a dramatised stage direction: what Webster envisages
here is a monumental tableau prefiguring the actual monument of act V.
Antonio himself picks up her impassioned image and gives it an elegant
complimentary twist – 'I will remain the constant / Sanctuary of your good
name' (I, i, 460–1) – presenting himself as a kind of living memorial to her
fame. His own action in kneeling before his bride as she puts the ring upon his
finger (l. 415) takes on a peculiar suggestiveness in the light of her evocation
of the statuary of tombs; and when the Duchess raises him, she does so in lines
which closely anticipate her own death speech:

Sir,
This goodly roof of yours is too low built,
I cannot stand upright in't, nor discourse,
Without I raise it higher.   (I, i, 415–8)

heaven-gates are not so highly arch'd
As princes' palaces, they that enter there
Must go upon their knees.   (IV, ii, 232–4)

'Heaven-gates' here are literally the portals of the grave, the tomb which the
Duchess must exchange for the high-roofed palace to which she elevated her
husband. By its exact and ceremonious reversal of the earlier ritual, her
gesture becomes more than a sign of simple Christian humility; it is an
emblematic recapitulation of one of the play's most insistent themes, the

opposition of the monuments of fame to the ephemeral architecture of worldly greatness.[22]

Tombs and monuments are, of course, deeply equivocal devices; while they may serve as images of fame's triumph over death, they may equally (as their inscriptions frequently remind us) act as reminders of the instability of all worldly achievement. Those double tombs which juxtapose their splendid portrait sculptures with rotting cadavers exploit this ambivalence to create a kind of sculptural anamorphosis. Webster creates a similar effect by constantly switching our attention from the monumental marble to its decaying contents.[23] So that even the Duchess's gorgeous palace, metamorphosed by turns to prison and madhouse, becomes reduced to a kind of charnel: the 'inconstant / And rotten ground of service' which Bosola finds in it (III, ii, 198–9) suggests a graveyard; while for the Duchess it becomes a kind of reliquary for her living remains –

> Why should only I
> Of all the other princes of the world,
> Be cas'd up like a holy relic?
> (III, ii, 136–8)

– an image which springs to grotesque life in her farewell to Antonio:

> your kiss is colder
> Than that I have seen an holy anchorite
> Give to a dead man's skull.
> (III, v, 88–90)

The sudden appearance of Ferdinand's waxworks in act IV, scene ii makes the palace into a bizarre funerary chapel; and for Cariola the Duchess, with her 'deal of life in show, but none in practice', begins to resemble one of its crumbling tomb sculptures: she is 'like some reverend monument / Whose ruins are even to be pitied' (IV, ii, 32–5). Bosola, who presents himself as her tomb maker, satirically instructs the Duchess in the art of composing such a monument:

> princes images on their tombs do not lie, as they were wont, seeming to pray up to heaven, but with their hands under their cheeks, as if they died of the toothache; they are not carved with their eyes fixed upon the stars, but as their minds were wholly bent upon the world, the selfsame way they seem to turn their faces. (IV, ii, 156–62)

It is a kind of instruction by negatives for the tableau she composes at her death. With the 'tomb maker's' gifts of '*coffin, cords and a bell*' and his 'talk fit for a charnel' (ll. 165–6), the palace becomes a place of 'mortification' in its most literal sense:

> *Call upon our dame, aloud,*
> *And bid her quickly don her shroud.*

> *Much you had of land and rent,*
> *Your length in clay's now competent.*
> *A long war disturb'd your mind*
> *Here your perfect peace is sign'd.*
>   (IV, ii, 80–5)

His dirge speaks the language of epitaph: it is as though she were already dead.

At other times the human form itself appears as a kind of living tomb. For Bosola, in his vein of melancholy satire, the body is not the lofty palace the Duchess's metaphor made of it, but already a corrupted corpse, given the semblance of life by the bravery of its decoration:

> Though we are eaten up of lice and worms,
> And though continually we bear about us
> A rotten and dead body, we delight
> To hide it in rich tissue: all our fear –
> Nay, all our terror – is lest our physician
> Should put us in the ground to be made sweet.
>   (II, i, 55–60)

– a conceit which gives a particularly concrete nastiness to his moral denunciations of Ferdinand and the Cardinal:

> You have a pair of hearts are hollow graves,
> Rotten, and rotting others.   (IV, ii, 319–20)

> And wherefore should you lay fair marble colours
> Upon your rotten purposes to me?
> Unless you imitate some that do plot great treasons,
> And when they have done, go hide themselves i'th'graves
> Of those were actors in't.   (V, ii, 297–301)

The human heart is secret as the grave, but like the grave the secrets it contains are only the grim truths of corruption. The Cardinal, with sadistic irony, finds in the painted body of his mistress, Julia, 'a grave, dark and obscure enough' to keep the secret of his complicity in the Duchess's murder (V, ii, 272–3). For Ferdinand, his sister's remarriage is a stroke which reduces his own body to a grave in which his heart is coffined:

> thou hast ta'en that massy sheet of lead
> That hid thy husband's bones, and folded it
> About my heart.   (III, ii, 112–14)[24]

As that telling 'hid' suggests, this is an image of secrecy as well as of morbidity: and what is hidden will not be fully revealed until, after the Duchess's death, 'The wolf shall find her grave, and scrape it up' (V, ii, 309). That wolf is to be none other than the demented Ferdinand himself, and the grave he digs in is, ultimately, his own morbid psyche. Lycanthropia is a monstrous literalisation not just of his passionate animality, but of his terrifying compulsion to exhume the secret corruptions of his heart:

> In those that are possess'd with't there o'erflows
> Such melancholy humour, they imagine
> Themselves to be transformed into wolves,
> Steal forth to churchyards in the dead of night
> And dig dead bodies up: as two nights since
> One met the Duke, 'bout midnight in a lane
> Behind St Mark's church, with the leg of a man
> Upon his shoulder; and he howl'd fearfully;
> Said he was a wolf, only the difference
> Was, a wolf's skin was hairy on the outside,
> His on the inside.   (v, ii, 8–18)

The inverted wolf-skin is both an image of secret viciousness and (in its recollection of the penitent's hair-shirt) of the hidden suffering that ensues from it. The imaginative connection between the horrors hidden in the grave and those within himself is underlined when the Duke is described as bidding his followers 'take their swords, / Rip up his flesh, and try' (ll. 18–19).

The scene envisaged here is clearly designed as a symbolic counter-point for Antonio's visit to the churchyard in the following scene. Both are grave-openings of a kind, reworkings of the *Visitatio Sepulchri* motif, in which the idea of resurrection is successively parodied and then (in a new secular fashion) triumphantly enacted. To the dazzled Ferdinand, with his 'cruel sore eyes' (IV, ii, 264; V, ii, 64) the grave offers up images of darkness and horror, tokens of that violated past which so haunts him; to Antonio it shows a luminous image of compassionate sorrow which 'lights the time to come'. For Antonio indeed, if not for Bosola, the Duchess's 'fair soul' is able to 'return ... from darkness' to lead him 'out of this sensible hell' (IV, ii, 342–3).

The full meaning of the echo scene is shaped by Antonio's moralisation on the ruined abbey:

>   I do love these ancient ruins:
> We never tread upon them but we set
> Our foot upon some reverend history.
> And questionless, here in this open court,
> Which now lies naked to the injuries
> Of stormy weather, some men lie interr'd
> Lov'd the church so well, and gave so largely to't,
> They thought it should have canopy'd their bones
> Till doomsday; but all things have their end:
> Churches and cities, which have diseases like to men,
> Must have like death that we have.   (v, iii, 9–19)

Here images of ruin and tomb come together to provide an emblem of vanity, its irony redoubled by Antonio's ignorance of who lies buried in this yard. When the mysterious echo chimes into his thoughts with '*Like death that we have*', it sounds the admonitory note of an epitaph ('As I am now, so shalt thou be ...'). Yet paradoxically its 'deadly accent', in sounding to Antonio 'like my wife's voice' (l. 26), challenges the simple *memento mori*, returning us from the mortal corruption of grave and ruin to the transcendent symbolism of monument.

'The ancientest *nobility*', Wester's dedication insists, is 'but a *relic* of time past'; inherited honour, as it were, makes a man but the tomb of an ancestor's glory, 'the truest *honour* indeed being for a man to confer *honour* on himself'; 'every worthy man' as Middleton's encomium puts it 'is his own marble'. *The Duchess of Malfi* enacts the debate on the nature of greatness foreshadowed in this prefatory material. At one extreme it presents the pride of lineage represented by the Aragonian brothers, for whom their sister's crime unpardonably taints 'our blood / The royal blood of Aragon and Castile' (II, v, 21–2); at the other it places the cynical subversiveness of Bosola, who (like many an alienated Jacobean intellectual) has made his Montaigne the bible of a degraded scepticism:[25]

> a duke was your cousin-german removed: – say you were lineally descended from King Pepin . . . what of this? search the heads of the greatest rivers in the world, you shall find them but bubbles of water. Some would think the souls of princes were brought forth by some more weighty causes than those of meaner persons – they are deceived, there's the same hand to them, the same reason that makes a vicar go to law for a tithe-pig and undo his neighbours, makes them spoil a whole province, and batter down cities with the canon.
>
> (II, i, 96–107)

It is in part Bosola's activity which brings Antonio to the despairing perception that '*The great are like the base; – nay, they are the same*' (II, iii, 51); just as it is Bosola who undercuts the Duchess's last attempt to proclaim her royal self:

> *Duchess.* Am not I thy duchess?
> *Bosola.* Thou art some great woman, sure, for riot begins to sit on thy forehead, clad in grey hairs, twenty years sooner than on a merry milkmaid's . . .
> *Duchess.* I am Duchess of Malfi still.
> *Bosola.* That makes thy sleeps so broken:
> *Glories, like glow-worms, afar off shine bright,*
> *But look'd to near, have neither heat, nor light.*   (IV, ii, 135–45)

Yet it is precisely at this moment that he chooses to cast himself in the ambiguous role of a tomb maker whose 'trade is to flatter the dead' (ll. 147–8). And there is another side to Bosola's cynicism which emerges, curiously enough, in the course of his attempt to persuade the Duchess to betray her husband. When she seeks to parry his effusive praise of Antonio with an evasive 'But he was basely descended' (III, ii, 258), Bosola comes back with what may at first appear to be a stock reply culled from the pages of *Arcadia:*

> Will you make yourself a mercenary herald,
> Rather to examine men's pedigrees than virtues?
>
> (III, ii, 259–60)

But the sentiment answers closely to his rankling sense of neglect in the world of courtly reward; and it is this which fuels his subsequent reflections on Antonio's fate with an emotion powerful enough to overwhelm the Duchess's caution. Her confession – 'O, you render me excellent music . . . / This good one that you speak of is my husband' (ll. 274–5) – while it tells Bosola what he most wants to know, at the same time deals a crippling blow to his cynical composure. His reply registers genuine wonder, astonishment at this profound shock to his construction of the world, as well as the simple excitement of discovery:

> Do I not dream? can this ambitious age
> Have so much goodness in't, as to prefer
> A man merely for worth, without these shadows
> Of wealth, and painted honours? possible?
>   (III, ii, 276–9)

It is true that there is a degree of comic exaggeration in what follows, as though the old sardonic Bosola were reasserting his ironic control:

>   you have made your nuptial bed
> The humble and fair seminary of peace:
> No question but many an unbenefic'd scholar
> Shall pray for you for this deed . . . .
> . . . . The virgins of your land
> That have no dowries, shall hope your example
> Will raise them to rich husbands: should you want
> Soldiers, 'twould make the very Turks and Moors
> Turn Christians, and serve you for this act.
>   (III, ii, 281–90)

But it is important, if Bosola's subsequent conversion is to seem convincingly motivated, that the irony be understood for what it is – self-mockery directed at an emotion as dangerous as it is unfamiliar.[26] It is telling that Bosola should be made to end the speech by reiterating the very theme announced in Webster's dedication:

> Last, the neglected poets of your time,
> In honour of this trophy of a man,
> Rais'd by that curious engine, your white hand,
> Shall thank you, in your grave, for't; and make that
> More reverend than all the cabinets
> Of living princes. For Antonio,
> His fame shall likewise flow from many a pen,
> When heralds shall want coats to sell to men.
>   (III, ii, 291–8)

For the audience, the irony is already disarmed by Webster's pen. Heraldry in this play is the art and property of madmen:

First Madman. I have skill in heraldry.
Second Madman. Hast?
First Madman. You do give for your crest a woodcock's head, with the brains
   picked out on't – you are a very ancient gentleman.   (IV, ii, 86–9)

That 'spirit of greatness' for which, in Cariola's eyes, her mistress seems to
stand (I, i, 504) is best defined, perhaps, in the fable which the Duchess offers
to Bosola after her arrest. Her persecutor, in the bitterness of his already
divided emotions, turns on Antonio, denouncing him as 'this base, low fellow
.... / One of no birth' (III, v, 117–19); the Duchess replies with a recapitulation of the very theme on which Bosola himself had earlier expatiated:

> Say that he was born mean:
> Man is most happy when's own actions
> Be arguments and examples of his virtue . . .
>
> I prithee, who is greatest? Can you tell?
>   (III, v, 119–23)

Her answer is the parable of the salmon and the dogfish:

> 'Our value never can be truly known
> Till in the fisher's basket we be shown;
> I'th'market then my price may be the higher,
> Even when I am nearest to the cook and fire.'
> So, to great men, the moral may be stretched:
> *Men oft are valued high, when th'are most wretched.*
>   (III, v, 136–41)

Her moral is precisely that with which Delio, confronted with the 'great ruin'
of the house of Aragon, will end the play:

> *Integrity of life is fame's best friend,*
> *Which nobly, beyond death, shall crown the end.*
>   (V, v, 120–1)

   The visible sign of this integrity is the Duchess's tomb, whose clear light of
fame illumines the dark world of 'these wretched eminent things'; while the
vanity of their 'quest of greatness' is expressed in the 'dead wall, or vaulted
graves' of the surrounding ruins, figuring forth the empty pride of that vast
pyramid to which Bosola compares the Cardinal.[27] But the Duchess's tomb is
itself only a cipher for the true monument which, Webster defiantly asserts,
will overtop and outlast the vain architecture of courtly grandeur. His
tragedy is a 'shrine' for that 'rich diamond', the Duchess, just as *A Monumental Columne* was for his beloved Prince Henry:

> For they shall live by them, when all the cost
> Of guilded Monuments shall fall to dust.

His *Duchess of Malfi* is the finely embellished tomb from which the echo of her
memory sounds.

NOTES

1. John Weever, *Ancient Funerall Monuments* (London, 1631), pp. 1–3, 18. Weever's book is the most extensive seventeenth-century treatment of the ideology of tombs. Weever begins his treatise by citing a whole series of *loci classici* for the trope of literature as monument, of which his own book is clearly meant as an exemplar, since it sets out to preserve for posterity a record of all those honourable men whose tombs Weever saw threatened by iconoclastic vandalism and the action of 'eating-times ruines'. Weever's 'To the Reader' is a long lament for the consequences of iconoclasm, 'by which inhumane, deformidable act, the honourable memory of many vertuous and noble persons deceased is extinguished, and the true understanding of divers Families in these realmes ... is thereby partly interrupted'. His book is thus in some sense both a work of heraldry and a work of history. Webster, on the other hand, opposes the monuments of art and the individual histories they record, to the vanities of heraldry.

2. Andrew Gurr, *The Shakespearean Stage, 1574–1642* (Cambridge University Press, 1970), p. 123.

3. See Glynne Wickham, *Early English Stages, 1300–1600*, 3 vols (London: Routledge & Kegan Paul, 1959–72), I, 244 and pl. XVI; II, i, 318 ff.

4. John Russell Brown (ed.), *The Duchess of Malfi*, The Revels Plays (London: Methuen, 1964). All citations are from this edition.

5. Glynne Wickham, 'Romance and Emblem: A Study in the Dramatic Structure of *The Winter's Tale*' in D. Galloway (ed.), *The Elizabethan Theatre III* (Toronto: Macmillan, 1972), pp. 82–99; 97.

6. Brown, *The Duchess of Malfi*; Robert Ornstein, *The Moral Vision of Jacobean Tragedy* (Madison and Milwaukee: University of Wisconsin Press, 1965); and the essays by Gunby and Baker-Smith in Brian Morris (ed.), *John Webster*, Mermaid Critical Commentaries (London: Ernest Benn, 1970), pp. 179–204, 205–28.

7. Gunby in Morris, *John Webster*, p. 181.

8. T. S. Eliot, *Selected Essays* (London: Faber, 1951), p. 117, makes the point negatively 'a very great literary and dramatic genius directed towards chaos'.

9. Inga-Stina Ekeblad (Ewbank), 'The "Impure Art" of John Webster' in G. K. and S. K. Hunter (eds), *John Webster*, Penguin Critical Anthologies (Harmondsworth: Penguin, 1969), pp. 202–21.

10. See Hereward T. Price, 'The Function of Imagery in Webster' in Hunter, *John Webster*, pp. 194–202.

11. Anne Lancashire (ed.), *The Second Maiden's Tragedy*, The Revels Plays (Manchester University Press, 1978), IV, iv, 42 s.d. Act V, scene ii of this play, in which the Lady's ghost appears beside her corpse, presumably required the services of the same waxwork artist who provided the figures for Webster's play. Perhaps he was that same Abraham Venderdorf who supplied the 'very curious-lie wrought' funeral effigy for Henry's hearse – see David M. Bergeron, 'The Restoration of Hermione in *The Winter's Tale*' in Carol McGinnis Kay and Henry E. Jacobs, *Shakespeare's Romances Reconsidered* (Lincoln and London: University of Nebraska Press, 1978), pp. 125–33 (p. 132). For further discussion of the *Second Maiden's Tragedy* tomb, see Bergeron. 'The Wax Figures in *The Duchess of Malfi*', *SEL*, 18 (1978), 331–9 (pp. 331–2).

12. Henslowe in Gurr, *The Shakespearean Stage*, p. 123.

13. For other examples see Michael Neill, '"Anticke Pageantrie": The Mannerist Art of *Perkin Warbeck*', *Renaissance Drama*, n.s. VII (1978), 117–50, and 'Massinger's Patriarchy: The Social Vision of *A New Way to Pay Old Debts*', forthcoming in *Renaissance Drama*, n.s. X (1981). Among *Malfi*'s encomiasts, Ford was to make elaborate use of the tomb motif in his own tragedy *Love's Sacrifice*, while Middleton was in all probability the author of *The Second Maiden's Tragedy* itself (see Lancashire's introduction to the Revels edition, pp. 19–23).

14. Middleton's reference to 'Death's cathedral palaces / Where royal ashes keep their court' will surely have evoked for Webster's readers Henry VII's Chapel at Westminster Abbey, where the King had recently interred his mother and eldest son. Middleton may have been responding to the play's own oblique allusion to these royal tombs – see below, pp. 76–7.

15. The subdued pun on *clarus* (clear / famous) picks up the significance of Webster's own 'clear light'.

16. See Brown's edition, pp. xvii–xviii, for discussion of the dating of the two works.

17. Citations from *A Monumental Columne* are from F. L. Lucas's edition of Webster's *Works*, 4 vols (London: Chatto & Windus, 1927).

18. For a similar view see M. C. Bradbrook, *John Webster Citizen and Dramatist* (London: Weidenfeld & Nicholson, 1980); pp. 3, 144, 147, 163.

19. See Wickham, 'Romance and Emblem', and Bergeron, 'The Restoration of Hermione'. Bergeron (p. 129) argues that Hermione's statue was probably mounted 'on some kind of tomb device'. *The Winter's Tale* may have been revised for its performance at Princess Elizabeth's wedding in the spring of 1613; and the connection between the two plays is strengthened by the possibility that Webster's Masque of Madmen in IV, ii drew on wedding masques written for the same occasion (see Brown's introduction, pp. xxxvi–xxxvii). Bergeron's description of the pageant-resurrection of Lord Mayor Farringdon in Munday's *The Triumphes of Golde* (1611) provides an interesting analogue for both plays. Both Bergeron, 'The Wax Figures' (pp. 332–3) and Joan M. Lord, '*The Duchess of Malfi*: "the Spirit of Greatness" and "of Woman"', *SEL*, 16 (1976), 305–17 (pp. 312–13) have seen a link between Hermione's statue and the waxworks of *Malfi*.

20. *The Duchess of Malfi*, I, i, 299; *A Monumental Columne*, ll. 4–5.

21. A further parallel with *The Duchess of Malfi* occurs at lines 162–5, where the presentation of Sorrow as a galley-slave and a victim of 'Court delaies' recalls Bosola's condition at the beginning of the play, and also the Duchess's speech at IV, ii, 27–30. See also Lucas's edition, II, 2 and III, 286–90. Brown (p. xxxv) traces the use of the echo itself to another elegy for the dead heir apparent, George Wither's *Prince Henry's Obsequies* (1612).

22. Ironically enough Ferdinand, in his parable of Reputation, Love and Death, ends by implicitly identifying himself with Reputation (III, ii, 130–6). The memorial function of the play is also noted by Bradbrook: 'If an overarching fable were to be sought for the whole play, it could be called a Masque of Good Fame' (*John Webster*, p. 164). Cf. Bergeron, 'The Wax Figures', p. 336.

23. Weever, *Funerall Monuments*, writes at length about the calculated ambiguity of monuments: of their epitaphs he says 'in them love was shewed to the deceased, memorie was continued to posteritie, friends were comforted, and the reader put

in minde of humane frailtie' (p. 9); the very Latin name for tomb, he maintains, points to this double aspect, since *sepulchra* is derived from *semi-pulchra* – 'halfe faire and beautifull; the externall part or superficies thereof being gloriously beautified and adorned; and having nothing within, but dreadfull darkenesse, loathsome stinke, and rottenesse of bones' (p. 9); and at the same time they were 'called by *S. Paul, Seminatio*, in the respect of the assured hope of resurrection' (p. 9). These ambiguities, for Weever, make the tomb especially valuable as an object of pious contemplation; and he even suggests that the contemporary taste for visiting not just the splendid royal monuments in Westminster Abbey, but the ruined and broken tombs in old monasteries, should be construed as a kind of spiritual exercise which 'puts us in mind of our mortalitie, and consequently brings us to unfained repentance' (p. 41). It is in exactly this spirit that Antonio visits the ruined monastery and its graves in Webster's play. For evidence of the continuing popularity of tombs and monuments as objects of resort, see Walter Pope, *The Life of Seth Lord Bishop of Salisbury* (London, 1697), p. 157: 'It is a Custom for the Servants of the Church upon all Holidays, *Sundays* excepted, betwixt the Sermon and Evening Prayers, to shew the Tombs, and Effigies of the Kings and Queens in Wax, to the meaner sort of People, who then flock thither from all the corners of the Town, and pay their Twopence to see *The Play of the Dead Volks*, as I have heard a *Devonshire* Clown not improperly call it' (cited by John Barnard in his edition of George Etherege, *The Man of Mode*, New Mermaids, London: Ernest Benn, 1979, p. 42).

24. Cf. Antonio at III, v, 91: 'my heart is turn'd to a heavy lump of lead'.
25. Brown cites the borrowing (Florio, II, xii) on p. 45.
26. Compare Flamineo's puzzled glimpse of an emotion he has systematically re-pressed in *The White Devil*: 'I have a strange thing in me, to th' which / I cannot give a name, without it be / Compassion' (v, iv, 113–15). Webster's interest in the consequence of unacknowledged or repressed feeling is most apparent in his treatment of Ferdinand's passion for his sister.
27. Cf. Joan Lord, '*The Duchess of Malfi*', p. 316: 'It is only from the Duchess's grave that an echo is heard . . . for her memory still reverberates in the minds of those who are left.'

The fate of the symbolic in *A Streetcar Named Desire**

KATHLEEN HULLEY

> To reconcile literature and theatre is not to compromise and lose something
> from each, but rather to understand what dramatic dialogue is and does, why
> words on the page are not the same in function as words on the stage. The
> methods of literary criticism may well be inappropriate by themselves: we are
> not judging the text but what the text makes the actors make the audience do.
> (J. L. Styan, *The Dynamics of Drama*)

Styan points out what we too often forget in writing about theatre: that
theatre does not exist except through the presence of an audience. Martin
Esslin tells us of an actress Max Frisch saw walking across a stage (see p. 3
above). She was simply walking, eating an apple, somewhere, anywhere.
However, because for Frisch she was walking across a stage, the moment
suddenly blazed with significance. For Frisch the important element was the
stage; for me, it is the presence of Frisch. If he had not been there, as
audience, the event would have had no meaning at all. The sacred powers of
the stage are utterly dependent on the presence of an audience which tacitly
agrees that what happens on the stage is *not* life but its magic simulacrum.

Because of this convention, the stage is the semiotic space par excellence.
Every artifact, every gesture, every word on the stage is symbolic because
nothing on the stage refers to itself; by its very presence on the stage, the
simplest chair becomes a symbol of reality, but is not reality. It gestures away
from itself and toward a world exactly like ours but elsewhere. The stage *re-*
presents reality; it doubles it, but it is not it.

Theatre is thus nothing but a system of signs, a crossroads through which
the symbolic functions. Nothing on stage has meaning except through the
presence of an audience. Thus the theatre is the space where we see functioning what O. Mannoni has called 'l'autre scène'.[1] The concept of *the other scene*
is useful because it uses the structure of theatre to demonstrate the structure
of desire in three ways. First of all, what is on the stage points to another
scene, just as desire must always be for what is absent. Secondly, the stage
points to that absent scene only because of the presence of the *other* – the

* A draft of this paper was read at the *Themes in Drama* International Conference on 'Drama and
Symbolism' held at the University of California, Riverside, in May 1980.

play's audience, the desired object – to whom the play, or desire, is directed. Finally, the distinction between the objects on the stage and the objects in the 'real' world is possible only because the members of the audience share a discourse, not their own, but that which makes of them an audience so that, like desire, they are created by a culture or ideology outside themselves. This last *other* is the language of codes and conventions into which we are born and which we acquire in learning to speak. It is through this discourse that we define ourselves as 'normal', 'male', 'female', 'audience', and so on. Without reference to the *other scene*, neither theatre nor desire exists.

Theatre demonstrates, therefore, that signs do not signify; rather, one sign points to another sign. Neither has meaning except in an ecology of relationships. Because of this ecology, the theatrical artifact functions as a 'trace' in the Derridian sense; it marks an absence, it makes possible what has not yet come into existence, it marks the *other scene*.

Derrida says of the 'trace':

> *The (pure) trace is differance* [sic]. It does not depend on any sensible plenitude, audible or visible, phonic or graphic. It is, on the contrary, the condition of such plenitude. Although it *does not exist*, although it is never a *being-present* outside of all plenitude, its possibility is by rights anterior to all that one calls sign . . .[2]

The sign on stage functions like the trace because its emptiness marks the possibility of desire so that desire may exist.

In *Streetcar* Blanche's neurotic symptoms do the same work as the trace in language: they have no meaning but they create the condition for meaning. Elia Kazan, the director of the first major production of the play, conceived of the character of Blanche as a series of roles and changing masks which called to the powers of belief in the characters around her.[3] But *Streetcar* is more than a series of changing masks; it is a series of productions or stagings in which each of the central characters – Blanche, Stella, Stanley – interchanges the positions of actor, director and audience. This interchange empties any sign or role of meaning and places meaning in the play's audience. Any 'reality' to which the stage refers is purely a construction of its audience.

Alvin B. Kernan points out that the 'play turns on a fundamental similarity between life and the stage, and the problem of an individual constructing a life and an author constructing a play'.[4] If this is so, the play leaves in suspension any solid base for meaning; both the scene and its points of reference (life) are 'constructions'. Because *Streetcar* makes this analogy between life and theatre specific, it represents, doubles, and thereby deconstructs the process by which meaning is produced.

The process is dramatized through a deconstruction of the forces controlling desire. The first of these Williams treats thematically through the relation between desire and hysteria. The second of these is the symbolic level of Williams's manipulation of our relation to the setting. The third is ideological as he represents the function of the audience's interpretation of desire.

The epigraph of *Streetcar* is from Hart Crane:

> And so it was I entered the broken world,
> To trace the visionary company of love, its voice
> An instant in the wind (I know not whither hurled)
> But not for long to hold each desperate choice.

This citation directs us to Williams's thematic and structural concerns: the brevity and incompleteness of desire. The poem reflects a fractured Platonism – the world we know merely shadows the traces of an ideal love which we grasp only in fragments. More importantly, that broken world is exactly analogous to theatre – a partial space we enter to watch a shadow play which represents some other desired space.

The thematic level – hysteria – gives rise to important issues of the play. Freud has suggested that hysteria produces signs or symptoms which are both signs of the disease and signs of the causes of the disease, but not, in fact, either.[5] Thus, a symptom, like the mask, points both away from and toward itself. According to Mannoni, hysterical symptoms, such as those that Blanche manifests, are a series of roles or masks which hide an absence. In *Clefs pour l'imaginaire*, Mannoni describes the close relation between the masks of hysteria and the masks of theatre:

> The subjects who are termed histrionic represent themselves 'dramatically'; they play the roles of love, jealousy, outraged honor as well as mourning or jubilation in order to defend themselves against an insufficiency in experience – against the feeling of their own nothingness.[6]

In theatre, on the contrary, even though the actor plays a number of roles, none of which is his own, the conventions of the stage allow the roles, which mark an absence, to assure us of the presence of *something* elsewhere. The actor playing love is not in love, but he assures us that love exists because it can be indicated. The difference between the absence behind the hysteric's roles and the absence behind the actor's roles lies not in the roles but in the *conventions* which govern the audience of theatre and the audience of hysteria.

It is precisely because of these theatrical conventions that the symbolic register of *Streetcar* begins with the initial setting of the play. We enter the play through a series of specifications which are ambiguously 'realistic': the street is named 'Elysian Fields', the streetcar named 'Desire'.[7] The house, 'weathered grey with rickety outside stairs and galleries', sits on a most unnatural street. The sky is tinted an artificial shade of 'tender blue, almost turquoise', and a blues piano provides unceasing background music, drowning out the more realistic sounds of the river and the railroad (both unseen).

Two women, one white one black, guard the entrance, and their opening dialogue overlays a surrealistic montage of disconnected, meaningless fragments – 'St Barnabus', 'Blue Moon Cocktails', 'Red Hots', 'Four Deuces', the sound of prostitutes tapping at shutters. This set is meant to indicate reality, but it increasingly functions as a mask.

Indeed, in scene iii, Williams heightens the artificiality, insisting that the set look nothing like reality but like a Van Gogh painting – a representation of a representation. This accumulating artificiality subtly disarms the viewer by a gradual shift toward unreality: we must disavow a realistic set just as we must disavow a real face – 'that is not me', we say, in relief; we do not feel impelled to disavow a mask. Thus, the set subverts our defenses against whatever it, in fact, does represent, as it allows the emotional and psychic symbols of the play to speak to us directly.

Finally, the artificial aspect of the opening scene has one other function; it creates the community of *otherness* among the members of the audience. The play calls to the audience from other texts – from mythology, from conventional symbolism, from poetic tradition. 'Elysian Fields', for example, is no more than a street sign, but because of the community of literary tradition it refers ironically to another text. This reference both unifies the audience and draws it into the construction of the scene.

The theme of hysteria and the set's artificiality are, indeed, both rhetorical devices which indicate 'this is just make-believe'; the play's reality lies, as Blanche knows only too well, in the audience. The meaning of the production devolves, therefore, on the ideology of another scene which gives the theatrical sign its power. This ideology also makes of the audience the functioning pivot between the paradoxical unity of the *signified* and its *signifier* on the one hand, and the impossibility of their identity on the other. The problem is that if the audience is the center of meaning, its power is contradictory, for the audience is both utterly subjective and utterly conventional. The subjective aspect of the audience runs the risk of allowing unlimited meaning while the conventional aspect runs the risk of tyrannizing meaning. Blanche's ability to shift masks is Williams's mode for exploring both the dangers and the freedom inherent in the audience's construction of meaning.

In *Jokes and Their Relation to the Unconscious*, Freud states that the pleasure we feel when suddenly released from the necessity to 'make sense' or behave within the syntax of convention can verge on ecstasy.[8] The unrestrained production of meaning, which the shifting categories of humor imply, allows a glimpse of perfect freedom – a moment of absolute revolt against the prevailing codes of order, that primal moment when the world is simultaneously unified and unbound.

However, the implications of the freedom Blanche enacts mirror the dangerous aspects of our own role as audience. For the hysteric's assertion that any role simply represents another role, which can signify yet another role in an infinitely opening series of reflections, suggests that the 'real' can never be reached, only signified. The origin of signification lies always beyond, absent, yet continually producing signs of its existence.

It is clear that both the symptoms in hysteria and the act of interpretation rest on the assumption that, in Mannoni's terms, 'one thing can always represent another'.[9] To interpret is to suppose that in the scene there is a meaning which lies beyond the scene. Commentary reveals not what is said but what was *meant* to be said, and echoes the convention that the signifier represents something other than itself. Theatre, hysteria and commentary spring from the same assumptions about the nature of meaning: that meaning lies beyond what is revealed, and is absent from what is present. These assumptions, once again, place the audience in the dominant position because they fill with significance the emptiness opened by the sign.

In *Streetcar* the shifting categories of meaning are carefully structured through a shifting series of texts and contexts, each of which displaces the other and each of which puts context-making into the forefront. The first *textual* context is Crane's epigraph, which makes of the reading a literary experience. The first *scenic* context is the rickety house framed by its street with its artificial name, the whole framed by the sounds of the street. The walls of the Kowalski house are organized like a stage within a stage – its two rooms the simultaneous scene of different productions, each played against the other. The bathroom suggests, ironically, a behind-the-scenes scene where various roles, lines, entrances and exits are prepared. The house itself is framed by illusory walls which dissolve in the climactic moment; while the stage frames the set, the audience frames the stage, and the world, to which the stage refers, bustles indifferently outside.

Blanche erupts into this claustrophobic setting like a wild atom from another molecular structure – that 'Belle Reve' which never was. But she has already been carefully placed in the opening scene. As the two women in scene i joke about Stanley and Stella, it is clear not only that Stanley 'has taught Stella to catch his meat', as Ruby Cohn so aptly puts it,[10] but also that this relation is communally fixed and ritualized. Blanche is an intruder in a functioning community. It is not her arrival, but the disjunction we are made to perceive between Blanche and the setting that unleashes the chain of action and sets the streetcar named Desire on its wild course.

It is this disjunction which threatens the boundaries of the permissible and puts the seat of power, both within and without the play, in jeopardy. Blanche is literally and symbolically dangerous because she is too multivalent to be contained; she opens too many possibilities.

Clearly she is disruptive because no matter what she is – fake or genuine, whore or puritan, even sane or insane – she multiplies desire. She herself wants too much – too many men, too much money, her irretrievable youth, purity, love, a home. She wants the reversal of time, two things at once, the impossible, the non-linear, the forbidden. Moreover, she multiplies desire in others: she makes Stella, for the first time, dissatisfied with Stanley; she offers Mitch escape from his sickly mother; she flirts with Stanley. While Williams creates tremendous sympathy for Blanche's longing for 'what *ought* to be true', he has Blanche explicitly equate uncontrolled desire with death – the ultimate loss of identity and meaning. Blank and uncontrolled herself, Blanche erases the marks and codes which make human community possible.

From the moment Blanche and Stanley encounter each other, the play becomes a struggle between them for control of these codes. They do not struggle for territory, but to define what territory will signify. They compete with one another to produce a staging which will elicit from Stella and Mitch the desired definition of territory.

Blanche walks into Stanley's set and begins rearranging his scene. Her trunk is full of costumes for her own varied parts, and she assigns roles to everyone else as well. Stella must become the discontented wife; Mitch, Blanche's 'Rosenkavalier'; the young boy, her 'prince from Arabian Nights'. Stanley, Blanche says, is 'simple, straightforward, and honest, a little on the primitive side', a 'man'. For Blanche, this is not an assessment, it is the role she assigns Stanley.

The success of Blanche's staging depends on her audience. If they believe, her play becomes 'what *ought* to be'; if they do not, it remains false. We have seen that the audience is an audience only by a set of conventions which are established by the codes of theatre. Therefore, while there are various possible interpretations of the signs emitted on the stage, the audience is bound to interpret those signs only within the codes of the play and the codes of theatre. As a result, the play balances not so much, as Kernan has suggested, on the 'difference between truth and falsehood, real and illusion',[11] as it does on the *discourse* about truth or falsehood, real or illusion. Consequently, the play dramatizes that meaning can be shifted when framed by varying social codes and conventions. Thus, the central issue of *Streetcar* is not merely meaning, but the structure of power that gives a sign a context which determines its meaning. Williams explores this structure by dramatizing the issue of contextual control in the theme of sexual control.

There is nothing new in this. Control of social context has always been an issue, in part at any rate, of sexual control. Lévi-Strauss has pointed out that, because the incest prohibition is universal, it is fundamental to any social order.[12] However what is important about this prohibition is not its context, but its negative function. The incest prohibition is the *NO* which bars desire from unlimited production; it is the law which makes social exchange, and therefore communication, possible. According to this theory then, the social contract, which makes meaning possible, is the map of permissible desire.

Stanley makes explicit the interdependence of contextual and sexual control when he transforms Blanche's 'make-believe' about the past into 'lies'. Furthermore, when he takes over the definition of Blanche's sexuality, he exchanges his role as audience to her play for the role of producer of his own. This interchange itself is a semantic act which limits the field of meaning where desire can function. Stanley maps out Blanche's area and determines her future.

However, Stanley's definition is more than simply one other possible meaning. Stanley lays down the *law* which makes meaning possible. Without law to mark the *différance*, the ecology of the sign collapses. Thus, when Blanche provokes Stanley's resistance, she invites the block which makes the symbolic function. Neither she, nor her symptom/symbols can continue to produce without limit; the end of such production is the end of meaning.

Nevertheless, though Williams has Stanley impose the law necessary to meaning, Williams does not necessarily support the meaning Stanley imposes. Indeed, as Stanley and Blanche wrestle for control of the context, they dramatize several possible strategies for dealing with the symbolic. Blanche's desire may be subversive, but she invites an imaginative interpretation which will form her flood of signs into some vision of the good and the beautiful. The illusions she creates call to the transformative powers of her audience. Indeed, she invites Mitch to share with her the creative moment which would have made love possible. Stanley's law, on the contrary, blocks creativity and puts an end to love. His vision is both anti-dialectic and anti-metaphoric. He restricts the powers of the symbolic function to their most socially expedient level.

Neither Blanche nor Stanley, therefore, is able to play in the interface between desire and the law. Each is excessive in need; neither grows toward a lucid relation to the construction of reality. Consequently, neither paradox nor contradiction has energy in Williams's world. Instead, in *Streetcar* Williams presents a fundamentally enraged vision of a sterile world where meaning has become merely a function of social use.

The power Stanley draws upon to fix meaning resides in three locations: in the characters, in the setting, and in the audience. These three loci determine the control of desire along socially useful lines and allow Williams to expose what he sees as the mechanisms of repression in the dominant system of meaning.

First of all, the characters who surround Blanche and Stanley – Stella, Mitch, Steve, Eunice, the poker players – function as the chorus. They witness events and elevate the quarrel between Blanche and Stanley to the level of ritual by making it significant to the surrounding community. But the choral function depends on stability. It is impossible for the chorus to make events significant without a fixed point from which to view the shifting possibilities. Its ceaseless demand for limits implies that when desire exceeds bounds, both the community and the function of the chorus disintegrate. Chorus and community are each founded on a principle of prohibition.

The chorus must construct the social myth of 'reality' and exclude any threat to that myth. In this function, the chorus dramatizes the conventional basis which creates the play's audience. Furthermore, the chorus deconstructs the hermeneutic function of convention; the chorus both extends meaning beyond the personal and limits that meaning.

When the chorus in *Streetcar* allows Stanley to exclude Blanche, it allows the exclusion of that which makes love and art possible. Instead, it limits the possible interpretations of Blanche's roles to their most fundamental level and destroys any rapprochement between the demands of art and the demands of community.

However, if Blanche and Stanley fail to resolve this issue, Williams does not. His setting functions in opposition to his theme by subverting the opening 'order' of the setting. The play begins with clear distinctions between inside and out, home and street, marriage and prostitution, black and white. But by scene iii Williams has already shifted the context of his set so that it no longer represents reality, but art. By the end of scene v, the set has moved entirely inward to represent Blanche's subjectivity. The set continues to fluctuate between representing 'reality' and 'unreality' until scene x when the walls dissolve and hellish flames shadow the room while the *Varsovia* of Blanche's memories dominates any exterior sound; all pretense of order disappears. Instead, nothing holds together and nothing holds apart.

The disintegration at the level of setting is thematically mirrored in Stanley's trangression. When he rapes his wife's sister, he too exceeds the limits of his world. At this climactic moment, every category is threatened; desire transcends bounds. Music, light, space collude in a cacaphony of disorder.

As the walls dissolve in scene x, the chorus loses its place; there is no longer an outside or an inside in which to locate, and the choral function shifts to the audience, which is, by convention, 'outside'. This is the crucial moment for the audience, the moment in which either it allows the disintegration to continue or it restores order. This is the moment when each member of the audience decides either that Blanche has gotten what she asked for, or that Stanley's insensitive dominance exceeds any sympathy. No matter which attitude we adopt, however, to choose is to carve space up once again into socially acceptable territories. Any judgement grants power to Stanley; even to hate him is to impose limits on the unbearable violation.

Stella, in the last scene, occupies a position analogous to the audience; she deconstructs the relation between the subjective and conventional limits of the symbol. Like the audience she has been watching a play performed for another – Blanche's 'play for' Mitch. Like the audience, she knows more about Blanche's play than does Blanche's intended audience. In this position

Stella can form the point of view which will allow Blanche's 'play' to continue, or which will terminate it.

When Blanche's play begins, Stella supports any production so long as she, Stella, feels secure. Judgements about truth or falsehood do not concern her at all. Her problem arises only when it becomes evident that Stanley is staging a different production for the same audience, and that she must choose. She cannot allow both meanings to go on simultaneously without putting her own *mise en scène* in jeopardy.

Stella is forced to take a position and thus frame a context for the conflict between desire and community which have been polarized by Blanche's and Stanley's relation to the symbolic. Unfortunately, Stella must destroy either her marriage or her sister. Furthermore to choose to believe Blanche is to choose desire but destroy the scene of its expression. To believe Stanley is to secure that scene but empty it of desire. Either choice is cruel; but the disorder created by Blanche and Stanley destroys Stella's privileged neutrality and demands action.

When she restores order by choosing, Stella unmasks the simultaneously repressive and creative function of our own interpretative position. Repression is dramatized by the isolation and expulsion of Blanche's boundless desire; creation lies in Stella's very choice. Though her security has been bought at the price of desire, the moment she chooses Stella begins staging her own drama – 'The Happy Marriage of Stanley and Stella Kowalski'.

Because her choice is responsible for the play's outcome, the play's ironic conclusion belongs not to Stanley but to Stella. 'I couldn't believe her story and go on living with Stanley', Stella cries. She is not deluded by Stanley; rather, her decision is the deliberate preservation of social order. No longer innocent or passive, she too adopts a mask, which by its very presence points ironically to the absence of what it represents.

The capacity of theatre to shift categories and contextual frames, which Brecht for example so consciously manipulated, is the same capacity more conventional playwrights have used, at least tacitly, to multiply meanings. The conventions of the stage by which a sign both is and is not what it represents depend entirely on the audience which allows the sign to point in two directions at the same time.

No message, of course, carries meaning without a receiver who shares approximately the same code and context as the sender. The strength of theatre as opposed to any other message system is that the audience which renders the semiotic system on stage significant has no existence as 'audience' except by a prior ideology which renders a 'real' person on stage an 'unreal' character. Thus, theatre functions within the same code that defines 'reality' and whatever lies beyond it, enabling us to examine the conventions of 'reality' in a way no other message system can.

Williams deconstructs this function of theatre by beginning with a set that signifies 'reality' and which poses little threat to the audience: the stage is 'there' and 'unreal', the audience is 'here' and 'real'. The life-like aspects of his set allow the members of the audience to remain unaware of the dramatization of their own role; they remain outside events, 'objective'. Taken strictly at the realistic level, *Streetcar* is about the triumph of Stanley's and Stella's desire.

But Williams undercuts the set's duplicitous surface and subverts the illusion of safety, first by transforming the set into an artificial, unreal space which functions like a mask to disarm the audience; second, by handing the choral function over to the audience; and finally, by using Stella to reveal that no audience is in fact 'safe'. We are all implicated in the play's meaning, whatever that may be.

Because *Streetcar* is a play about conflicting theatrical productions by the various characters, the action on the stage mirrors the action of the audience watching the play. By doubling that action, the play *re*-presents the audience/stage relationship and brings into evidence the conventions by which the audience creates the distinction between 'life' and 'theatre'. At this level, *Streetcar* is not about the wild triumph of desire, but about desire's destruction. Desire is simply another form of theatre, dependent on social convention for its existence, and therefore in bondage to its social function.

Desire is, indeed, replete at the end of the play. Stella is pregnant; family and community will continue. But as Stanley fumbles at Stella's blouse, he has lost his virile stature and seems like a child at his mother's breast; Stella's luxurious weeping is not a lapsing back to the darkness of desire, but grief at her irrevocable loss. The streetcar which brought Blanche to the Kowalski household is not named 'Desire', it is named 'Cemeteries', and its destination is the land of the dead.

Streetcar draws analogies between the social control of desire and the conventional functioning of theatre in order to represent the death of desire. The problem Williams presents is that to limit the productive power of the symbol is repressive, while to allow the symbol unlimited power is chaos. By representing the either/or categories of contextual control through the death of desire, Williams surpasses the issues of 'sane' or 'insane', 'truth' or 'illusion' to expose the ambivalent social law which makes those terms significant.

NOTES

1. O. Mannoni, *Clefs pour l'imaginaire ou l'autre scène* (Paris: Editions de Minuit, 1967).
2. Jacques Derrida, *Of Grammatology*, trans. Gayatri Chakravorty Spivak (Baltimore and London: Johns Hopkins University Press, 1974), p. 62.
3. Elia Kazan, 'A Notebook for *A Streetcar Named Desire*', in *Directors on Directing*, ed. Toby Cole (Indianapolis: Bobbs Merrill Co., 1963).

4. Alvin B. Kernan, 'Truth and Dramatic Mode in the Modern Theatre: Chekhov, Pirandello, and Williams', *Modern Drama*, 1 (Sept. 1958), 113.

5. Sigmund Freud, *Dora: An Analysis of a Case of Hysteria* (New York: Collier Books, 1963), pp. 149–57.

6. Mannoni, *Clefs pour l'imaginaire*, p. 302. My translation. The original text reads: 'Les sujets qu'on appelle *histrioniques* ... représentent ainsi dramatiquement l'amour, la jalousie, l'honneur outragé, mais aussi le deuil ou la jubilation, parce qu'ils se défendent contre l'insuffisance de ce qu'ils éprouvent, contre le sentiment de leur néant.'

7. Friends of mine from the south tell me there are both a street named 'Elysian Fields' and a streetcar named 'Desire'. Nevertheless, to those of us who live outside that linguistically fanciful region, and despite the fame of the Champs Elysées, those names are both literary and ironically symbolic.

8. Sigmund Freud, *Jokes and Their Relation to the Unconscious* (New York: Norton Library, 1963), p. 118.

9. Mannoni, *Clefs pour l'imaginaire*, pp. 202–3.

10. Ruby Cohn, 'The Garrulous Grotesques of Tennessee Williams', *Dialogue in American Drama* (Bloomington: Indiana University Press, 1971), p. 106.

11. Kernan, 'Truth and Dramatic Mode in the Modern Theatre'.

12. Claude Lévi-Strauss, *The Elementary Structures of Kinship*, trans. James Harle Bell, John Richard von Sturmer, and Rodney Needham (ed.) (Boston: Beacon Press, 1969), p. 25.

Memory and betrayal: the symbolic landscape of *Old Times*

ARTHUR E. McGUINNESS

Phenomena in Harold Pinter's plays vibrate with overtones of otherness, but one is hard put to fix a single symbolic 'meaning' to any of them, the way one can to Tennessee Williams's glass menagerie or Eliot's cocktail party. And yet the rooms, the dumb waiter, the statue of Buddha, Jack Straw's Castle, Bolsover Street are all clearly more than objects and places. The problem of symbolic interpretation is especially acute in *Old Times*, perhaps Pinter's most enigmatic play. *Old Times* has a full measure of potentially symbolic phenomena – Anna's villa in Sicily, the menacing park near which the two girls worked as secretaries in London, Kate's baths, the exchange of under-wear, the old songs, the film *Odd Man Out*, the softness of the seaside as against the hard lines of the city. Conscious of the fact that any interpretation will somewhat compromise the quality of tentativeness which Pinter values, this essay will propose as a plausible meaning a deep structure in *Old Times*, a structure of psychological games played to the death. Places and objects in the play illuminate this deep structure.

Anna, Kate and Deeley belong to Pinter's walking wounded. Mortally afflicted with psychological obsessions – lesbianism, voyeurism, sado-masochism – they seek dominance and the momentary satisfaction it brings through what might be called 'creative memory'. Each offers a version of the past which triggers perverse psychic energies. Each exists entirely alone, though part of a complex sexual trio. The aggressors, Anna and Deeley, become the prey at the end of the action. Kate, the dormant intended victim, is roused by acts of betrayal to dominate and even 'kill' her own victims. Anna and Deeley, hunters turned hunted, are psychologically satisfied at the end of the play by Kate's compulsive acts of vengeance.

One can never be sure in *Old Times* about the reality of the reported past. It may be entirely a fiction made up to induce psychic states, or it may be true. As Anna says mid-way through the play, 'There are some things one remembers even though they may never have happened. There are things I remember which may never have happened but as I recall them so they take place.'[1] One could conclude from statements about the past in the play that Kate and Anna were once intimate in ways going beyond normal 'friend-

ship'. Anna refers to Kate as a 'parson's daughter' with Brontëesque needs for
passion and secrecy (p. 64). Though their giddy social lives as young London
secretaries twenty years before make them appear quite conventional types,
their private lives involved fetishism and voyeurism. Anna wore Kate's
underwear and reported back to her 'shy' roommate the behavior of those
like Deeley who had 'gazed' up her thighs. But Anna made the mistake of
falling in love with Deeley (p. 70). To punish her, Kate seduced Deeley and,
though she had no feelings for him, married him. Now Anna, unhappily
married herself, has returned to seek a rapprochement with Kate.

Deeley and Anna at first believe they can master Kate and they compete
for her attention. Kate, a vacant and powerless dormouse, seems an unlikely
object of their efforts. Before the dimly present Anna formally 'appears' on
the scene, Deeley queries Kate about her relations with Anna during their
'old times' in London. Deeley learns that the two 'lived together' (p. 18) and
that Anna used to steal Kate's underwear. Kate functions entirely as an
object mirroring Anna's and Deeley's sexual fantasies. As Kate puts it
toward the end of act 1, 'You talk of me as if I were dead ... you talk about
me as if I *am* dead. Now' (pp. 34–5). Neither Anna nor Deeley experiences
Kate as an actual person. They merely want her to keep alive their quite
different fantasies of sexual intimacy in the 'old times'.

Kate's self-image belies these perverse sexual fantasies of Anna and
Deeley. She does not wish to become a clearly defined object, preferring to
languish in her own fantasy of indefiniteness. She has moved out of the bustle
of the city to a country house near the sea. She perceives herself as a creature
without defined limits, someone who would be happier in a culture where
the lines of individuality were not so sharply drawn.

> *Kate.* .... I like living in the country. Everything's softer. The water, the light,
> the shapes, the sounds. There aren't such edges here. And living close to the
> sea too. You can't say where it begins or ends. That appeals to me. I don't
> care for harsh lines. I deplore that kind of urgency. I'd like to go to the East,
> or somewhere like that. .... The only nice thing about a big city is that when
> it rains it blurs everything, and it blurs the lights from the cars, doesn't it,
> and blurs your eyes ...   (p. 59)

Kate shies away from 'urgency', the sort of obsessive energy directed at her
by Anna and Deeley.

The nature and structure of these energies are suggested in an apposite
series of love songs which Anna and Deeley sing to Kate, the songs themselves being a bit of 'old times'. The familiar lyrics accomplish two things in
the play. First, they distinguish Deeley's and Anna's fantasies about Kate.
Deeley's male fantasy involves possession and dominance. Anna's female
fantasy has a subtler character, a desire for spiritual intimacy rather than
physical possession. Second, the songs foreshadow the major revelation in
the play as the aggressive bravado of the two hunters is revealed to be the
thinly-disguised cries of lonely and desperate people.

Deeley. Blue moon, I saw you standing alone . . .
Anna. The way you comb your hair . . .
Deeley. Oh no they can't take that away from me . . .
Anna. Oh but you're lovely, with your smile so warm . . .
Deeley. I've got a woman crazy for me. She's funny that way.
       [*Slight pause*]
Anna. You are the promised kiss of springtime . . .
Deeley. And someday I'll know that moment divine,
       When all the things you are, are mine! . . .
       . . . .
       When a lovely flame dies . . .
Anna. Smoke gets in your eyes.
       [*Pause*]
Deeley. The sigh of midnight trains in empty stations . . .
       [*Pause*]
Anna. The park at evening when the bell has sounded . . .
       [*Pause*]
Deeley. The smile of Garbo and the scent of roses . . .
Anna. The waiters whistling as the last bar closes . . .
Deeley. Oh, how the ghost of you clings . . .

                                                        (pp. 27–9)

These bright romantic illusions darken as the songs go on and the con-
tingencies of time are revealed. Time passes. A lovely flame dies. The station
empties, 'the last bar closes'. The romantic moments are 'old times' which
exist only in memory.

Memory, then, becomes in *Old Times* a means of ordering the random
ephemerality of life. But memory provides no reliable exposition in this play.
After the songs, which express generalized, conventional memories, the three
characters get down to what will be the major business of the play, namely, a
contest of memories to determine whose fantasy will be most fully played out,
whose 'old times' will prevail. First, one hears Deeley's memory of the time
he went to see the movie *Odd Man Out* and met Kate. He also 'remembers'
meeting Anna in the Wayfarer's Tavern. Anna first 'remembers' the time
when she and Kate were 'innocent secretaries' in London, and then 'remembers' a sobbing man in the bedroom she and Kate shared. Kate, at the
end of the play, 'remembers' quite a different version of their shared past.
Each of these versions of the past sounds plausible. One never knows for
certain what actually happened, but one infers from the devastating impact
Kate's version has on the other two members of the trio that her 'memory'
contains the deepest truth about exploitation and betrayal.

The least aware of the three, Deeley, recalls what he takes to be an act of
male dominance, picking up a girl at a movie. 'I thought Jesus this is it, I've
made a catch, this is a trueblue pickup' (p. 30). In fact, when one later hears
the memories of Anna and Kate, one realizes that Deeley has very likely been
'picked up' himself, in the sense of being exploited for another's sexual needs.
His memories do not include Anna's adventures wearing Kate's underwear,

Kate's eagerness to share Anna's exploits vicariously, or Kate's feelings of betrayal when Anna falls in love with a man who has gazed up her thighs. Anna and Kate have shared 'old times' long before Deeley enters their lives.

There is much enigmatic detail in Deeley's speech, his longest in the play (pp. 29–31). He recalls seeing the movie *Odd Man Out* in a neighborhood which he closely associates with his father, where his father bought him his first tricycle. He also recalls two usherettes in the foyer of the cinema, one of them stroking her breasts and moaning, the other looking on and calling her a 'dirty bitch'. (p. 39) After the movie, a girl comes out and the 'pickup' occurs.

The speech suggests the structure of Deeley's troubled ego. One hears from Anna later in the play that she and Kate also went to see *Odd Man Out*, and one learns later that it was Kate whom Deeley picked up, Kate making a move in the perverse sexual game she and Anna are playing. Deeley is surely 'odd man out' in his relations with Anna and Kate; he is excluded from their feelings and baffled by their actions. His association of the cinema's location with his childhood and his father suggests strong super-ego injunctions against unorthodox sexual attitudes and behavior. He recalls, but does not comment on, the usherette fondling herself in the foyer. His own instinctive response would no doubt have been 'dirty bitch'. Later in the play, as the sexual game between Anna and Kate becomes more apparent, Deeley retreats into clichés, jokes, and other vaudeville routines. He cannot grasp the complex sexual needs of Kate, the parson's daughter who requires disapproval to experience sexual pleasure.

Pinter also uses *Odd Man Out* to foreshadow the major theme of *Old Times*, betrayal. The film concerns an IRA gunman on the run in Northern Ireland who is betrayed to the police by his friends and then shot. Anna and Deeley betray their intimate moments with Kate. Anna had earlier betrayed her friendship with Kate by seeking a male sexual partner. Kate responds to these betrayals by psychologically killing Anna and Deeley at the end of the play.

In the second major memory passage in the play, Anna counters Deeley's male chauvinist version of his seduction of Kate with another episode in their shared past which will challenge Deeley's dominance of Kate, namely, the strange behavior of a man in Kate and Anna's bedroom. The episode reveals more deeply the real psychological needs of the three characters. A precise re-enactment of this revealing interplay occurs at the end of *Old Times*, this time unfolding as a ritual. Deeley's presumed dominance of Kate is undercut by Anna's remarks. For the remainder of act 1 Anna maneuvers close to Kate until she manages to revive a memory about their 'old times' at the end of the act. Deeley cannot keep Kate from her drift toward Anna.

The sudden introduction of the man-in-the-bedroom memory reveals an undercurrent of desperation in the trio's relations.

Anna. This man crying in our room. One night late I returned and found him
sobbing, his hand over his face, sitting in the armchair, all crumpled up in
the armchair, and Katey sitting on the bed with a mug of coffee and no one
spoke to me, no one spoke, no one looked up.   (p. 32)

Pinter again withholds crucial exposition which is not provided until the end
of the play. The episode in fact constitutes part of Kate's punishment of
Anna for violating their special relation by being attracted to Deeley. Anna
brings up the episode to shake Deeley's hold on Kate by reminding him of his
humiliation in the bedroom. But once begun, Anna's 'memory' flows on to
reveal her own vulnerability and shame. Her voice becomes defensive and
hysterical as she mechanically denies any feelings for Deeley.

Anna. The man came over to me, quickly, looked down at me, but I would have
absolutely nothing to do with him, nothing. . . . He looked at us both, at our
beds. Then he turned towards me. He approached my bed. He bent down
over me. But I would have nothing to do with him, absolutely nothing.
                                                              (p. 32)

Virtually silent since Anna and Deeley began their contest for her attention, Kate reacts to both the *Odd Man Out* memory and the man-in-the-
bedroom memory with a remark which foreshadows her ultimate marshal-
ing of her own memory against Deeley and Anna. 'You talk of me as if I were
dead. . . . I said you talk about me as if I *am* dead. Now' (pp. 34–5). Kate
resents being made an object, and finally rises against both exploiters to
reveal their weakness and their desperate need for companionship. Ignoring
Kate's protest, Anna and Deeley continue their struggle for 'possession' of
her. Anna betrays more of her intimacy with Kate. 'I'm looking down at you
now, seeing you so shyly poised over me, looking down at me' (p. 35).
Affecting a music-hall stage-Irish voice to lure her from her drift toward
Anna, Deeley reveals more of his Kate-fantasy, his image of her as a vague
and indecisive person, one obviously needing a strong male companion. He
calls her 'a slip of a girl not long out of her swaddling clothes whose only
claim to virtue was silence but who lacked any sense of fixedness, any sense of
decisiveness, but was compliant only to the shifting winds. . . . A classic
female figure' (pp. 35–6). Anna challenges this male-chauvinist perspective
by asserting that Kate 'never did things loosely, carelessly, or recklessly'
(p. 36). Kate responds to this truer awareness of her character by ignoring
Deeley's meaningless clichés and moving into Anna's emotional orbit.

In the long dialogue between Kate and Anna which concludes the first act
of *Old Times*, more of Kate's personality is revealed and she in no way
resembles the timid soul of Deeley's fantasy. One gradually discovers that
Kate is a tigress, very protective of her territory, and that she has a complex
sexual character. The dialogue with Anna reveals Kate's independence as
well as a very dependent Anna. The lines seem to go back to their London

days before the arrival of Deeley. They are remembering 'old times' together. Anna is terrified of leaving the flat, fearful of going into the park nearby where all sorts of monsters may be lurking.

> *Anna.* The park is dirty at night, all sorts of horrible people, men hiding behind trees and women with terrible voices, they scream at you as you go past, and people come out suddenly from behind trees and bushes, and there are shadows everywhere, and there are policemen, and you'll have a horrible walk, and you'll see all the traffic and the noise of the traffic and you'll see all the hotels, and you know you hate looking through all those swing doors, you hate it, to see all that. (pp. 43–4)

Kate has no fear of walking outside into the park. But Anna is terrified by the boundless spaces outside, and needs the security of a familiar room, an intimate space. 'You'll only want to come home if you go out. You'll want to run home ... and into your room ...' (p. 44). In their 'old times' Anna was clearly the servant who willingly and affectionately waited on Kate: 'Would you like me to ask someone over?' (p. 45); 'Shall I run your bath for you?' (p. 46). Kate continues to assert her independence by telling Anna she will run her own bath. The bath, simple naturalism at this point, becomes richly symbolic in the second act where it becomes a means for a prudish parson's daughter to wash away the 'dirty bitch' of her own libidinousness.

The enigmatic 'all that' which ends Anna's desperate speech about monsters in the park may be made somewhat clearer by drawing the reader's attention to a poem titled 'All of That' which Pinter published at the time he was writing *Old Times*.[2] The poem is quoted in full.

> *All of That*
>
> All of that I made
> And, making, lied.
> And all of that I hid
> Pretended dead
>
> But all of that I hid
> Was always said,
> But, hidden, spied
> On others' good.
>
> And all of that I led
> By nose to bed
> And, bedding, said
> Of what I did
>
> To all of that that cried
> Behind my head
> And, crying, died
> And is not dead

The unconscious and, more specifically, sexuality seem likely meanings for 'all of that'. The first two stanzas could pertain to each of the trio who has repressed psychological trauma, but then discovers the wounds surfacing in odd and unpredictable ways. The poem as a whole seems most suited to Kate, who is pretending that her bizarre past is dead, who plays the voyeur to Anna's adventures, and who leads the bewildered Deeley not only to bed but to marriage.

Deeley tries to bring Kate back into his psychological orbit early in the second act by discrediting Anna by means of his 'memory' of an experience with her at the Wayfarer's Tavern. These events, which occurred before the *Odd Man Out* or the man-in-the-bedroom episodes, presumably constituted the first meeting of Anna and Deeley. Deeley's revelation of such humiliating secrets indicates his level of desperation, or perhaps the masochism which is the reverse side of his efforts to dominate. Bringing these experiences 'to light' makes Deeley and Anna much more vulnerable and allows Kate her full measure of revenge. Anna tries to escape the psychological consequences of Deeley's remarks by suggesting they are merely his fantasies. Not until the end of the play can the audience be certain that Anna and Deeley had a sexual encounter.

> *Anna.* Oh, it was my skirt. It was me. I remember your look ... very well. I
> remember you well.   (p. 71)

Her admission generates Kate's final devastating punishment of this betrayal.

Ignoring Anna's protests, Deeley recalls the details of their 'old times' at the Wayfarer's Tavern. Anna and Deeley are alone on stage at this point; Kate is taking her bath. But the bathroom door is just up left in the bedroom set and one can imagine Kate's ear at the door. Deeley remembers Anna as 'the darling of the saloon bar' in her 'black stockings'. One night at an after-hours party in Westbourne Grove he and Anna had a Bloom/Gerty en-counter, the gazer and the gazed upon.

> *Deeley.* You sat on a very low sofa, I sat opposite and looked up your skirt. Your
> black stockings were very black because your thighs were so white. That's
> something that's all over now, of course, isn't it, nothing like the same
> palpable profit in it now, it's all over. But it was worthwhile then. It was
> worthwhile that night. I simply sat sipping my light ale and gazed ... gazed
> up your skirt. You didn't object, you found my gaze perfectly acceptable ...
> nobody but I had a thigh-kissing view, nobody but you had the thighs which
> kissed. And here you are. Same woman. Same thighs.   (p. 55)

The word 'gaze' has been used by Anna earlier in the play but without the sexual meaning it has here. When Anna introduces the term it seems merely part of an affected upper-class vocabulary which Deeley resents.

> *Anna.* She was quite unaware of my gaze.
> *Deeley.* Gaze?
> *Anna.* What?
> *Deeley.* The word gaze. Don't hear it very often.   (p. 26)

In the context of Deeley's revelations at this point in the play, however, 'gaze' belongs to the erotic vocabulary of the voyeur and his 'victim'. 'I ... gazed up your skirt ... you found my gaze perfectly acceptable' (p. 51). The word is used six times in this exchange between Deeley and Anna.

The duel for Kate in the second act is structured very similarly to the duel in the first act. Pinter even introduces a few more 'old songs'. The possessiveness of Deeley and Anna toward Kate here centers on Kate's bath and the fantasies each of them has about drying her off and powdering her after her bath. Both husband and friend are excited by the fantasy. But, once again, Kate reveals her independence. Just as she decides to run her own bath at the end of act I, so in act II she resists efforts to dry her off.

As was indicated earlier, Kate's present self-image belies the 'Kate-fantasies' of Deeley and Anna. She resents their efforts to shape her into an object to satisfy their psychological needs. She experiences herself as a floating, undefined being, free of 'urgency', free of the possessiveness which 'memory' triggers. Her emergence from the bath leads Anna to exclaim: 'She floats from the bath. Like a dream' (p. 54). And Deeley has earlier also experienced Kate's 'floating' quality. 'Sometimes I take her face in my hands and look at it.... Then I kind of let it go, take my hands away, leave it floating' (p. 24). Kate does not retain this undefined quality much longer. Anna's and Deeley's advances force her to shape her 'memories' in order to protect her own ego and then to strike out against these assaults.

The duel for possession of Kate intensifies when Kate emerges from the bath. One soon realizes, however, that she has more psychic power than either Deeley or Anna, that her version of their 'old times' will prevail. Deeley's retreat into clichés has already shown the shallowness of his character; Anna's fear of the park has revealed her psychological vulnerability. Both of them behave aggressively toward Kate, but both have a need for her to be the aggressor, to achieve dominance over them. The structure is sado-masochistic, with Anna and Deeley the ones needing to be punished and goading a reluctant Kate into a role of dominance.

Kate's bath represents an effort on her part to preserve her soft, 'floating' character. Her speeches up to this point have been responses to Deeley's and Anna's intrusive 'memories'. Now she begins to affirm more of her own personality and she delivers the long speech about a fondness for the soft, blurred quality of the country and the seaside as against the hard lines of the city. The country is passive, yielding, undemanding; the city is active, aggressive, urgent. She wishes she could live in the east where individual identity is less important than being part of the whole of life. Kate makes several attempts to persuade Deeley and Anna about the pleasures of indefiniteness. She offers gentleness and sensitivity as attractive personal qualities. But both are deaf to the psychological alternative of passivity, even though at a deep level this is what they desire. Yet neither can accept the structure in its positive, gentle form. They must experience it as dominance.

Anna's and Deeley's efforts to unleash Kate's aggressiveness become more desperate after her bath. More 'old songs' are sung, but the tone is darker. 'The way you haunt my dreams . . . The way you hold your knife . . . The way you've changed my life . . . No, no they can't take that away from me' (p. 58). They affect the servant roles which at a deep level both desire.

> *Anna.* I could do the hem on your black dress. I could finish it and you could try it on.
> *Kate.* Mmmnn.
>   [*Anna hands her her coffee.*]
> *Anna.* Or I could read to you.
> *Deeley.* Have you dried yourself properly, Kate? . . .
>   . . . .
>   [*Kate smiles.*]
> *Deeley.* See that smile? That's the same smile she smiled when I was walking down the street with her, after *Odd Man Out*, well, quite some time after.
>   (pp. 60–1)

Kate tries to bring Deeley and Anna into awareness of her 'eastern' values of sensitivity, patience, gentleness in the lines which follow Kate's smiling (pp. 62–3). She tells Anna and Deeley of someone she likes 'best', someone called Christy. Kate remarks 'He's so gentle, isn't he? And his humour. Hasn't he got a lovely sense of humour? And I think he's . . . so sensitive' (pp. 62–3). Christy sounds Christ-like, a model of non-aggressive 'eastern' values.

But Anna and Deeley return to the war of 'memories' and continue the betrayal of their intimacy with Kate.

> *Anna* [*To Kate*]. You're still shy, aren't you?
>   [*Kate stares at her.*]
> *Anna* [*To Deeley*]. But when I first knew her she was *so* shy, as shy as a fawn, she really was. When people leaned to speak to her she would fold away from them, so that though she was standing within their reach she was no longer accessible to them. She folded herself from them, they were no longer able to speak or go through with their touch. I put it down to her upbringing, a parson's daughter, and indeed there was a good deal of Brontë about her.
>   (p. 64)

One soon experiences the 'Brontë' in Kate, the unleashing of destructive psychic forces which have hitherto been repressed by this 'parson's daughter'.

The most devastating betrayal of intimacy which follows finally pushes Kate over the edge and she fights back. Anna reveals details about borrowing underwear, going to parties, and returning to tell Kate details about voyeurs like Deeley – 'a man at the party had spent the whole evening looking up my skirt' (p. 65). Deeley joins in the betrayal of intimacy, trivializing his relation to Kate by describing in a boorish music-hall manner his voyeuristic pursuit of Anna.

> *Deeley.* Yes, we met in the Wayfarer's Tavern. In the corner. She took a fancy
> to me. Of course I was slimhipped in those days. Pretty nifty. A bit squinky,
> quite honestly. Curly hair. The lot. We had a scene together. She freaked
> out. She didn't have any bread, so I bought her a drink. She looked at me
> with big eyes, shy, all that bit. She was pretending to be you at the time. Did
> it pretty well. Wearing your underwear she was too, at the time. Amiably
> allowed me a gander. Trueblue generosity. Admirable in a woman.
>
>   (p. 69)

Kate responds to this double betrayal of intimacy by allowing one more opportunity for responding to her positive power before destroying Deeley and Anna. She describes Deeley's affair with Anna as something beautiful: 'What do you think attracted her to you? ... She found your face very sensitive, vulnerable. . . . She wanted to comfort it, in the way only a woman can. . . . She was prepared to extend herself to you. . . . She fell in love with you' (p. 70). Deeley and Anna can perceive only a more limited and perverse relation, one which does not admit love.

> *Deeley.* But I was crass, wasn't I, looking up her skirt?
> *Kate.* That's not crass.
> *Deeley.* If it was her skirt. If it was her.
> *Anna* [*Coldly*]. Oh, it was my skirt. It was me. I remember your look ... very
> well. I remember you well.   (p. 71)

Kate's vengeance first on Anna, then on Deeley reveals the parson's daughter with Brontëesque passion. It represents a devastating application of Anna's earlier remarks about memory: 'There are things I remember which may never have happened but as I recall them so they take place' (p. 32). Kate, the compulsive taker of baths, the one forever trying to clean herself of the 'dirt' of her sexual needs, 'kills' Anna by 'remembering' her as dirty.

> *Kate.* I remember you dead. [*Pause*] I remember you lying dead. You didn't
> know I was watching you. I leaned over you. Your face was dirty. You lay
> dead, your face scrawled with dirt, all kinds of earnest inscriptions, but
> unblotted, so that they had run, all over your face, down to your throat.
> Your sheets were immaculate. I was glad. I would have been unhappy if
> your corpse had lain in an unwholesome sheet. It would have been graceless.
>
>   (p. 71–2)

Kate's killing of Anna concludes, she recalls, with a cleansing bath. 'I had quite a lengthy bath, got out, walked about the room, glistening, drew up a chair, sat naked beside you, and watched you' (p. 72).

Deeley is also dirtied through Kate's memory, 'plastered' with dirt to symbolize Kate's rejection of his sexual advances. Kate has used 'little tricks' to seduce Deeley away from Anna, but she refuses to have sexual relations with him.

> *Kate.* But one night I said let me do something, a little thing, a little trick. He lay there in your bed. He looked up at me with great expectation. He was gratified. He thought I had profited from his teaching. He thought I was going to be sexually forthcoming, that I was about to take a long promised initiative. I dug about in the windowbox, where you had planted our pretty pansies, scooped, filled the bowl, and plastered his face with dirt.

(p. 72–3)

Deeley responds to Kate's dominance and humiliation of him by proposing marriage. Kate has met his deepest psychological needs, a factor far more important than satisfying his conventional sexual needs.

Kate prevails at the end of *Old Times*, though aggressiveness and betrayal are not things she admires in herself. She needs to cleanse herself from such 'dirtiness'. In the symbolic tableau which ends the play, Kate retains the superior position, sitting in a chair. Deeley first lies in her lap, then slumps in a chair. Anna lies on the divan beneath Kate. The scene almost exactly repeats the opening arrangement of the characters and enacts as well the man-in-the-bedroom episode. But the symbolism of these gestures and positions, satisfaction of the needs of two of the characters to be dominated and of the third character, somewhat reluctantly, to dominate, only becomes clear through the complex interplay of memories which constitutes the deep structure of *Old Times*. The places and things which are introduced in the play, the menacing park, the film *Odd Man Out*, the old songs, Kate's baths, all of these function symbolically in relation to this deep structure.

NOTES

1. *Old Times* (New York: Grove Press, 1971), pp. 31–2.
2. *The Times Literary Supplement*, 11 Dec. 1970.

The void in *Macbeth*: a symbolic design

DANA SUE McDERMOTT

In 1921 Robert Edmond Jones designed *Macbeth* for Broadway. The set was the first extreme example of abstract symbolism offered in the commercial American theatre, and it outraged the majority of the newspaper reviewers. Because the critical reaction was so extraordinarily violent, the production closed after only twenty-eight performances, and the aura of reprehensible failure established limits for the degree of abstraction in symbolic design on Broadway. Jones at the time was recognized as the first American stage designer of genius and the rejection of his *Macbeth* was a matter of principle – even of moral principle. In America, as in Europe, symbolism has been generally welcomed only as a qualifying influence on drama which retains a strong interest in portraying concrete reality. Jones's career, in particular his work on *Macbeth*, indicates some important truths about the development of American theatre, and also about the complex ways in which experimentation with symbolism has influenced twentieth-century production.

The *Macbeth* production was one of a long continuing series of collaborations with Arthur Hopkins, and the second in which they worked together on Shakespeare. Hopkins as producer and director was unique on Broadway in that he was committed to 'art theatre'; with no other producer would Jones have been given such free scope and no other director could have been more open to Jones's visionary zeal.

The Apollo on West 42nd Street had been built in 1910 and was a conventional gilt-and-plush proscenium-arch theatre.[1] When the curtain rose, the audience was confronted by the first open-space use of a Broadway stage. With black drapes and selective lighting Jones created a void rather than a set. Into this black hole came abstract grey fragments and shafts of light. For the witches' scenes three large silver masks loomed over the void with white light streaming from the eyes (see plate 8). In the final scenes the fragments suggesting arches lurched threateningly, 'expressionistically' portraying the disintegration of Macbeth's inner world.

Critics vehemently denounced this violation of traditional staging practice. One reviewer noted that *Macbeth* received a 'tribute of ... damnation ... unprecedented in volume' and suggested the production would have been

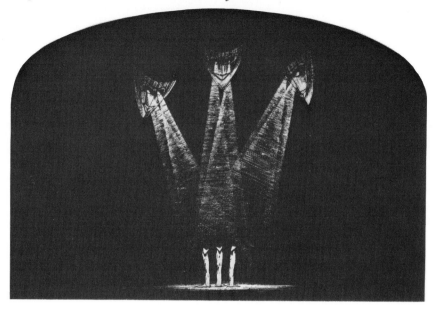

8   Robert Edmond Jones: design for *Macbeth*, 1921, the silver masks

playing to full houses months after the actual closing date if everyone who
gave 'detailed damnations of *Macbeth*' had actually seen the play.[2]
Alexander Woollcott, drama critic for the *New York Times*, was appalled by
the production and described the settings in highly derogatory terms:

> Jones has set upon his stage certain cubistic properties which, not in them-
> selves, but in their present association, are quite horrible imaginings. An
> Inverness that looks like a fiercely extracted tooth, a Dunsinane that suggests
> wastebasket cuttings strewn through space, a path for the sleepwalker that
> threads its way through gewgaws which may strive to suggest the graveyard of
> her hopes but which actually suggest a forest of giant snowshoes battered by
> storm.[3]

In other reviews Woollcott carried his comparison with modern art further,
stating that Jones's *Macbeth* was 'like the "Nude Descending a Staircase"
with the figure cut out and a fine detailed photograph of James K. Hackett as
Macbeth pasted in its place'.[4] He felt that abstraction might be quite
acceptable in painting, but that it had no place in the theatre where the live
actor was going to appear amidst the scenic elements.

Other reviewers were equally unsympathetic toward Jones's expressionistic approach to *Macbeth*. They believed that the appropriate manner for
staging Shakespearian plays had been established during the nineteenth
century and that any production which moved too far from the accepted
realistic practices threatened to violate a sacred tradition. Broadway audi-

ences were accustomed to seeing Shakespeare's texts chopped up and re-shaped according to the preferences of star performers and the practicality of changing heavily-dressed, elaborately ornate settings. A number of stock companies had experimented with a bare-boards staging, but this had no effect on commercial practice. Productions of Shakespearian plays followed as closely as possible the conventions set for modern prose plays.

Prior to the work of Robert Edmond Jones, David Belasco's productions had epitomized the ideal in stage settings: 'realism' was valued above all else. Belasco provided this with, for example, an imported garret including furnishings and wallpaper stripped from a Parisian dwelling, and a function-ing Child's restaurant: programs emphasized the origins and 'authenticity' of the objects used on stage. Across the nation producers emulated his detailed stage pictures. Into this milieu Jones introduced the European concept of 'the new stagecraft'. Following his reading of Gordon Craig and his observation of Max Reinhardt's work, Jones presented American theatre with a new symbolic approach to design. His 1915 design for Anatole France's *The Man Who Married A Dumb Wife* marks the beginning of this new movement in the United States: Jones did not try to reproduce or even suggest a medieval town, but used bold colors and geometric patterns to convey the essential atmosphere of the play.

Jones saw himself as a revolutionary who would follow in the footsteps of his European mentors and help rouse the American theatre from its stodgy realism. While he was a student at Harvard, he became aware of Gordon Craig's writings and was exhilarated by the potential of these new forms. For his first production, the Patterson Strike Pageant held in New York City at Madison Square Garden, 7 June 1913, Jones followed Craig's principles and created a huge silhouette of silk mills at the back of a stage which accom-modated 2,000 players. Using ingenious lighting, he caused the mills to come alive at various moments.[5] The design did not attempt to re-create the factories but rather suggested their emotional impact on the workers who struggled there daily under such intolerable conditions that they were forced to strike. Throughout his career Jones was concerned not with the depiction of actual places but with capturing the emotional essence of a situation through the careful use of objects, color, and light.

After the Patterson Pageant, Jones went to Europe to study the avant-garde work being done in theatre design, and to reach a fuller understanding of the symbolist techniques being used there. When he went abroad in 1913 he hoped specifically to study with Gordon Craig; however, Craig had recently quarreled with Mabel Dodge, Jones's hostess, and refused to accept the young artist as a student. Jones then met a member of Max Reinhardt's company and traveled to Berlin to observe the production process at the Deutsches Theater.[6] The outbreak of World War I forced him to return to America.

In the designs Jones created from 1915 to 1920 European influences were quite apparent: spare settings characterized by bold colors, exaggerated proportions, and carefully arranged lighting were quite typical. His designs for the Shakespearian scenes of *Caliban by the Yellow Sands* (1916) showed the combined influences of Reinhardt, Craig, and Appia. With Hopkins he continued this approach creating such memorable productions as *Redemption* (1918), which was a stage version of Tolstoy's story 'The Living Dead', *The Jest* (1919), and *Richard III* (1920). Each of Jones's designs prior to *Macbeth* was accepted as a valuable contribution to the developing art of American theatre.

The design for *Richard III* (1920) did not adhere closely to the traditional 'realistic' standards; nonetheless, it was hailed by the critics. Alexander Woollcott recalled the magnificence of *Richard III* and contrasted it with the *Macbeth* design:

> Mr. Jones is unquestionably the foremost conjurer of light and color in the history of the American theatre and all that has been or may be said here of the tricks he has played *Macbeth* is set down by one who believes his *Richard III* was incomparably the most beautiful Shakespearean investiture this country has ever known.[7]

Like the *Macbeth* design, that for *Richard III* was based on a central symbol; but the crucial difference in the two concepts and hence in the audience's response to them was in the nature of the symbol. For *Richard III* Jones created a unit setting in which all the scenes occurred inside or outside the Tower of London. Since clear references are made in the text to Richard's use of the Tower to imprison his enemies, the audience easily accepted this location for all the scenes. Unlike his *Macbeth*, Jones's *Richard III* was based upon a representational rather than an abstract symbol; the audience responded positively to this production because it was innovative and beautiful while maintaining close connection with the world as they perceived it.

When Jones created the *Macbeth* production, he was the most respected designer in the United States; he had just completed a series of successes and seemed to be at the height of his powers. At this moment, when apparently anything he attempted would be accepted, Jones ventured to bring a very personal view of a Shakespearian play to the theatre.

Around 1920–21 Jones's conviction about the importance of symbolism in art was reinforced by his contact with the theories of Carl Jung. At that time Jones was in analysis with Dr Smith Ely Jelliffe, an early eclectic New York psychoanalyst, who combined Freudian, Jungian, and Adlerian theory.[8] The impact of psychology on the artistic life of Robert Edmond Jones cannot be overestimated; like his friend Eugene O'Neill, Jones was fascinated by concepts of subconscious and unconscious states of mind. The attempt to express deep levels of the human psyche is the basis of the most innovative work of both Jones and O'Neill.

Jones opens his book *The Dramatic Imagination* with a discussion of the importance of modern psychology, saying that this new means of looking into man's 'inner life' has become not only an accepted part of our intellectual endeavors but also an influence on art:

> In the last quarter of a century we have begun to be interested in the exploration of man's inner life, in the unexpressed and hitherto inexpressible depths of the self ... The concept of the Unconscious has profoundly influenced the intellectual life of our day. It has already become a commonplace of our thinking, and it is beginning to find an expression in our art.[9]

Jones's personal response to modern psychology and especially to Jung's concepts was not merely intellectual excitement; in the theories of Jung he found keys for resolving his own deepest personal conflicts. Jung's teachings became one of the most important influences in his life. After spending approximately two years in analysis with Dr Jelliffe, Jones again experienced psychological difficulties in 1926. This time the situation was quite severe and he was ready to leave the theatre permanently. He went to Zurich for a year of analysis with Jung, after which he was able to return to the theatre and work productively for another twenty years.[10] In 1946, nine years before his death, Jones wrote to a friend saying that he had always tried to live by what Jung taught him.[11]

Jung's theories of art and life rely heavily on the concept of symbol. In *Man and His Symbols* he explains that:

> What we call a symbol is a term, a name, or even a picture that may be familiar in daily life, yet that possesses specific connotations in addition to its conventional and obvious meaning. It implies something vague, unknown, or hidden from us.[12]

In other writings he refers to the symbol's connotations as *numinosity* – a meaning or emotional significance greater than its own properties – and says that through the amplification of symbols human beings have access to their own personal and also to the universal unconscious. For Jung art has one main purpose: to express the contents of the unconscious in symbolic form. Through the creation and sharing of symbols the artist, who has more direct contact with the unconscious realm than the average person, gives shape to emotions and sensations which exist in every person but rarely find expression. Within society the artist's role is to share his perceptions so that individuals less closely attuned to the inner workings of the psyche may experience a greater integration of conscious and unconscious material. Through the assimilation of subconscious and unconscious material, individuals move closer to the self-realization which is Jung's ultimate goal for the mature person.

For Jones the work with Jung and the ensuing process of self-realization allowed him to continue functioning as a designer and to articulate the essence of his art. He defined the stage designer as '*an artist of occasions*',[13] and gave the primary characteristic for this special type of artist as one of temperament:

> a temperament that is peculiarly sensitive to the atmosphere of a given occasion, just as the temperament of a musician is peculiarly sensitive to the characteristic qualities of a muscial composition. Stage designers, like musicians, are born and not made. One is aware of atmospheres or one isn't, just as one has a musical ear or one hasn't.[14]

This awareness of atmospheres which Jones considers essential for the designer is a characteristic dominant in his own personality. While in Zurich, Jones wrote to Kenneth Macgowan saying that his friend would understand him better if he read Jung's description of the 'Extraverted Intuitive Type' in *Psychological Types*.[15] Jung's explanation begins:

> Whenever intuition predominates, a particular and unmistakable psychology presents itself. Because intuition is oriented by the object, a decided dependence upon external situation is discernible . . .[16]

Dependence on the external situation is the foundation of Jones's work as a designer; it is the key to his temperament as an artist and the cornerstone of his method of working. Jones read a text, intuited the atmosphere of the play, then searched for objects which embodied that same essential quality. He worked from the stimulation of the text to an intuitive understanding of it and then turned back to the external world to look for objects which could embody and communicate the same essential feeling. After these objects – works of art, pieces of furniture, architectural elements – had been found, he began to adapt them for the stage. Jones transformed his source materials by stripping them of all unnecessary detail and emphasizing the elements which conveyed the essence of the object. In this manner he created symbols for the stage which expressed the central emotion he found in the text.

This process, which characterizes Jones's method of working, is very close to T. S. Eliot's classic expression of the modern symbolist theory of art:

> The only way of expressing emotion in the form of art is by finding an 'objective correlative'; in other words, a set of objects, a situation, a chain of events which shall be the formula of that *particular* emotion; such that when the external facts, which must terminate in sensory experience, are given, the emotion is immediately evoked.[17]

Eliot suggests that two elements are essential in a successful work of art – appropriate objects, situations, events and a formula by which they are arranged to elicit the desired response. The components of Eliot's 'objective correlative' – objects, situations, events – function in a manner very similar to Jung's symbols. Eliot argues that the artist creates a pattern of symbolic elements which will elicit an emotional response in the audience related to the emotions expressed by the artist. Jung never goes so far as to suggest how individual symbols are shaped into a powerful, persuasive whole. He does state that the artist is in touch with the unconscious realm and that symbols spring from that connection; he even says that the artist may refine the products of the unconscious through conscious choices, but he does not move from the artist into the work of art as Eliot does to discuss the most effective arrangement of symbols for the desired effect.

Eliot and Jung were working in the same milieu of symbolism: Eliot wrote his essay on *Hamlet* in 1919 and Jung published his epoch-making *Psychological Types* in 1921. Both defined art in terms of symbolism, but they approached the subject differently. Jung, a psychologist, was concerned with the creation and use of art for the psychic well-being of the individual and society; Eliot, as an aesthetician, was concerned with the question of *how* the created piece functions as a thing in itself quite independent of the artist.

In order to understand Jones's approach to *Macbeth*, it is helpful to consider Eliot's brief discussion of the play. Eliot juxtaposes *Macbeth* and *Hamlet*, using the former as an example of 'Shakespeare's more successful tragedies', arguing that the artistic success of *Macbeth* depends upon the symbolic medium: a state of mind is communicated by an 'accumulation of imagined sensory impressions' and there is a 'complete adequacy of the external to the emotion'.[18]

Lady Macbeth is obsessed by the imagined sight and smell of Duncan's blood

> Out, damned spot! . . . who would have thought the old man to have had so much blood in him? . . . What, will these hands ne'er be clean? . . . Here's the smell of the blood still. All the perfumes of Arabia will not sweeten this little hand. (v, i)[19]

and by her memory of the dreaded sound on the murder night

> There's knocking at the gate. Come, come, come, come, give me your hand! What's done cannot be undone . . . (v, i)

The character's situation, the stage design, the actress's costume, 'props', gestures and words communicate a complex and unique state of mind. Likewise, Macbeth's emotional response to his wife's death is expressed with consummate particularity: he speculates on the nature of existence, the deceptive promise of tomorrow, and the unnoticed passing of time:

> Life's but a walking shadow, a poor player
> That struts and frets his hour upon the stage
> And then is heard no more. It is a tale
> Told by an idiot, full of sound and fury.
> Signifying nothing. (v, v)

Macbeth has been promised kingship by the witches, has followed Lady Macbeth's urgings to murder Duncan, then out of his own fear has had Banquo assassinated and the wife and children of Macduff slaughtered. At this moment in the play Macbeth is steeped in blood and his castle is under siege. In responding to the very complex 'objective correlative' created by poet, director, designer and actor, the audience is carried along in the play's emotional sweep. The messenger arrives to say that Birnam Wood is advancing on Dunsinane; and he is followed by Macduff 'from his mother's womb/ Untimely ripped' (v, viii). Through Shakespeare's formula of prophecies, urgings, murder, remorse, further killings, madness, and suicide we are led to empathize with his protagonist. Jones sought to complement the element of 'artistic "inevitability"' in Shakespeare's text by creating a design which fitted his response to the emotion of the play. For Jones *Macbeth* was about possession and fatalistic determination; he constructed an environment in which the protagonist had no choices in life but was compelled by inner and outer forces beyond his control. Macbeth is moved toward destruction by an uncontrollable destructive impulse. Jones believed this fate was possible for any man and his design was intended to enhance our identification with and pity for Macbeth: in the dreadful void he found a means to convey the psychological situation of Macbeth, who existed in a vacuum, adrift in a world seemingly without boundaries. There was no form of stability in his life; he was pushed and pulled by the coincidence of chance events and prophecies with his own inner desires; there was no reality against which he could gauge his responses. The audience was to be led to appreciate that Macbeth and his Lady had no control over their lives; they functioned in a trance or dream-like state.

When Jones and Arthur Hopkins created the *Macbeth* production both were in analysis with Dr Jelliffe,[20] who used the interpretation of dreams as a psychoanalytic tool. Donald Oenslager, a close friend of Jones, discusses the dream motif in the design and the connection with analysis:

> At that time Jones was deeply concerned with psychoanalysis and his brief suggestions of these scenes for *Macbeth* resembled personified abstractions – indications of place seen through the mind's eye of the characters of the play. In the Letter Scene ... Lady Macbeth found her way, as in her own dream world, between twisted and tormented frames.[21]

When Hopkins describes his first response to Jones's design, he refers to it as a dream:

> When we saw his sketches we were enthusiastic. They permitted an expanse of ominous witch-infested space. Figures came out of the dark into the light and were enveloped by the dark again. There was the quality of an evil dream in which visible objects had a nightmarish distortion. There was no sense of reality. The whole was pervaded by the poisonous brew of the witches' cauldron.[22]

Then in his defense of the production in the *New York Times*, Hopkins speaks of Macbeth as 'one in a dream'.

> We find Macbeth, a man of whom there has been no ill account, walking along a road. A hand reaches out and touches him. From that moment on he becomes as one in a dream. He is possessed. He is picked up and whirled through a torrent of blood and agony.[23]

Out of Jones's and Hopkins's shared concern for understanding the deepest human impulses and motivations came their decision to create a production of *Macbeth* in which the protagonist is caught in a nightmare.

The erratic quality of the banquet scene directly reflected Macbeth's state of mind (see plate 9). Lady Macbeth moved through the black space and grey structures wearing first a robe of intense red heightened by a red follow-spot, then for the sleepwalking scene a gown of pure white (see plate 10). For the witches' scenes three large silver masks hung over the bare, black stage. Pools of white light streamed from the eyes of the masks to the red-clad witches below. The lighting plot reveals that Jones lit the entire production with cones of light; he did not use general illumination or overlapping areas.[24] Stark Young described the effect: 'Vast daggers of light poured down, crossed, pierced, and flooded the scenes of the witches.'[25]

The void represents dead nature; the fragmentary structures are man's institutions. The large masks are the fates; the witches, who wear smaller versions of the same masks, are their envoys. Man exists in a dark, desolate place; his attempts to shape his environment are futile; his destiny is controlled by fate. The void portrays the unknowable realm within which man lives; the structures illustrate his attempt to shape that void. Their malleability and apparent fragility suggest the transitory, ineffectual nature of man's endeavors.

By creating a landscape of the psyche on stage Jones sought to provide an external equivalent of his response to the emotion of the play. However, the general audience could not accept the abstract, 'expressionistic' symbols and could not respond as Jones, Hopkins, and various members of the art-theatre community were able to; they dismissed the production as eccentric and meaningless. Elizabeth Sergeant, who interviewed Jones, describes the effect of this public rejection on him.

> The power of dream abstractly has dangers of its own . . . Undoubtedly he was moved largely by his own creative urge, and by his need to experiment in a new and unfamiliar form when he tumbled into his first and only cataclysmic failure – *Macbeth* . . . The artist had to digest his failure; in the process many of his cerements of ice melted away. He saw that messages from the unconscious must be censored before they become popular art.[26]

Jones was made to realize that abstract symbolism is acceptable to a very limited number of people.

9   Robert Edmond Jones: design for *Macbeth*, 1921, the banquet

10   Robert Edmond Jones: design for *Macbeth*, 1921, the sleepwalking

The following year for *Hamlet* Jones returned to the semi-representational mode that had been so successful in *Richard III*: he again created an architectural unit set. The structure was characterized by high stone-like walls, a huge central arch, and a large flight of steps. Unlike the *Richard III* setting this design does not seem to be derived from the study of an actual building, but combines the complex stair-unit known as *Jessnertreppen*, which Jones had recently seen in Germany,[27] with elements of romanesque architecture. Nevertheless, the overall effect is similar: in both designs Jones creates a single setting which is recognizable as a castle-like structure and is a symbolic embodiment of the mood of the play. In *Hamlet* the setting is dark and brooding, completely enfolding the action; these characteristics reflect Hamlet's state of mind.

Jones's later Shakespearian designs, *Othello* (1934 and 1943), *Richard III* (1941), and *Henry VIII* (1944), followed the 'representational symbolic' precedent set by *Richard III* (1920) and *Hamlet*. Most of his other designs, for example, *Desire Under the Elms* (1924), *Green Pastures* (1930), *Mourning Becomes Electra* (1931), *The Philadelphia Story* (1939), *Lute Song* (1946), and *The Iceman Cometh* (1946), also drew upon the representational tradition, but presented ordinary objects in a highly stylized and symbolic manner. After *Macbeth* Jones continued to experiment with color, lighting, varying spatial relationships, and open staging, but he never again created such an abstract design.

The Jones–Hopkins's *Macbeth* was the first open-stage expressionistic staging of a Shakespearian play on Broadway, and some members of the art-theatre community hoped this would be the beginning of highly abstract design in commercial theatre. However, the critical response was so extraordinarily negative that it put an end to such hopes. One influential history of the modern theatre argues that 'it was so controversial that it seems to have turned Jones and others back to a simplified realism as a basic mode'.[28] I would suggest that the failure of *Macbeth* defined the limits for design on the commercial stage, making it clear that abstract symbolism was not acceptable but leaving Jones and others free to develop designs based on symbols drawn from the recognizable world.

In the early twentieth-century American theatre the standard style of scenic design moved from Belascoesque 'realism' to a flirtation with highly abstract scenery which reached its extreme in the designs for *Macbeth*, *The Hairy Ape*, and *The Adding Machine*. These controversial productions set certain limits; designers discovered through audience response that an intermediate style which might be called 'symbolic realism' was more acceptable. By the middle of the century designs such as those for *Death of a Salesman* and *A Streetcar Named Desire* by Jo Mielziner were considered entirely appropriate.

In recent years there have been continuing experiments with non-representational concepts and environmental stages. In 1973 both the

American Shakespeare Festival and the Juilliard School American Opera Center presented *Macbeth* in extremely abstract settings; these received much better responses than their predecessor fifty years earlier. However, in 1974 when the first exhibition of American design was organized, the vast majority of the projects shown were based upon representational elements.[29] This is not surprising when one considers the evolution of American drama. Our three major playwrights – Eugene O'Neill, Tennessee Williams, and Arthur Miller – have all created highly stylized plays, but their most successful pieces have invariably been drawn from the close study of daily life. *Long Day's Journey into Night*, *A Streetcar Named Desire*, and *Death of a Salesman* make important use of symbolic techniques, but they are rooted in the familiar world of Tyrone's second-hand Packard, Stanley Kowalski's seven-card stud, and Willy Loman buying seeds in a hardware store on Sixth Avenue: at its best, American drama is tied to the actuality of daily American life.

In the 1920s Jones and other practitioners of the 'art theatre' introduced European traits to the American theatre public and explored the degree to which abstraction in design and drama might be developed. Abstract symbolism was rejected, but its influence made possible the development of a form which fused close imitation with ambitious symbolism. This style of symbolic realism continues to dominate the American commercial theatre.

NOTES

1 Mary C. Henderson, *The City and the Theatre* (Clifton, New Jersey: James T. White, 1973), p. 206.
2. Raymond M. Weaver, 'New Plays and Old', *Bookman*, 53 (1921), 273.
3. Alexander Woollcott, 'A Rebellion Against the Emperor Jones', *New York Times*, 27 Feb. 1921, sec. 6, p. 1, col. 1.
4. *Ibid.*
5. Mabel Dodge Luhan, *Movers and Shakers*, vol. III of *Intimate Memories* (New York: Harcourt, Brace & Co., 1936), pp. 204–5.
6. Robert Edmond Jones, Letters to Kenneth Macgowan, 1913–14, Kenneth Macgowan Papers, University of California, Los Angeles.
7. Woollcott, 'A Rebellion'.
8. Nathan G. Hale, Jr, *Freud and the Americans: The Beginnings of Psychoanalysis in the United States, 1876–1917* (New York: Oxford University Press, 1971), pp. 383–6.
9. Robert Edmond Jones, *The Dramatic Imagination* (New York: Duell, Sloan & Pearce, 1941), pp. 15–16.
10. Robert Edmond Jones, Letters to Kenneth Macgowan, 1926–27, Kenneth Macgowan Papers, University of California, Los Angeles.
11. Robert Edmond Jones, Letter to Mary Foote, 12 April 1946, Private Collection of Mrs Franz M. Oppenheimer, Washington, D.C.

12. Carl G. Jung, 'Approaching the Unconscious' in *Man and His Symbols*, by Carl G. Jung, M. L. von Franz, Joseph L. Henderson, Jolande Jacobi and Aniela Jaffe (New York: Dell, 1968), p. 3.

13. Jones, *Dramatic Imagination*, p. 69.

14. *Ibid.* p. 70.

15. Robert Edmond Jones, Letter to Kenneth Macgowan, *c.* 1926, Kenneth Macgowan Papers, University of California, Los Angeles.

16. C. G. Jung, *Psychological Types*, trans. H. G. Baynes, rev. trans. R. F. C. Hull, vol. v of *The Collected Works of C. G. Jung*, exec. ed. William McGuire, (1956; repr. Princeton University Press, Bollingen Series, 1970), p. 464.

17. T. S. Eliot, '*Hamlet*' in *Selected Essays* (New York: Harcourt, Brace & World, 1964), pp. 124–5.

18. Eliot, '*Hamlet*', p. 125.

19. Quotations are from *Macbeth*, ed. Sylvan Barnet (New York: New American Library, 1963).

20. Arthur and Barbara Gelb, *O'Neill* (New York: Harper & Row, 1962), p. 565.

21. Donald Oenslager, 'Introduction to the Second Edition', *Drawings for the Theatre by Robert Edmond Jones* (1925; repr. New York: Theatre Arts Books, 1970), p. 16.

22. Arthur Hopkins, *To A Lonely Boy* (Garden City, New York: Doubleday, Doran, 1937), p. 224.

23. Arthur Hopkins, 'The Approaching "Macbeth"', *New York Times*, 6 Feb. 1921, sec. 6, p. 1, col. 1.

24. Herman David Middleton, 'The Use of the Design Elements in the Stage Designs of Robert Edmond Jones and Lee Simonson', Diss. University of Florida, 1964, pp. 89–90.

25. Stark Young, *Immortal Shadows* (New York: C. Scribner's Sons, 1948), p. 100.

26. Elizabeth Sergeant, 'Robert Edmond Jones: Protean Artist' in *Fire Under the Andes* (New York: Alfred A. Knopf, 1927), pp. 44–5.

27. In the spring of 1922 Jones and Kenneth Macgowan had gone to Europe to observe the theatre work being done there. *Continental Stagecraft* (New York: Harcourt, Brace & Co., 1922) was the result of that trip. Macgowan wrote the text; Jones provided the illustrations of the productions they had seen. In Germany they saw Jurgen Fehling's *Masse-Mensch* and Leopold Jessner's *Richard III*. Both productions used the flights of steps and connecting platforms, which came to be known as *Jessnertreppen*.

28. Oscar G. Brockett and Robert R. Findlay, *Century of Innovation* (Englewood Cliffs: Prentice-Hall, 1973), p. 496.

29. Elizabeth B. Burdick, Peggy C. Hansen and Brenda Zanger (eds), *Contemporary Stage Design U.S.A.* (Middletown, Connecticut: Wesleyan University Press, 1974).

In praise of particularity*

BEN MADDOW

As an artisan rather than a philosopher, let me raise, for my craft, a disagreeable question: is symbolism in film necesary or even desirable? The very word has a dryish taste to most of us. We associate it either with worship, where we are meant not to know quite what it means; or with public statuary, where we know too easily what it means. We have often read complex and delicate analyses of our own films, and put them on file with amused tolerance; we wonder whether the symbol, so industriously discovered, is substantial skeleton or merely Platonic shadow. By its ubiquity, the cinema has become a rich dig for the symbolist critic. And this intellection has infected some film makers, too.

There are at least three kinds of symbol used, and misused, in film. One sort appears in a movie such as *Le sang d'un poète*, where Cocteau creates images whose meaning is deliberately vague; they can be translated only by a personal dictionary: are the angelic cyclists the leather boys of his desires? In this respect the symbols are like deaf mute language, or Linear B, strangely fascinating if impenetrable but banal when explained.

A second sort of symbolic image can be illustrated by the scene in Stroheim's *Foolish Wives*, in which the hero entices the heroine to a forest hut, and while he waits for her to undress, looks in a convenient mirror, in which a goat is reflected back at him from a neighboring pasture. It is a sort of visual pun. Eisenstein has many of a similar kind in *Ten Days that Shook the World*; we see the Tsar's statue, pulled down with ropes in the early part of the film, spring back to its pedestal in reverse motion, on the accession of Kerensky as Prime Minister.

A third sort of symbol is formed by the poetic compression implied in the image itself. A successful example, also in *Ten Days*, is where the failure of the old bureaucracy is denoted by a single cut: a disorderly pile of typewriters at the doorway beside an armed sentry. Yet even this kind of symbol can easily become ludicrous, like Dovzhenko's galloping horses (in *Arsenal*) talking

* This paper is part of a continuing series of contributions to *Themes in Drama* in which distinguished artists discuss their own work in detail. Mr Maddow's contributions to the cinema as both writer and director have been very highly acclaimed.

sonorous Russian verse. Indeed, one is hard put not to distrust all three kinds of symbol: they are all effective and they are all shallow.

But is there not a fourth kind? Where the symbol is clothed by living particulars? In Bertolucci's *Last Tango in Paris*, is the empty apartment merely a symbol of the vacancy of a rented and temporary world, where fewer and fewer people have a fixed set of values? Are the two protagonists carnal – all too carnal – symbols of a generation that believes only in the present? I am afraid that is precisely what Bertolucci meant; and like any other sort of pornography, it lies in that peculiar zone between boredom and fascination. It does not have the complex interest I would urge is vital: the irrational truth of real characters. Falstaff, Othello, Hamlet; their character is beyond category.

Is the discovery of symbols only a game, or does the labor of analysis uncover a deeper truth? This is a cultural question: for men (and certain apes, and possibly even pigeons, goldfish, and worms) treat signs as real. The illusion is built into our heads. The earliest symbols we know are numerical: the signs for animals counted in trade, stamped on bits of baked clay and sealed in a pot. Counters like these were elaborated into a system of hiero-glyphics; by the dark connections of the mind, they acquired more than their precise meaning: they became co-ordinates of emotion and association. Take a symbol such as the word 'hair'. It means, literally, a dead fiber excreted by certain cells of the skin. But it has what one might call an umbra: a zone of meanings larger and vaguer than the central one. 'Hair' also means any thread-like object; or wider still, any tiny measure. But beyond this, the word has a penumbra: a broad zone of emotive meanings, many of them sexual, the touch and scent of experience. When we read the four letters h.a.i.r. on a page, the whole complex flings itself open in our mind.

But now let us condense 'hair' into a movie image: a woman combing her long dark hair with a white plastic comb. Here, too, we have the literal: a person combing hair. We have the umbra: it is morning or it is night, the woman is dressing or undressing. And the penumbra: who is watching? Is he still in bed? Has she risen or is she about to join him? Why does she keep combing? Is it after love? Is it the delay of love? In any case, it is still sensuous, sexual. But what it is, with all its vaporous meanings, will be defined not only by the story in which this image is embedded, but by the limits and associations of our own lives, our personal reality – not too different, the film maker is obliged to think, from anyone else's.

But wait: isn't reality itself a symbol? Isn't visual experience, in particular, no more than a two-dimensional diagram on the tiny screen of our retina, of an infinitely complicated and ultimately inconceivable universe of quarks, waves, photons, etc.? In spite of the Zen masters, it is not; and that is simply because any image is a great deal more than a mere representation. The work of such physiologists as James Gibson has shown that the flat image on the plate of our retina is not a true model of how we see. The brain picks up not merely variations in light and shade, but the pattern of moving variations, which it transforms at once with the colors of the viewer's endowment and experience. We see everything through the rich vegetation of our own lives, to which, nicely enough, the film now adds a thicket or two:

> How can we characterize these memory structures?
>
> Since it is not easy to describe memory representations literally, we often resort to metaphors that may be misleading. For example, virtually everyone can form what we call a 'mental picture' of a square. But this does not mean that somewhere in the brain there is a two-dimensional region describable in terms of points, edges, and surfaces, isomorphic to the square. It is hard to imagine a mechanism for manipulating (for example, rotating) or make inferences about such a physical structure in the brain.
>
> More likely is the proposal, supported by gradually accumulating evidence, that human memory consists of a complex organization of nodes connected by links, called a 'list structure'.[1]

This structure is the very opposite of symbolization. The square on the page is a simple sign, but the reality set free in our heads, conscious and unconscious, is far more complicated; all the squareness of things is implied in those four simple lines; in that sense no symbol, except possibly one just invented half a second ago, is wholly pure. I will argue that drama, and film as a peculiarly hypnotic form of drama, deals with precisely these vast, vague, glowing internal structures of experience, emotion, and character. Symbols are unstable, perishable, ultimately unsatisfying. But the intense complexities of human drama are permanent. The story of Job in the Old Testament, or of David and Bathsheba, are dilemmas co-eval with the human spirit; they will last as long as we do.

Is it a contradiction to admit to a force, say, of a Cycladic Venus, a stone smoothed down to the hieroglyphic of abstract breast, folded arms, lifted head, and the universal triangle of sex? Or of the fat, abstract labia of an African carving? Or, with heads universally inclined, all the robed Marys of medieval stone? Or the voluptuous brasses of Brancusi or Lachaise, or indeed the woman sawn in three by the hand of Henry Moore? These are all Women, not a particular Woman; is their power derived from their universality, from a symbol so deep that it is common to mankind, running like a hidden river from generation to generation?

Yes, they are symbols; and no, their power does not spring from their simple meaning. They affect us because the emotion, the experiences of being a child and a lover are common to all of us. There is no such thing as a blank human being, not even while it kicks in the womb. It has already experienced warm liquidity, if nothing else.

There is nothing mystic about this fact. The very earliest sculptures are abstractions, true; but their power derives not from their sign, but from their association. As the skill of the artist became greater and subtler, he urged himself closer to reality. The great sculptures of fifth-century Greece were painted, and their eyes inlaid with blue stone; the object was to make them as alive as possible; belief and emotion were compressed into one striding object. This is just as true of the so-called archaic period; certainly of the much older Egyptian figures; and even in Neolithic times, a profile on a bit of bone has, I suppose, the same symbolic value as the bison in the cave of Altamira – but what a difference in power and emotion!

We can see the same development, the same distinctions, in the work of the theatre. That great drama in the Gospel of St Matthew may be merely cosmic to the theologian, but to the non-Christian like myself it is far more, far deeper; the 'pity and terror' of its tragedy lies in the artistry of its human detail; when Christ cries out from the Cross, 'My God, my God, why hast Thou forsaken me?', the writer may have quoted, for symbolic and doctrinal reasons, from Psalm 22 of the Old Testament, but the effect is not sectarian; it is powerfully and fully and commonly human: the detail of a great dramatist.

Speaking from the inside as a workman in the field, I would say that symbolism does not elevate a drama; nor degrade it, either; it is only irrelevant. It is easy enough to derive a matrix of symbols for *The Pilgrim's Progress*; a lot harder for *The Canterbury Tales*. Rabelais and Homer are almost impossible. They are too elaborate, too wild, too human. Hector dragged through the dust by Achilles; or Gargantua squatting down to banter with the pretty courtesans: neither of these can be bent into symbols. They are too particular. On the other hand, some of the plays of Shakespeare have certainly been ground up, digested, diluted, and redistilled into a symbolic structure. The process may be interesting, but the fact is that it is irreversible. No statement of what a Shakespeare play is or means can regenerate the play. Indeed, any dramatist who would try to construct a play or film from a set of symbols is either cracked, mediocre, or more usually (and there are numerous examples) both.

Even *Oedipus Rex* has not been spared the hindsight of the critics. Why, they say, did Oedipus blind himself instead of committing suicide? Isn't this proof that the eyeballs were symbolic of organs hung rather lower? This thought is fascinating, and irrelevant. With regard to what happens to him, Oedipus the King is not representative: he is too particular, too prone to accident; imagine someone who is left to die as an infant, is happily rescued by peasants, grows up and meets a man in a chariot and kills him, not knowing the man is his own father, and then goes on to answer the clever riddle of the Sphinx, and as a curious consequence, marries a widow queen who turns out, against all the rules of probability, to be his mother. These five strange events can. hardly happen again; certainly not to the same person; hence the drama can never be knitted into a plausible symbolic structure; it refutes generality by its particulars. But what it has (like the early and late Pietàs of Michelangelo) is a powerful commonality of emotion. The distinction is crucial.

Now films, especially and intrinsically, resist the nice traps of symbolism. They have order, of course, but their great power is in their specificity. At the risk of self-exposure, let me elaborate at this point and consider three films which I helped to create. They are not great films, but they are good and interesting. And each of them, because they deal with a corrosive social problem, would seem to be open to symbolic analysis. But I speak as a craftsman when I ask: is such analysis true, and not merely clever; and, where true, does it clarify our enjoyment of films?

Intruder in the Dust, very succinctly, is the story of a black man in Oxford, Mississippi, accused of shooting a white man, and threatened with an old-fashioned southern lynching. His proud refusal to aid in his own defense might be seen as symbolic of the rural southern black in the 1920s. But Lucas Beauchamp wears a gold watch, carries a gold toothpick, wears a pale hat, a long coat and a pistol; he is hardly a typical tenant black; he is far too idiosyncratic to be filed on the spike of 'symbol' in that sense of the word. As the reluctant lawyer Stevens says, 'Lucas, has it ever occurred to you that if you just said Mister to white people, and said it like you meant it, you might not be sitting here now?' So the black farmer Beauchamp is a maverick, too large to be a symbol.

Stevens himself might be construed to be 'symbolic' of the white gentry, the old power-structure of this backward county, descendant of the patrician slave-owners, who knew (Faulkner implies) and valued their blacks, indeed were nursed by them as babies, and slept with them as adults – the men, anyway. The boy Chick Mallison is, in fact, a distant cousin of Lucas Beauchamp; it is part of his dilemma. For miscegenation is the obsessive bloody thread in many of Faulkner's novels; in this he reflects the southern conscience of his time. Only Stevens has a narrow enough character to be truly representative; he expresses Faulkner's curiously naive view of politics; and in fact was meant to replenish Faulkner's thin bank account by working as the hero of a projected series of detective novels. But Chick is much too specific to fit any scheme; a white boy brave enough to disinter a buried body to prove a black's stubborn point: this is an act of private courage. Then there is the old, genteel Miss Habersham, who helps Chick and his young black friend Aleck dig up a white man's grave; this is very particular indeed. And even the Gowrie clan, who might be said to represent the poor and dispossessed rednecks, are a father with one arm and his sons who are twins, rather exceptional persons.

That, precisely, is the point. The tragedy that nearly happens is a par-ticular exception to the normal order. Exceptions illuminate, and par-ticulars are what make a story possible. Indeed, one of the few rules of serious drama is that there should be a disequilibrium, a violation of the normal societal structure, that elaborate compound of habits and morals. Yet I speak as a workman when I repeat that even such generalities are uneasy and awkward in practice. What is exceptional and specific is exactly what makes the engine of the drama start and run.

It has been caustically said that the history of any film has been measured to be about ninety-seven times as long as the film itself. The 'symbolic' final scene of *Intruder in the Dust* is an illuminating instance of the damage that can be done by symbolization. In the present ending, the boy and his lawyer uncle are looking down from a second story office into the public square on a Saturday afternoon, when both black and white come in to shop. I quote:

> MEDIUM LONG SHOT – PAST CHICK AND STEVENS *in the f.g., looking down from the railing of the upper gallery, watching Lucas as he goes away, through the crowded, seething square. Lucas' pale felt hat is lost among the heads and faces of an ordinary Saturday afternoon.*
> *Chick.* They don't see him. As though it never happened.
> *Stevens.* They see him.
> *Chick.* No. They don't even know he's there.
> *Stevens.* They do. The same as I do. They always will. As long as he lives.
>
> MEDIUM CLOSE TWO SHOT – CHICK AND STEVENS
> *Stevens.* Proud, stubborn, – insufferable: but there he goes: the keeper of my conscience, – [2]

But in the original script this rhetorical and sentimental scene had a somewhat different meaning – because it was not the final scene; it was the last but one. In the final episode Lucas Beauchamp came up the stairs from the street to pay a final visit to the lawyer. Now Stevens may be moral and 'symbolic', but not Beauchamp: he has lived too long and too hard. He pays Stevens for the repair of the lawyer's broken pipe: a dollar bill and assorted small coins out of a paper bag. Then:

> MEDIUM CLOSE SHOT – STEVENS, LOOKING DISGRUNTLED
> *He opens his drawer, sweeps the money into it, shuts it, looks up at Lucas. Puts his pipe into his mouth, picks up a book and begins to read. Lucas stands waiting.*
> *Stevens* [*angrily*]. Now what? What are you waiting for now?
>
> CLOSE SHOT – LUCAS
> *Lucas.* My receipt.[3]

This is the natural, instinctive, particular, dramatic place to end the film. But Dore Schary, who was then production head at MGM, insisted on putting the moral at the end; the old curse of the documentary had struck again.

Then what about documentary films? Aren't these heavily dependent on symbols and a symbolic nexus? Mostly they are, and they are often therefore exciting and even convincing in the season they are made, when they can

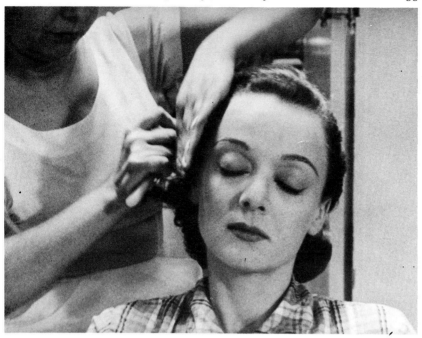

11   *The Savage Eye*: the divorced heroine having her hair done

move an audience already on their side; but they become increasingly dull and false as the years pass, when the symbols common to the audience will have unfortunately changed.

An instance in which I was concerned involved certain striking images of immense, smoking industrial chimneys in a feature-length American documentary, *Native Land*. At the time it was finished, in 1941, these tall stacks represented high employment and a full lunch pail and economic justice. But when this film was revived some thirty years later, the contemporary audience hissed and booed: to them the smoke was the symbol of establishment poison. Their scorn was shallow, but correct. The error was in the aesthetic of film makers who dealt in symbols, not in the complexities of character and life.

The Savage Eye, a partly-enacted documentary of more enduring influence, is another interesting case. I had first written it as a gloss on certain Hogarth prints, with parallels between contemporary Los Angeles and eighteenth-century London. The original script was full of symbolic shots, as one might expect from such a cerebral idea. Luckily, it did not work; meantime, filming proceeded over a period of three years. The material, in its crude form, was a kind of anthropological journey through the American lower middle class.

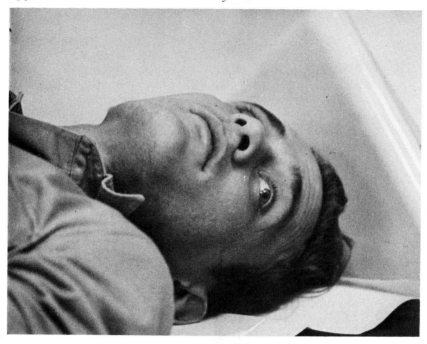

12   *The Savage Eye*: skid-row man lying down to sell his blood

The problem was how to deal with footage so monstrous, strange, moving, and particular. Five scripts followed, each less symbolic than its predecessor; the seventh script was simply the journal of a year in the life of a divorced woman. Frightened, curious, vulnerable, bitter, her character was allowed to experience the lewd, raucous and powerful extravaganzas of ordinary American life. The conflict, in fact, was often between the misty symbol and the glaring reality:

Kirts and Judith leave.
Woman. New Year's morning. I knew I was lost. We drove to my place.
FREEWAY
   He opened the door. I did nothing. I sat on a chair, shivering. He made
   coffee and turned out the lights.
Poet. Were you sad?

FREEWAY – ANOTHER ANGLE
Woman. No. I turned off the key in my head. It was all mechanical. I opened
   the window. He left. There was a siren ...

STOP SIGN
   ... rising and falling. The sky smelled of cigars and ...

RAG MAN
   ... coffins. I was a thousand years old. Zero, zero. No one loves no one.[4]

13   *The Savage Eye*: spectator taunting wrestlers with baby's feeding bottle

And this passage, about halfway through the film:

PEANUT VENDOR
Poet. On the morning of the sixth day, the stars declined, and the sun rose, and
   out of a handful of fire and dust, garbage and alcohol, God created Man.
Woman. He made a big mistake.[5]

And finally, perhaps the best example, are the words cried out by an old sick
woman to the preacher at the healing ceremony; these were words never
written, never imagined, indeed unimaginable; in fact, the words themselves
mean little on a page; it is the tone, the anguish that counts. The scene, a
generation later, is still electrifying. It is exact, not symbolic; it is human, not
logical.

   The Asphalt Jungle is an equally tempting subject for symbolic analysis. The
original novel, as its author W. R. Burnett points out in his afterword to the
printed script,[6] began with the crime news coming over the Police
Commissioner's radio while the Commissioner gives a group of newsmen a
moral lesson. Thus the crime and the criminals can be construed as a
violation of the good order of society. The script I wrote with John Huston
discarded this frame. Instead it placed the main emphasis on the personalities of the criminal group, on the violent or ingenious mechanics of the

14 *The Savage Eye*: drunk woman at New Year's party

crime itself. It ended, of course, in tragedy. But it was not the tragedy that must come inevitably to violators of public order; instead, it was the tragedy of ambitious men with a fine plan thwarted by a corrupt police. It was as if the order, the logic, of criminal life was primary; and the moral order of society was a tragic disruption.

The film itself appears to make such a general point. The crooked lawyer, Emmerich, is talking with his wife:

Mrs Emmerich. Why, you're as pale as a ghost. What's the matter?
Emmerich. I heard some bad news. Man who was working for me got killed.
Mrs Emmerich. Oh, Lon, how awful! Was it an accident?
Emmerich [*shakes his head*]. No. it was an intentional killing.
Mrs Emmerich. What was his name?
Emmerich. Brannom. He had a private detective agency.
Mrs Emmerich. Do they know who did it?
　　[*Emmerich shakes his head.*]
　Lon, when I think about all those awful people you come into contact with –
　downright criminals – I get scared.
Emmerich. There's nothing so different about them.
　　[*Something in his tone strikes her as queer. Watching him, she frowns slightly.*]
　– After all, crime is only a left-handed form of human endeavor.[7]

We tend to forget that this is not meant as universal and cynical truth, but simply the platitude of a particular character. Because he runs a respectable business, he must seek to justify his investment in crime. Nevertheless his speech has been taken to be the symbolic theme of the film; it is not: it is the rationale of one character, and only that. Just so, Nora's final speech in Ibsen's *A Doll's House* has been misinterpreted as the message of the play, and even of the playwright; but it is simply Nora speaking, and no one and nothing else. The longer a play or a film has existed, the more subject it becomes to the playful infection of the symbol. In *The Asphalt Jungle*, is Dix symbolic of the plain American? He was certainly not conceived in so simple a manner; he was not merely 'a small time hooligan who's crazy for horses'. Dix is alternately violent and sentimental; but more than that, he has a taut sense of personal honor: 'I just can't be in Cobby's debt and keep my self-respect.' And then there is his girl, Doll. She has begged to go with him back home to Kentucky. He's badly wounded:

EXT. MEDIUM TWO-SHOT PROCESS DOLL'S CAR – NIGHT
SHOOTING THROUGH THE WINDSHIELD TOWARD DOLL AND DIX
Dix is behind the wheel, Doll seated beside him. The car is not moving: they're at a grade crossing, waiting for a long, slow freight to pass. They watch in silence.

INT. MEDIUM CLOSE TWO-SHOT DOLL'S CAR *behind Doll and Dix and toward the dark masses of freight cars as they move slowly by.*
Doll. How are you feeling now, Dix?
Dix. All right. Cold. It didn't use to get cold, this time of the year.
Doll. Dix, why don't you let me drive for a while?
   [*There's a pause before Dix answers.*]
Dix. You don't know the way. I'd just have to keep telling you.[8]

Is this the American Woman? Not if we believe Jung:

As a basis for the analysis of the American way of life I am now treating a young American (doctor). Here again the mother-complex looms large (cf. the *Mother-Mary cult*). In America the mother is decidedly the dominant member of the family. American culture really is a bottomless abyss; the men have become a flock of sheep and the women play the ravening wolves – within the family circle, of course. I ask myself whether such conditions have ever existed in the world before. I really don't think they have.[9]

   Certainly one can imagine films, and some fine directors have made them, that are mostly the clever manipulation of symbolic puppets. *Metropolis*, if one is kind enough to pardon its peculiar story, is a vast mummery of ponderous mass abstractions. *The Cabinet of Dr Caligari* (1919) is a stiff and classic bore; the Yoda in *The Empire Strikes Back* is a fashionable doll; and Brando in *Apocalypse Now* is yet another dreadfully symbolic Alienated Man. On the other hand, the woman's erotic monologue in Bergman's *Persona* is worth all the knee-deep Scandinavian profundity of Death playing chess. Sculpture, painting, even certain kinds of theatre can deal with symbols without too much embarrassment. But the film is natively cruel to abstractions, and this for a very simple reason: it is too close to reality. It is a composite of many moving photographs, and a photograph by its nature gives us an infinity of information; such details correspond, one-to-one, to a Cantorian infinity of detail in the visual world.

Such richness, such specificity, is the opposite of symbolism; and this marvelous fact has given the cinema its inner quality: the exact which is also the unique. One thinks of such brilliant, instinctive scenes, irreducible to anything but pale descriptions, as the young gangsters in a Kurosawa film, fighting in a mess of spilled white paint in a hallway under repair; and from the same director, the great, static funeral banquet in *Ikiru*; the assault down the Odessa steps – a pure invention by Eisenstein; Stroheim who had Zazu Pitts squirming in a bed of gold coins in *Greed*; Buster Keaton, in a diving suit, in *The Navigator*, washing his hands before lunch, three feet under water: or the great shaven-headed close-ups in Carl Dreyer's *Joan of Arc*. The child in *The Tin Drum* may be construed as the observing artist, innocent and selfish; but the hypnotic force of this performance comes from his actual, photographed presence, from the specific words he says. There are critics who assert that there was a sad loss of symbolic depth when movies changed from silent to sound. Once again, they underestimate the connection of the photographic image to the complexities of life; furthermore, there is not all that great a distinction, because even the silent films used language with the printed word.

Are there no dangerous effects to this heavy reliance on physical reality? Have photography and cinema begun to confuse our sense of life? Susan Sontag has argued that they have. There is a certain truth to this charge. I know a grandmother, who, on being complimented on the beauty of her granddaughter, said, 'Oh, that's nothing! You should see her pictures.' Yet we all know, unless we are truly mad, the difference between life and art. That difference is the very tension of drama. Still, we no longer see as we saw 150 years ago. Both photography and cinema are not merely new arts, but new windows of consciousness. They are still arts, but of a special kind: one of their unique qualities is that they are resistant, because of their detail, to every sort of generality.

On the other hand, is there not something good and interesting in the play of symbols? It is an intelligent game, after all; and one feels engrossed by its equations, just as one does in reading kabbala: the extraction from tiny black marks on a page, of vast, heady premises, the meaning inside the meaning. One finds it as fascinating as the analysis of dreams, particularly of one's own.

Does not the serene stripper in *The Savage Eye* represent Cybele, Astarte, Venus, the avatars of the divine feminine, the primary Mother? In *The Asphalt Jungle*, does not 'Doc' Riendenschneider represent the Intellectual, the man armed only with theory, who succumbs to the intellectual's Achilles heel, voyeurism? And does not the very grave in *Intruder in the Dust*, dug up once in the film, but four times in the novel, represent the hidden crime of the south – not slavery, but miscegenation? Or can one not, most generally, regard all film, but particularly those shown on a large screen to a darkened audience, as an essentially religious ritual, or a pageant intended to dramatize a set of values? The dramatic challenge of an alien and wicked order defeated by a native and conservative order that draws its guns at last? True or not, all this sort of symbolic analysis is witty and intriguing; except that it does not distinguish a dud from a masterpiece.

And this, to be blunt, is the tool the craftsman needs every day of his working life: a criterion that will help him judge his own art. There is no such certain measure, of course; the world and its images are too complex; for one thing films are embedded in social judgments, scene by scene, from start to finish. One is obliged to wrestle and charm the audience at the same time; it is like the struggle between Jacob and the Angel. No extra machinery ought to burden the artist. All symbols, however clever, should be banned from the armament of the artist. He does not need them: he has troubles enough already. The real, changing world awaits his grasp.

NOTES

1. Jill Larkin, John McDermott, Dorothea P. Simon and Herbert A. Simon, 'Expert and Novice performance in Solving Physics Problems' *Science*, 20 June 1980, p. 1,337.
2. Regina K. Fadiman, *Faulkner's Intruder in the Dust, Novel Into Film, The Screenplay by Ben Maddow as adapted for film by Clarence Brown* (Knoxville: University of Tennessee Press, 1978).
3. *Ibid.*
4. Ben Maddow, *The Savage Eye*, unpublished ms. in possession of the author.
5. *Ibid.*
6. *The Asphalt Jungle, a screenplay by Ben Maddow and John Huston, from a novel by W. R. Burnett* (Carbondale: Southern Illinois University Press, 1980).
7. *Ibid.*
8. *Ibid.*
9. Letter from C. G. Jung to Sigmund Freud, 8 Nov. 1909, printed in *The Freud/ Jung Letters* (Princeton University Press, 1974).

Russian *pagliacci*: symbols of profaned love in *The Puppet Show**

The author of *The Puppet Show* is a veritable wizard of theatricalism. (Vsevolod Meyerkhold)[1]

The collaboration of Aleksandr Blok and Vsevolod Meyerkhold in the production of Blok's playlet *The Puppet Show* was a milestone in the development of modern Russian drama. For Blok it was a public declaration of his break with the mysticism of his youthful poetry. For Meyerkhold it was a declaration of his break with the Naturalistic Theatre and the Theatre of Mood of Stanislavsky's Moscow Art Theatre[2] and the perfect opportunity to apply his new theory of stylized acting. (A translation of the play is printed at the end of this paper, p. 171.)

Recognized at once by some as a masterpiece and a radical departure from traditional theatrical fare, the play made a tremendous impact upon the theatrical world of *fin de siècle* Russia. In the words of Georgy Chulkov, a close friend of Blok and a member of the first-night audience which was studded with the elite of the St Petersburg intelligentsia: 'Never, either before or since, had I witnessed such implacable opposition and such admiring ecstasy in the theater auditorium. The violent whistles of enemies and the thundrous applause of friends mingled with shrieks and howls.'[3]

The fortunate combination of Blok's symbolic *pagliacci* and Meyerkhold's stylized theatre launched a new episode in the history of Russian culture, the 'Petrushka' era.

As the Soviet scholar A. V. Fyodorov points out, Aleksandr Blok was the first to introduce the stock characters from what Fyodorov chauvinistically calls the theatre of masks[4] into a Russian play. He was the first Russian playwright deliberately to stress the theatricality of his work, as opposed to any attempt to 'represent life'. In his introduction to the volume which contained *The Puppet Show* and the other plays with which it formed a trilogy, Blok says:

---

* A draft of this paper was read at the *Themes in Drama* International Conference on 'Drama and Symbolism' held at the University of California, Riverside, in May 1980.

15 Blok's *Lyrical Dramas*: book-cover by K. Somov, 1908

Is it possible to describe all the complexity of the modern psyche, enriched by the impressions of history and present-day life, enfeebled by doubts and contradictions – a psyche which suffers long and agonizingly when it is miserable and dances, acts the buffoon, and blasphemes when it is joyful, forgets unrestrained deep suffering and unrestrained vibrant joy?

Keeping all of this in mind, I consider it essential to specify that the three little dramas brought to the readers' attention are *lyrical* dramas, *i.e.* the kind in which the feelings of an individual psyche – the doubts, passions, failures, and blunders – are just represented in dramatic form. I draw no ideological, moral nor other conclusions here.[5]

Blok disassociates himself from the tendentiousness of nineteenth-century literature, and offers his audiences lyrical dramas which reflect his own mood and that of his times.

It is difficult for me to understand why neither Soviet nor western scholars have chosen to analyze this highly symbolic playlet on the basis of its origins – the *commedia dell'arte* as it had evolved throughout the centuries and been absorbed into early twentieth-century Russian culture. It is far too common a failing of students of Russian literature to treat it as an isolated phenomenon, ignoring the fact that pre-revolutionary Russia was well integrated into the whole European cultural community. Educated Russians kept themselves abreast of the latest developments in the intellectual and artistic life of the rest of Europe. Those who choose not to discuss the obvious ties which *The Puppet Show* has with the *commedia dell'arte* overlook an important key to an understanding of the play.

A number of interpretations of the play have been offered. Soviet specialists in the theatre of Blok view *The Puppet Show* as an expression of Blok's repudiation of the social values and political views held by his fellow Russian Symbolists. His turnabout was caused, they feel, by the disillusionment Blok experienced after the abortive revolution of 1905. Disciples of the philosopher Vladimir Solovyov who counted Blok as one of themselves construed it as a deliberate blasphemy – a malicious, spiteful distortion of the mystical longings and metaphysical quests found in his first cycle of verse, 'Poems about the Beautiful Lady'. To those who had shared Blok's perceptions and dreams, it seemed a slanderous misrepresentation of their philosophical and ethical beliefs.

Another theory which grew in retrospect was related to a personal drama involving Blok, his wife Lyubov, and Andrey Bely. Bely was the vital force behind a 'collective' of disciples of Vladimir Solovyov. The little group consisted of Bely, Blok, Lyubov Blok, and the minor poet Sergey Solovyov, nephew of the philosopher. Part of the credo of the 'collective' was a longing for the Divine Sophia, principle of the 'Eternal Feminine'. Lyubov Dmitrievna Blok was treated as the incarnation of this concept. What had begun as a worshipful fantasy, in which the young Madame Blok was practically adored as the embodiment of Sophia, developed into a more earthly physical attraction between Bely and Lyubov Dmitrievna. This *amitié amoureuse* was only in its initial stages at the writing of the play; nonetheless, contemporaries attributed the following roles to the principals of the real comedy of morals. Blok was Pierrot, Bely was Harlequin, and Lyubov Dmitrievna was the fickle Columbine. Some scholars[6] see the play as Blok's attempt to exorcise his obsession with duality. They interpret it as yet another manifestation of the 'double' theme which frequently appears in Blok's lyrics. According to this theory, Pierrot and Harlequin are alter-egos of the poet.

Prior to discussing the play itself, I would like to consider the source of *The Puppet Show*, the history of its development, and its various productions.

The Puppet Show was written in January 1906; it took only twenty days to complete the final version of the text. Blok had undertaken the project at the request of Georgy Chulkov, who was at that time editor of *Fakely* (Torches), the organ of a society of the same name which was dedicated to symbolist theatre. Blok was asked to expand the following poem[7] which he had written in 1905.

The Puppet Show

Look, they've opened a puppet show
For happy, good children,
A little girl and boy watch
The ladies, kings, and devils.
And that infernal music resounds,
And a doleful violin bow whines.
A terrifying devil has grabbed a chubby little child,
And cranberry juice trickles down.

Little Boy:
'He escapes black wrath
With a sleight of his white hand.
Look: flames are approaching from the left ...
Do you see the torches? Do you see the puffs of smoke?
That is the queen herself no doubt ...'

Little Girl:
'Ah, no! Why are you teasing me?
That is the retinue of hell ...
A queen would walk in broad daylight,
All garlanded with roses,
And enamored knights would carry her train,
Clanking their swords.'

Suddenly a *pagliaccio* bends over the footlights
And yells: 'Help me!
I'm bleeding cranberry juice!
I'm bandaged up with rags!
On my head is a cardboard helmet!
In my hand a wooden sword!'

The little girl and boy begin to cry,
And the happy puppet show closes down.

16   1914 stage set for *The Puppet Show*

The poem, written in the summer of 1905, was later published in a collection
entitled 'Unexpected Joy' (1907). The play was the first of three 'lyrical
dramas' which were all written in 1906. The second was *The King on the Square*
(*Korol na ploshchadi*) written in the late summer–early fall of 1906, and the
third was *The Unknown Woman* (*Neznakomka*) written in November of that
year. *The Puppet Show* was given its première on 30 December 1906 at the
Kommissarzhevsky Theatre in St Petersburg. The other two plays were
never commercially produced, although *The Unknown Woman* was staged at
the studios of S. V. Khalyutin's acting school in Moscow in 1913, and at
Meyerkhold's acting studios in St Petersburg in a double program with *The
Puppet Show* in 1914 (see plate 16).

The Puppet Show ran for a total of three weeks after its first night.
However, it was subsequently produced several times by Meyerkhold – once
on tour with his repertory group in 1907 at the Hermitage Theatre, Moscow,
and at his Petersburg acting studios. It was also given abroad by theatre
companies: Georges Pitoeff produced it with his troupe in Geneva in 1915
and again in Paris during the 1923–24 theatre season. The American
Commedia dell' Arte Theatre gave an English version in New York City in
the spring of 1923. The popular comedian James Watts took the role of
Pierrot, originally played by Meyerkhold himself.[8]

Blok introduces an ironic twist to one of the standard situations from

17   Portrait of Vsevolod Meyerkhold as Pierrot. Drawing by N. Ulyanov, 1908

commedia dell'arte repertoire – mistaken identity, or the heroine in disguise. The first section of two in the play, which is not formally separated into acts, unfolds during a seance of mystics. Pierrot, ignored by them and glaringly out of place, is present. When a beautiful young woman appears mysteriously on stage, the mystics take her to be Death for whose advent they have convened their meeting. Pierrot, on the other hand, recognizes her as Columbine. There is an exchange of views in which the mystics accuse Pierrot of being mad. Pierrot, however, contradicts them, speaking what

18   Columbine at the mystics' seance. Lithograph by N. Dmitrevsky, 1922

seems to him the simple truth. Here, yet another theme based on nineteenth-century versions of the *commedia dell'arte* is introduced – the seduction of Columbine by Harlequin and her fickle abandonment of Pierrot.

During the course of the play several interruptions are made by the Author. The first takes place during the mystics' seance and the second at the initial encounter between Pierrot, Columbine, and Harlequin. The Author appears a third time at the play's conclusion. Such interventions, too, can be traced to improvisational techniques from *commedia dell'arte*.

The second section also draws upon characters and situations from Italian comedy, more specifically, as it was absorbed into the customs of the eighteenth-century Russian court in the form of masked balls and costumed processions. At such occasions the participants often dressed in costumes from the *commedia dell'arte*. Here we find Pierrot seated to one side of the ballroom scene, once again utterly divorced from the actions going on around him. At first the spotlight is upon him, but later the attention of the audience is drawn to three pairs of lovers who, each in turn, carry on meaningful dialogues.

Some comic relief is supplied by a *pagliaccio* who teases the most pompous of the lovers. Towards the end of this final section, Harlequin once again appears as the master of ceremonies of a torchlight parade. At this point, the theme of Columbine's double identity is resumed. The guests at the ball take her for the figure of Death, while Pierrot once again welcomes her as Columbine. And, indeed, the figure loses its deathly pallor and becomes Pierrot's young fiancée. However, the figure of the bumbling Author thwarts their joyful reunion even as he attempts to join the lovers. The play ends quite abruptly when the players and scenery suddenly disappear as if by a puppeteer's hand. Poor Pierrot, alone on the stage, provides the concluding remarks of the play in a sad monologue.

Blok's directions for the staging of the play are quite explicit. However, he admitted that they leave ample leeway for individual interpretation as we can see from the following description of Meyerkhold's rendition. Meyerkhold chose to keep the background very stark: 'The entire studio is draped along the sides and across the back in dark blue cloth; this dark blue expanse serves as a background and accentuates the color of the decorations of the "little theatre" which has been constructed on stage.'[9] He had the idea of having a miniature theatre built right on the stage to stress the artificiality of the production and to give the impression of a puppet theatre. At his instructions, 'The "little theatre" is to have its own stage, its own curtain, its own prompter's booth, its own doorways and borders. . . . In front of the "little theatre" there is to be a free space extending the entire length of the footlights.'[10] Meyerkhold's treatment of the mystics' costumes provided another means of preventing any sense of 'realism'; he specified that:

> In the first tableau . . . On the stage placed parallel to the footlights there is to be a long table covered to the floor with black cloth. At the table the mystics are to be seated in such a way as to make only the upper part of their bodies visible to the audience. Frightened by some remark or other, the mystics are to lower their heads so as to give the impression that around the table there remain torsos without heads or hands. The contours of their figures are to be cut out of cardboard and their frock-coats, shirt fronts, collars, and cuffs are to be colored on with chalk and charcoal. The actors' hands are to be stuck through the circular holes cut in the cardboard torsos, and the heads are just to be placed up against the cardboard collars.[11]

The cast of the play is relatively small, and it is sharply divided into two groups – the *pagliacci* and the actors in contemporary dress. Pierrot, Harlequin, Columbine, and the Author share most of the spoken text. The chairman of the mystics' seance has several lines to say; some of the mystics say a few words; and each pair of lovers converses for a short time. The other lines are spoken by one unnamed *pagliaccio* during his exchange with the pompous knight. There are a number of other members of the cast who have no lines to speak – mystics at the seance, guests at the ball, torch-bearers, and the shadowy double of the second lover.

Before I consider the symbolic meanings Blok infused into *The Puppet Show*, it is necessary to give a short account of the history of the *commedia dell'arte* in Russia and of its indigenous predecessors, the wandering players and minstrels known as *skomorokhi*. The *skomorokhi* were first mentioned in the old Russian chronicles of 1068. They functioned simultaneously as comedians, dancers, singers, and musicians. They gave presentations depicting current issues which could include comic songs, dramatic scenes, skits, social satires, and burlesques. They wore masks and special costumes. Their instruments of accompaniment were bagpipes, dombras (a Russian lute-like instrument) and old Russian prototypes of flutes and oboes. Highly characteristic of their presentations was the element of improvisation. Remarks were directed at the audience, which was sometimes invited to participate in the sketch.

The *skomorokhi*'s activities were linked to the old Russian observances of pagan rituals. After the Christianization of Russia, these performers preserved the lore of folk ceremonies – vestiges of pagan beliefs which still prevailed among the populace. *Skomorokhi* were called upon by Russians to direct and participate in such ceremonies as weddings, funerary rites and special holiday festivities. They reached the height of their development in Russia from the fifteenth to the seventeenth centuries, at which time they formed large companies consisting of dozens of members. The tsars invited such groups to their courts where the *skomorokhi* presided over the same kinds of ceremonies enjoyed by simpler folk and where they also served as court jesters.

Due to the *skomorokhi*'s strong ties with pagan practices, their lewd behavior during performances, and their outspoken criticism of the mores and ethics of the ruling classes, the Church and State joined forces to suppress them during the reign of Aleksis Mikhailovich Romanov. At that time, their troupes were dispersed, and the players were exiled to the peripheries of Russia. They were denied the right to use the musical instruments, garb, and paraphernalia of their trade. As a matter of fact, public spectacles were arranged to burn these theatrical implements ceremonially.

The first appearance of an operatic troupe from Italy was in 1731, when singers and musicians were sent to the Empress Anna Ioannovna from the Polish court. She commissioned them to perform plays and operas for her court. However, the empress's and her courtiers' ignorance of the Italian language forced the players to limit themselves to pantomimes from the repertoire of the *commedia dell'arte*. Unfortunately, their efforts met with little success, and they left that same year.

A second attempt to establish a court troupe was made in 1733, but this second group left after two years without taking root. Other troupes arrived at the end of the eighteenth century and found a more favorable reception in the very different milieu of the petit-bourgeois theatres and circuses. From that time on, characters, plots, and techniques were absorbed into the popular culture via the marionette theatre. There is even some speculation that the Russian equivalent for Pierrot – Petrushka – has its origins in a *commedia dell'arte* jester Pietro Miró, nicknamed Petrillo, who enjoyed great popularity in Russia.[12]

Some of the traditions of the *commedia dell'arte* combined with those of the *skomorokhi* were retained in the form of masked balls and triumphal parades at the courts of the eighteenth-century Russian empresses. During such festivities, the tsarinas and their courtiers and guests impersonated characters from the *commedia dell'arte* as well as other historical or mythological personages. Sketches from the *commedia dell'arte* were sometimes directly translated, but more often, Russian audiences saw Russian adaptations of the characters and situations from Italian comedy. They were also exposed to the transformations of *commedia dell'arte* plots in the plays of the French comic playwrights, especially Molière.

As we learn from Robert Storey's book *Pierrot: A Critical History of a Mask*, the Romantic movement in France contributed greatly to a resurgence of interest in and affection for the characters from the *commedia dell'arte*.[13] However, this was not the case in Russian literature and drama of the nineteenth century, because authors tended to dwell primarily upon national issues. There seemed to be no place for the particular style of buffoonery and comic situation characteristic of this type of comedy. In the second half of the century, the focus of literature and drama was mainly upon psychological and social problems which were given realistic treatment. It was only at the end of the nineteenth century that Russian writers and artists rediscovered the rich offerings of old Italian comedy – its theatrical techniques, its major characters, and the romantic interest attached to them by the French Symbolists.

There were three factors which spurred such an interest among Russian artists, writers, and composers. The first was a re-evaluation of the art and culture of the eighteenth century, both in Russia and France. It was sparked off by the graphic reproductions of English and French artists depicting that century in Sergey Diaghilev's magazine *Mir Iskusstva* (The World of Art), and the Russian Symbolists' journal *Vesy* (The Scales), by the verbal evocations of eighteenth-century life in French Symbolist poetry, and by several

THE
PIERROT
OF
THE
MINVTE.

19   Aubrey Beardsley, cover design for *The Pierrot of the Minute*, published by
John Lane

art exhibits devoted to that era. The most outstanding was one organized by Diaghilev on historical paintings and portraits by eighteenth-century Russian artists in 1905.[14]

The second factor which served to heighten interest in the eighteenth century was the promulgation of French Symbolist poetry in Russian literary journals and in translated editions. Foremost in transmitting images from the *commedia dell'arte* was the poetry of Paul Verlaine particularly in his 'Fêtes galantes', and of Jules Laforgue, whose verses in 'Complaintes et imitations de Notre Dame de la lune' are peopled with characters from the *commedia dell'arte*.

Foreign comedies were also sources of inspiration for the enchantment with characters and situations from the *commedia dell'arte* at the turn of this century. There were revivals of plays from the repertoire of the eighteenth-century Comédie Française. The opera *I pagliacci* came to Russia in September 1896 and enjoyed enormous success, going on to become a perennial favorite of both the St Petersburg and Moscow operas.[15] Russians were acquainted through reviews with such plays as J.-K. Huysmans' *Pierrot sceptic* and Albert Giraud's *Pierrot lunaire*. The ballet *Harlequinade* by Richard Drigo premièred in the 1899–1900 season and enjoyed great success in Russia until the revolution.[16]

Finally, there was a great enthusiasm in Russia for the graphic art of Aubrey Beardsley, who was particularly enchanted with the character of Pierrot, more moderately so with other *commedia dell'arte* figures and with the eighteenth century in general. Reproductions of his works available to Russians ranged from copies of his drawings for *The Savoy* and *The Yellow Book* and his illustrations for Ernest Dowson's *Pierrot of the Minute* to his designs for *ex libris* and calling cards for England's literati and socialites.

Lists of new publications featured in Symbolist journals from the turn of the century show that original editions of Beardsley's works were to be found in Russia. Bely refers to Blok's play, linking it with Beardsley's drawings (letter of 10–11 August 1907).[17] An entire issue of the major Symbolist journal *Vesy* (XI, 1905) was devoted to Beardsley's art. It predated the writing of *The Puppet Show* by only a month or so. There can be no doubt that Beardsley's art left many artistic and literary traces in Russia.[18] Not the least of these was the rising popularity of the characters from the world of old Italian comedy.

In light of the historical information offered above, I shall turn to a discussion of the symbolism of *The Puppet Show*. First, it is necessary to recall some of the more commonly held interpretations of Russian *skomorokhi* (a term applied by critics to the characters of Blok's play) and of European *commedia dell'arte* characters. In both east and west, they shared many similar traits, no doubt because they shared the same origins as descendents of the ancient Greek and Roman mimes. Throughout the ages, these co-

20   Aubrey Beardsley, design for the end-paper of *Pierrot*

medians were viewed by their detractors and admirers alike as critics of
mores, ethics, and the social order. Fathers of the Church, whether Roman
or Eastern Orthodox, inveighed against them as blasphemers and perverts.
Their audiences adored them for their ribald humor and sly social commentaries. We must also keep in mind the original theatrical functions of
ancient mimes, medieval jesters, and *commedia dell'arte* players. In classical
times, their skits provided comic interludes for the tragedies. In the Middle
Ages, they provided some lighthearted moments in between the serious
messages of the mystery plays.

Improvisation is perhaps the most important distinguishing feature of the
art of the *skomorokhi* and the Italian comedians. In studying the dynamics of
the original troupes, one learns that the actors were not given scripts, but
rather simple outlines of the plot. It was then up to the actors to provide
dialogues for given situations. The only constant elements were the standard-
ized gestures taught all members of the troupe. The humor of their presentations was based upon ridicule of accepted values or social conventions by
rendering them amusing or grotesque.

It is also necessary to provide an explanation of the significance which is
generally attributed to the principal characters from the *commedia dell'arte* at
the time when Blok wrote *The Puppet Show*. By the turn of the century, Pierrot
had evolved from a rather minor servant, Pedrolino, to a major romantic

21 Aubrey Beardsley, the death of Pierrot

figure in European theatre and poetry. By the time Blok made use of this character, his personality was greatly colored by the new psychological significance given Pierrot by nineteenth-century romantics and subsequently developed by the French Symbolists. Sociological interpretations colored his role so that he was seen as a representative of the downtrodden and misunderstood – a social pariah.[19] On a psychological level, he came to be associated with the related concepts of the rejected lover or the cuckolded husband. For the French Symbolists he became a symbol for the poet.

> A mirror and a mask: Pierrot functions as both for the poet. To look upon one was to see the other, the reflection within the disguise, and vice-versa. That Verlaine, like Hamlet, could both conceal and reveal himself within an antic disposition goes far towards explaining Pierrot's immense appeal to the artists of the late nineteenth century. Mediating as he does between public truth and private fantasy, comedy and pathos, the Self and the Other, he offers one small but effective key to this *parade sauvage*.[20]

Pierrot as the poet can also be tied in with the Nietzschean concepts of the poet–dreamer and the comic embodiment of the *principium individuationis*.[21]

The character of Columbine, like Pierrot, evolved from the buxom maid of coarse beauty to a more refined character in her eighteenth-century representations. At that time, she often achieved the status of an *inamorata*. Throughout the history of the Italian comedy, however, she was always involved in comic love episodes. In her various roles, Columbine usually retains certain traits: she is clever, changeable, very attractive, and frequently of easy virtue. Blok envisions her as the symbol of femininity or an incarnation of the 'Eternal Feminine': 'For all three [heroes of Blok's trilogy] the beautiful life is the embodiment of the image of the Eternal Feminine: for the one it is Columbine, the shining fiancée who is transformed into a "cardboard fiancée" by the sick and idiotic imagination of Pierrot ...'[22] Finally, it should be noted that she, like Pierrot, is from simple stock.

Harlequin is also a figure of great complexity. There have been many discussions of this beloved character, yet his origins are still debatable. Since Evgeny Anichkov's discussion of this rascal in his article on the *commedia dell'arte* for the Encyclopedic Dictionary[23] was readily available to Blok, I shall summarize his views. Anichkov believes that the name Harlequin is etymologically linked to the Germanic folk demon, the Erlkönig, who was immortalized in Goethe's poem of the same name. He also mentions Alichino as a source. He is one of the demons patroling a lake of pitch in Dante's *Inferno* (cantos 21–2). Russians, like other Europeans, attributed demonic powers to the seemingly frolicsome character. Vsevolod Meyerkhold envisions him thus: 'Harlequin is the foolish simpleton, the foxy servant, seemingly always so happy. But have a look at what his mask conceals. Harlequin is a mighty sorcerer, spellbinder and enchanter. Harlequin is the representative of the infernal powers.'[24] Blok seems to imply this connection between Harlequin and hell in the second scene, where he has him leading a torchlight parade. This group is none other than the hellish retinue imagined by the little girl in the poem 'The Puppet Show'. The stress laid upon the dripping tar might well point to Alichino's abode in *The Inferno*. Like his antithesis, Pierrot, Harlequin can be seen to reflect a Nietzschean element, in this case, the Dionysian which is also related to hell.[25]

The *pagliaccio* who pops out from among the other masked dancers at the ball scene enlivens a boring discourse of the pompous knight by his comic antics. Devoid of the pathos which Blok has given to Pierrot and Harlequin, he represents the classic interpretation of the *zanni* (comic servants) of the original comedies. As was often the case in the traditional scenarios, the *zanni* introduced an element of realism and common sense into the plot. Here, it is the *pagliaccio* who expresses the central idea of the play. He speaks out following his scuffle with the self-satisfied knight after he has interrupted the latter's dull musings. His cry 'Help! I'm bleeding cranberry juice!' draws attention to the artificiality of the whole performance and, by inference, the illusory nature of the actors and their concerns. Those whom Blok was caricaturing in this satire found this line particularly offensive and meaningful. Andrey Bely recalls: 'For years I could not forgive him for the "cranberry juice": for the sceptical irony directed at himself. And how cruel we were then!'[26]

I have been able to find one direct precedent for the role of the Author as participant in the comedy: this is in Rossini's *The Turk in Italy*, an *opero buffa* based on the *commedia dell'arte*, where the poet enters into the drama he is concocting. *The Turk in Italy* is a later, Romantic variation of the comedy within a comedy (Locatelli's *La commedia in commedia*). Of course, another famous but tragic variation of the 'comedy within a comedy' is to be found in Leoncavallo's *I pagliacci*. Blok uses the Author to indicate the fact that there are three different spheres of action and therefore three different levels of interpretation unfolding before the audience. Blok offers an ironic twist to the themes of the 'comedy within a comedy' and the author as player, and Meyerkhold's stage directions for *The Puppet Show* forcefully underline Blok's intended meaning.

The symbolism of *The Puppet Show* begins with its title. In Russian, it is a single word, *Balaganchik*. This is a diminutive form of the word *balagan*, the meanings of which range from the concrete to the figurative. It can signify the wooden trestles upon which the pantomimes, popular shows, and marionettes were presented at street fairs. It can refer to the open-air shows themselves. Finally, it has the abstract meaning of comic antics and nonsensical behavior like that seen at such shows. *Balaganchik*, used for both the title of the play and the poem, would seem to me to refer to what was happening on stage rather than the stage itself. It is what is happening in both the poem and the play which interests Blok, not the stage structure. Therefore I have chosen to translate the title as 'The Puppet *Show*' rather than 'The Puppet Booth', 'The Fairground Booth', or 'The Puppet Theatre' as other translators have rendered it. Blok's contemporaries correctly interpreted his play's title to mean that their 'religio-philosophical' societies, their mystical yearnings, and dreams of a rosy future were mere buffoonery.

Not only did Blok make use of characters from the Italian comedy, but he also drew upon its acting techniques when placing his actors in certain positions and having them perform certain actions. Allardyce Nicoll briefly touches upon the use of certain stock phrases and speeches of the *commedia dell'arte* in his book *Masks, Mimes and Miracles*. Termed *uscite* (exits) and *chiusette* (closings), these were soliloquies usually uttered out of context for a comic effect.[27] This is precisely the way in which the figures of Pierrot and Harlequin function within the play. What they have to say is unrelated to the other activities on stage, yet their words serve to ridicule what other actors are saying. It is only the appearance of Columbine which draws them into the mystics' meeting and integrates them into the ball scene. Pierrot's parting soliloquy corresponds to the *chiusetta*, although his final words are presented not in the form of a couplet, but rather in four stanzas of four alternating rhymed verses.

Blok seems to have been familiar with another standard comic device called the *lazzi* – verbal or physical comic interruptions to enliven scenes which were becoming dull or too lengthy. He makes adroit use of such antics throughout the play. The attempts of the Author to intervene in the performance of the play is one example. The shock effect of Harlequin's sudden exit is another. Finally, the scrap between the knight and the *pagliaccio* provides the most faithful enactment of a typical *lazzo* to be found in the play.

I pass now to a discussion of the two scenes in the play in relation to some of the facts about the *commedia dell'arte* mentioned above. If one were to analyze the plot from the standpoint of the techniques of the Italian comedy, one would have to conclude that the principal events unfolding on stage are the mystics' seance and masked ball – not the encounter between Pierrot, Columbine, and Harlequin. In the two separate parts of the play, the major function of the *pagliaccio*, as always, is to reveal the true value of the conversations, actions, and beliefs of the pretentious mystics, and masked lovers. From Blok's instructions, it is clear that *all* of the characters are cardboard puppets. However, the *pagliaccio*'s actions, language, and perceptions of reality come closer to life than do those of the mystics and couples. To underscore the fatuity and credulity of the mystics, Blok has them speak in a stilted, affected manner, employing archaisms and mystical jargon. The three sets of lovers in the second scene speak in an elevated, romantic style. Pierrot, Harlequin, and Columbine, on the other hand, speak the common idiom (with the exception of Pierrot's banal romantic clichés).

As I mentioned at the beginning of this paper, one of the unanimously accepted interpretations of *The Puppet Show* is that this play is a travesty of Blok's former involvement in the little group of disciples of Vladimir Solovyov. However, I do not think that Blok had in mind only his personal friends. Their 'brotherhood' was far from unique. It seems to me more probable that Blok had a whole category of turn-of-the-century intellectuals in mind. The early years of the twentieth century in Russia were rife with mystics, occultists, spiritualists and serious scholars of ancient, oriental, and folk religions. Probably most familiar to western readers from among the ranks of Russians of this ilk are Helen Blavatskaya and Peter Uspensky. The author of *The Puppet Show* was known to turn up at meetings of the 'Religio-philosophical Society', an organization of clergymen, scholars, and politicians who hoped to effect changes in Russia's political system through the co-operation of Church and State officials (an ideal formulated by Vladimir Solovyov for an ecumenical society). Blok also attended meetings of the organization 'Fakely' (Torches) dedicated to the study of the Eleusinian Mysteries and to ancient Greek drama. Andrey Bely, who had occasion to observe his friend at such gatherings, noted the discomfiture of Blok, who rarely spoke or participated and seemed to view the proceedings with an air of scepticism.[28]

Many critics agree that it was Andrey Bely and Sergey Solovyov who attributed mystical aspirations to what was probably nothing more than the romantic outpourings of an ardent young poet, couched in the language of the medieval romances so popular at that time. When the two young enthusiasts (Bely and Solovyov) pointed out the similarities between Blok's 'Beautiful Lady' and Vladimir Solovyov's Divine Sophia, Blok and his wife passively acquiesced.

Bely points out that Blok was experiencing great emotional turmoil during the summer of 1905 and that he seemed to be drawing away from the 'brotherhood'. When the former tried to resume their enraptured discussions of the summer before, Blok seemed bored and annoyed. This led to Bely and Solovyov falling out with Blok. Bely patched things up with Blok, but Solovyov was never on friendly terms with him again. In his memoir *Vospominania o A. A. Bloke* (Reminiscences of A. A. Blok), Bely cites examples from Blok's poetry of that period to show how the themes reflect Blok's inner conflicts. Particularly noticeable are motifs of blasphemy, hidden passions and sensuality.[29]

In the first scene of *The Puppet Show* one can see a number of messages emerging. The most widely applicable tells us that the 'mystics', i.e. those who espoused the myriad cultic beliefs of the time, were blinded to the realities of life. Narrowing the perspective, Blok relates the theme of the mistaken identity to one group – his friends Bely and Sergey Solovyov. Columbine can be construed as the profanation of the concept of the Divine

Sophia. Blok himself, in his introduction to the 1907 edition of his lyric dramas calls her the incarnation of the 'Eternal Feminine' for Pierrot. In Solovyov's philosophy, the advent of the Divine Sophia or Feminine Principle would herald a new era in human progress. What more ironic contrast to the romantic and sublime image of Sophia could Blok find than Columbine, the comely, simple, but wily servant girl who was far from scornful of earthy pleasures.

To focus even more closely upon Blok's personal life, he seems to be announcing publicly that the object of the worship of Sophia, his wife Lyubov Dmitrievna, was far from being a celestial and perfect being, but resembled far more closely the fickle object of a clownish dreamer's affections. It is quite interesting to note that when Bely sought to reconcile with the Bloks after they fell out in July 1905, the three of them agreed to improvise like the players from the *commedia dell'arte*: 'no philosophers of the future ... were going to teach us about life any more; the creation of life which we affirmed originated in improvisation, in a new *commedia dell'arte*. . . . instead of the mystery of transforming the world, we would dream of the mystery of transforming the moment'.[30]

Bely saw the figure of Pierrot as Blok's irreverent self-portrait. Mouthing stock romantic phrases in verse form, Pierrot, with his guitar, is the debased image of the medieval troubadour with his lute, composing verses to the exalted image of his lady fair. One can interpret Pierrot's first verses, where he addresses his absent lover, as a plea from Blok to his wife to join the ranks of normal couples: he points out that she is not some supernatural being as a reminder that, like Columbine, she is all too human. The helplessness of Pierrot, who flops over at the slightest touch, seems to echo Blok's own feelings of inadequacy. He was very stiff and shy with those outside his immediate circle; Bely recollects that when things were getting rather serious between himself and Lyubov Dmitrievna (late winter–early spring of 1906), Blok seemed to stand passively by. Both Bely and Lyubov Dmitrievna were quite frustrated with his lack of action. Bely says they would have been vastly relieved if he had been challenged as a rival.[31] It is ironic that Blok actually foretells the involvement which had not yet developed when he was writing the play.

The appearance of Harlequin at the end of the first scene has a definite function. He is suddenly there in the midst of the dispute between Pierrot and the mystics as to the true identity of Columbine. Harlequin serves the purpose of seconding Pierrot's perceptions of the situation. He shows the audience that Columbine, true to her designated role in the *commedia dell'arte*, runs off with Harlequin, as she usually does. She leaves us no doubts that she is who Pierrot thinks she is and not Death, as the mystics believe. Her departure with Harlequin pointedly underlines the frailty of her nature and her complete disassociation with both the figure of Death awaited by the

22 Columbine, Pierrot and Harlequin in the streets. Lithograph by
N. Dmitrevsky, 1922

mystics and the incarnation of the Divine Sophia. Harlequin promises to
take her out to the highways and byways – hardly the suitable abode for the
Eternal Feminine principle.

It was not difficult for friends and acquaintances mutual to both Blok and
Bely to see even a physical resemblance between the figure of Harlequin and
Bely, who was noted for his lithe form, quick movements, and his propensity
for dancing. He says in his reminiscences of those months that he was 'a
whirling dervish'. In the second scene, when Blok has poor Harlequin leap

out of a window into an abyss, he rather wickedly parodies Bely's symbolic jargon in an article originally entitled 'Okno v vechnost' (A Window to Eternity) then renamed 'A Window to the Future,'[32] in which Bely discourses on Nietzschean interpretations of drama and music. Bely writes of the illusory nature of our life *vis à vis* the Great Void or the Unknown. He points out that our glimpses into the Unknown or what he calls, 'scissures into the incomprehensible' are 'called a *window*' (Bely's italics).[33] Bely seems to have been fond of this theme, for he brings it up again in a letter to Blok of December 1905, where he speaks of flying in the blue ether, along the horizon to eternity. Although Blok does not repeat the ardent outpourings of Bely's letter, he reifies them in Harlequin's actions, and he eerily mimics Bely's impassioned style in Harlequin's speech just prior to his undignified exit.

It is not difficult to view the role of the Author as Blok's jab at those who tried to direct his and Lyubov Dmitrievna's lives. Foremost among those were Sergey Solovyov and Andrey Bely. Blok's two 'brothers' desperately wished that the Bloks completely share their beliefs and play the parts Solovyov and Bely had imagined for them. Bely, in some telling passages from his memoir, confides to his readers that he was quite taken aback upon first meeting Blok and his wife, for they did not correspond at all to his mental picture of them. At one point in his reminiscences, Bely admits that he and Sergey Solovyov (Bely lays most of the blame upon Solovyov) had transformed Lyubov Dmitrievna into a symbol, for which Madame Blok later reproached him. He paraphrases one of her remarks '. . . she is a person, not a doll or a symbol'.[34] Bely's descriptions of the young couple at times have the romantic aura of Russian folk heroes and heroines. As time passed both Bloks became acutely aware of this mythification of themselves and began to find it intolerable.

At first glance, the play's two different parts seem to have no logical connection. The audience is transported from a stark setting in which a mystical seance is taking place in hushed tones to the colorful and lively scene of a masked ball. Pierrot remains the only visible transitional link between the two sections of the play. Eventually he participates in the scene after the other *pagliacci* from the first scene make their appearances. The same triangle is formed with Pierrot, Harlequin, and Columbine with a different but equally tragic outcome. There is continuity, too, in the repeated theme of Columbine's mistaken identity which is presented under somewhat different circumstances.

Even though there seems to be little in the ball scene that can be directly associated with the mystics' seance, we shall see that the first and second halves of *The Puppet Show* are organically linked. It is my contention that the first scene dramatizes Blok's repudiation of the philosophical ideal of the 'Eternal Feminine', or Vladimir Solovyov's 'Divine Sophia', as well as his general condemnation of the pretentious and shallow mysticism of his contemporaries. The second scene, on the other hand, reflects Blok's radical change of heart. He is no longer the romantic troubadour, the knightly admirer of an unattainable feminine ideal, but a man deeply troubled by his sexual appetites. He presents us with a cruel caricature of himself on three different psychological levels, and he openly abjures the romantic world-view of his first book of poetry, 'Poems about the Beautiful Lady'. (The word used by Blok in this title, *prekrasnaya*, may also mean perfect.)

One of the organic links between the first and second parts of the play is the pervading impression of timelessness. Blok is able to achieve this through his use of characters from the *commedia dell'arte* and by his choice of settings. Nothing but the barest of essentials are shown in the first half. There is a conspicuous lack of stage props by which an audience normally identifies the historical underpinnings of a play. Emphasis is laid upon the theatricality of the production and its estrangement from real life. All that can be related to life at the turn of the century is Blok's directive that the mystics wear fashionable clothes, and even this is counterbalanced by his having the mystics look as wooden and unreal as possible. It is interesting to note here yet another echo from Bely's article, 'A Window to Eternity'. He speaks of his contemporaries who are so wrapped up in everyday concerns that they are not attuned to the mysteries of the Eternal, and he seizes upon their black frock-coats as a metonymical symbol for them. He fantasizes about what might happen if they caught a glimpse of the eternal values: 'The black contours of frock-coat wearers and their masks become transparent. Everything is submerged in the age-old universal void which eternally shapes its dreams and spins its suns.'[35]

The feeling of suspended time is evoked in a different manner in the second section of *The Puppet Show*. The masked ball, where the actors are dressed in costumes from many epochs and social strata, creates an air of temporal ambiguity (see plate 23). We are not permitted to identify any one historical moment in time, because such balls have been popular at least since the Renaissance period.

However, the eighteenth century stood out in the minds of poets and artists at the turn of our century as the heyday of the masquerade ball. Novels, paintings, and memoir literature from that era inform us that such gatherings offered the perfect occasion for avoiding social taboos and obliterating class barriers. It was at masquerades that illicit lovers met, dallied, and planned future assignations. At such balls, the anonymity of the masks equalized all of the guests. Yet another reason for the vogue of masquerades in Russian Symbolism was the prominence given to the theme of masks by Nietzsche in *The Birth of Tragedy* – in particular, the idea that masks disguised a void or Dionysian chaos.

In Russia as in western Europe among the favorite disguises at masked

23 Costume designs for the masquerade in *The Puppet Show*,
by N. Sapunov, 1906

balls were costumes derived from the *commedia dell'arte*. Perhaps the popularity of such attire lay in its direct association with the relaxed attitudes about love reflected in the Italian comedies whose main themes revolved around sexual dilemmas and whose dialogues forthrightly and humorously dealt with love.

The decadent aspects of eighteenth-century life were favorite themes of the French Symbolists and later of a number of Russian Symbolists. For the Symbolists, the *personae* from the *commedia dell'arte* became symbols of the pursuit of pleasure in both its comic and tragic aspects. There is much evidence to show that turn-of-the-century Russians perceived both French and Russian court life of the eighteenth century through its portrayals in French Symbolist poetry.

Of particular interest are the comments of V. Vsevolodsky-Gerngross, an early Soviet historian of Russian theatre who matured intellectually at the height of the Russian Symbolist movement. In the first volume of his *Istoria russkogo teatra* (A History of the Russian Theatre) under the chapter heading 'The Decadence of the Eighteenth Century', Vsevolodsky-Gerngross describes eighteenth-century decadence in terms of its theatre.

> The splendor of Louis XIV's era gradually tapered off, and its scope diminished. Grandeur was supplanted by the elegance, pleasure, and refinement of the sensual delights of Louis XV. The life of the court and the aristocracy consisted as it had before of continuous festivities. But its character changed. Instead of powerful, grandiose sentiments, there appeared effeminateness and languor. Love as pleasure wrested primacy from patriotic love, and the sentiments of duty and honor gave way to erotica, amatory games, flirtation and coquetry. The gallant century surrounded itself with the recherché ornamentation of rococo and its openwork. The solemn ode was replaced by coquettish little songs about kisses, roses, and shepherdesses. People became interested in novels relating amorous exploits, betrayals, seductions, and orgies.[36]

Certainly, decadence is another underlying theme which unites both the first and second sections of the play. In the first, Blok ridicules the intellectual decadence of his mystical contemporaries (often called the 'Decadents' in the press). In the second scene, Blok uses the theme of decadent love to reject the naive idealism of his first book of poems. He reduces images and concepts once sacred to him to blasphemous caricatures of his former values. The knights in search of holy ideals and the Platonic admirers of irreproachable maidens become maudlin Pierrots, silhouettes, and knights in cardboard helmets.

There is some justification in saying, as do the Soviet scholars, that the 1905 revolution was the catalyst which jolted Blok out of sharing the unrealistic utopian yearnings of his associates. However, since Blok never went on to militancy and rarely lent support to overtly political movements, its major effect probably was to have made him more aware than he had been previously of urban life and its social consequences. This new concern is quite evident in the letter of 25 June, 1905 to one of his closest friends, E. P. Ivanov, in which he talks about how he hates St Petersburg for its vice, filth and squalor.

The first scene is placed within an urban context where the mystics, symbolically isolated from the rest of the world in a tiny room, await the advent of 'Death'. In contrast to the mystics, the *pagliacci* have come from or go directly into the city streets – the milieu in which they were placed by the nineteenth-century Romantics and the French Symbolists. Blok's message here seems to me to be that the mystics are indulging themselves in day-dreams, while the concerns, joys and sorrows of the common man rep-resented by the *pagliacci* are incomprehensible to them.

The second scene focuses on the three pairs of lovers. Each couple is contrasted with the one preceding it and with the triangle of Pierrot, Harlequin, and Columbine. Each couple can be interpreted as different aspects of Blok's writings about or personal experiences of love. For example, the first couple is clothed in blue and pink, the predominating colors of Blok's 'Poems about the Beautiful Lady', and their conversation describes scenes and echoes the vocabulary of that cycle. Many of Blok's poems about the poet's quest for the Beautiful Lady take place in a church or chapel and there are numerous descriptive details about the architecture and ecclesiastical furnishings of churches. The couple in blue and pink use the same quaint expressions and elevated style found in that first cycle of poems, and the emotional tone of their dialogue is the same.

Each of the three couples is quite distinct from the others. The first couple is dreamy and pure and the second embodies carnal desires: they are characterized by their quick, passionate movements; they 'burst forth' from amidst the other dancers, their cloaks whirling about them; the two costumes complement each other, she in red with black and he in black with red – colors which signify passion and death. These lovers reveal Blok's own emotional upheaval and its reflection in his lyrics written around the same time as the play.

In exploring the urban milieu which had begun to fascinate him, Blok discovered the world of prostitutes, gypsies, and actresses. It was at this time that he embarked upon a whirlwind of excesses – both alcoholic and sexual – which engulfed him for many years. Many of his poems of this period (1905–1907) reflect Blok's inner turmoil. He was deeply disturbed to note the strength of his passions and torn between his former values and alliances and his new obsessions. He agonized over the views others had of him based upon his idealistic poetry and contrasted those views with what he felt himself to be.

When the male partner speaks of his fiancée and the fact that he is promised to her, it is not difficult to infer that Blok has his own marriage and his lack of fidelity in mind. Yet Blok is honest with his audience and readers. When the lover attempts to lay the blame for his passion upon his partner, calling her an enchantress, she retorts: 'You yourself wanted to step into my enchanted circle.'

Related to the theme of passions, and distinguishing the second couple from the others in yet another way, is the shadowy double of the passionate lover. Blok was haunted by this concept, and his poetry contains many references to doubles. They began to make their appearance as early as the 'Poems about the Beautiful Lady'. Andrey Bely and Evgeny Ivanov, close friends of Blok from different camps, concur in their analysis of Blok's recurring spectre. Bely tells us that already at the end of 1904 Blok tried to convince him that there was a 'dark' side to his character, that terrible, stormy feelings lurked in him which even he was at a loss to explain.[37] Ivanov also records a similar but more detailed conversation of October 1905 in which Blok speaks of the dichotomy between people's opinion of him as being 'luminous', when in reality he was 'dark'. Ivanov relates that Blok confessed that he greatly feared the heritage from his father's dark side. He relates to his friend how his father was '... Satan and tortured my mother with Satanism'.[38]

Before passing on to the third couple, I would like to discuss one funda-mental concept which permeates the whole play but which is openly ex-pressed in the dialogue of the male partner. This theme is linked to that of the double, because it deals with the duality of our nature and the fact that we often are not what we seem. One of the most influential sources of this idea is Nietzsche's *The Birth of Tragedy*. The Russian Symbolists wrote at length about the Nietzschean revelation that masks were devices invented by man to obliterate the horrors of chaos lurking within us. Another novel dealing with the problem of duality and with Chaos or the Void concealed behind our masks is H. G. Wells's *The Invisible Man*, which inspired a number of stories by Russian Symbolists. This is pointed out by E. P. Gomberg and A. M. Bikhter, commentators to E. P. Ivanov's 'Zapiski ob Aleksandre Bloke' (Notes on Aleksandr Blok), who use the term 'spiritual bankruptcy' to describe modern man's sense of emptiness.[39] Wells combines the concepts of disguise with a reification of the Void in *The Invisible Man*, and he relates these ideas to the themes of duality and doubles. Just as in nineteenth-century literature a hero's double acts out his hidden desires and fantasies, so the Invisible Man is completely free to realize his fantasies without the restrictions which visibility places upon him.

What connection does *The Invisible Man* have with *The Puppet Show* and Nietzschean Chaos? It is clear from the reminiscences of both Bely and Evgeny Ivanov that the metaphysical problems raised by Nietzsche and Wells were uppermost in Blok's mind. Deeply shaken by his own duality, he began to question the very origins of his being. Evgeny Ivanov recounts a very dramatic moment, when he and Blok were chatting in October of 1905: 'I was talking of what I had gone through, and of my feelings about myself as a windbag, a hypocrite, an imposter, a cardboard nonentity . . . We talked of such things. . . . As he was saying good-bye, Al. Blok asked, "Zhenya, do I exist or not?"'[40] This profoundly metaphysical question echoes several statements made by Bely in 'A Window to Eternity': 'The tragic mask looking at us with the smile of Medusa provokes bewilderment. What is looking out at us from behind the mask? Is it not emptiness staring at us? What would we do if, tearing off the mask, we found out that no one could hide beneath it?'[41] Several pages later in the article he elaborates further on this theme when he talks about the facades we all put on for one another: 'You know, it is not one superficies approaching another, but two black gaping holes from the abyss, covered by masks.'[42]

Blok's persistent reflections upon these questions are echoed in the words of the second lover. 'Watch out enchantress, I shall take off my mask and you will see that I am faceless. You swept away my features and led me off to obscurity where my black double nodded, nodded to me!' He joins the concept of facelessness or emptiness with that of the double in the parting dialogue of the impassioned lover: 'But it is three who will take the ominous path: thou, and I and my double!'

The final pair have fewer lines than the first two pairs. It seems to me that this couple represents the poet and his muse. The knight looks back at what has already happened in the play and reflects upon its meaning. His muse merely echoes his words, yet he attributes not only a knowledge and understanding of the past to her but also the ability to foresee the future and interpret symbols. 'You know everything that was and will be. You have understood the significance of the circle which was outlined here.'

It is interesting to note that of all the couples, Blok is most unkind to the third. The first is treated with delicacy. There is a poignancy and pathos in the directness with which Blok exposes his personal feelings through the second couple. However, the third pair is depicted with a great deal of irony – much of it directed at the knight. He is pompous; his costume is ridiculous and makeshift; he is teased by the *pagliaccio*; he gets entangled with his sword at the appearance of Death in the final moments of the play. His partner fares no better; she seems capable only of echoing her lover's thoughts.

As I mentioned earlier, Blok was very conscious of his stiffness and shyness. Contemporaries often mention the wooden way in which he spoke with a nasal, monotonous voice. He was noted also for his extreme formality and for his old-fashioned turns of phrase. These traits are all caricatured in the person of the knight.

The three couples present a contrast to the triangle formed by Pierrot, Harlequin, and Columbine. It is Pierrot, of course, who introduces the theme of lovers when he is the first to speak in the second scene. He describes

Harlequin's abduction of Columbine and his own anguished pursuit of the errant pair. In this, he foreshadows the double who follows the second lover. His anguish turns to laughter when Columbine becomes a cardboard doll. Then he and Harlequin wander off quite amiably together through the streets. Harlequin at one point even says that they are brothers. In Pierrot's monologue, Blok subtly introduces the double theme which is later developed in the second couple's dialogue.

The concluding moments of *The Puppet Show* artfully combine the ideas and symbolism of both parts while underscoring one of the major philosophical questions preoccupying Blok and his contemporaries. This is the problem of the deceptiveness of appearances. The figure of Death is not what it seems to the mystics. Columbine is not a real girl, but a cardboard figure – or is she? Pierrot is not an actor playing the role of a *pagliaccio* but a helpless flopping puppet. Harlequin is not a happy-go-lucky scamp but a demonic sorcerer. The mystics are nothing more than false fronts. The lovers are disguised by their costumes, so they are not who they seem. The dancers and other *pagliacci* are like 'dolls from an ethnographic museum'. And the finale makes it clear every one of the protagonists is a puppet. The props are arranged to stress the fact that they are false representations of reality (the emphasis on staginess for the first scene and the bench left over from *Tannhäuser* and the paper background for the second scene), and even they disappear into thin air at the end.

The double theme is but another manifestation of the notion that our empirical perceptions are illusory. People pretend to be or are taken for what they are not. Our exteriors and outward behavior often hide our true personalities and intentions. All of these verities can be symbolized by the double. Here again, I feel that Blok uses Andrey Bely's article 'A Window to Eternity' as a frame of reference for the last moments of *The Puppet Show*. The surprising conclusion intensifies our impression of the illusoriness of the whole production. Here is a passage which Bely uses twice in the above mentioned article: 'Then everything will disperse. The known will be engulfed by the unknown, and this city with its buildings, palaces, and temples will vanish like an old illusion which has disturbed the tranquility of eternity more than once.'[43] Several paragraphs later, Bely unites the themes of illusion and the masquerade in the following passage:

> The masquerade resumes. Dresses rustle. One mask asks another: 'Well, what (do you think)?' One mask answers another: 'Amazing.'
> Lively speeches and gestures which are too abrupt.... The frock-coats jump up. Their coat-tails flap. –
> – The ominous dance of those in masks goes on over the ever present abyss.[44]

The Puppet Show was, along with Stravinsky's *Petrushka*, Russia's major contribution to the renaissance of the *commedia dell'arte* reflected in the drama, art, and music of the turn of the century. Aleksandr Blok's choice of characters and plots from the Italian comedy for his play was inspired by a number of factors. He sensed that *pagliacci*, as he knew them – the romantic types popularized by the French Symbolists and by *fin de siècle* dramatists and composers – would be particularly appropriate mouthpieces for his symbolic messages. The lightheartedness and irreverence so characteristic of the traditional *pagliacci* and *skomorokhi* would set the tone for his ironic self-portrait, for the caricatures of his contemporaries, and for the blasphemous parodies of his own works and those of other Russian Symbolists. The pathos attributed to the *commedia dell'arte* players by the French Symbolists and their predecessors in Romantic literature is perfectly suited to the lyricism and passion of Blok's play in verse. Stereotyped roles of the original Italian comedians and their masks lend themselves to abstraction and symbolic interpretation. Finally, the blatant theatricality of the comic productions and puppet shows featuring the *pagliacci* are the perfect medium for creating the air of illusion which is so important for the message of the play. To be aware of the relationship between *The Puppet Show* and the *commedia dell'arte* opens the way to a deeper understanding of the symbolism of this genial play.

NOTES

1. Vs. E. Meyerkhold, *Stati, pisma, rechi, besedy. Chast Pervaya. 1891–1917* (Articles, Letters, Speeches, Conversations. Part One. 1891–1917) (Moscow: Iskusstvo, 1968), p. 208.

2. Introduction, *Meyerhold on Theater*, ed. and trans. Edward Braun (New York: Hill & Wang, 1969), pp. 20–1. See also Allardyce Nicoll, *The World of Harlequin* (Cambridge University Press, 1963), p. 218.

3. G. I. Chulkov, 'A. Blok', *Kultura teatra* (The Culture of the Theatre), 7–8 (1921), 20.

4. A. V. Fyodorov, *Teatr A. Bloka i dramaturgia ego vremeni* (The Theatre of A. Blok and Drama of His Time) (Leningrad University Press, 1972), pp. 41–58. Fyodorov uses the term throughout his chapter, 'Around *The Puppet Show*'. Nor is Fyodorov alone. Another Soviet expert on Blok's theatre, Tatyana Rodina, refers to the *commedia dell'arte* as 'ancient folk comedy' or 'the theatre of masks'. See references to her work below.

5. Aleksandr Blok, *Sobranie sochineny* (Collected Works), IV (Moscow–Leningrad: GIKhL, 1961), 434.

6. Among those holding this view are Tatyana Rodina, *A. Blok i russky teatr nachala XX veka* (A. Blok and Russian Theatre at the Beginning of the Twentieth Century), (Moscow: Nauka, 1972) and Irene Masing-Delic, 'The Mask Motif in A. Blok's Poetry', *Russian Literature*, 5 (1973), 79–101.

7. This poem, like the appended play, is translated into prose. The original Russian text is taken from Blok's *Sobranie sochineny*, II, 67–8.

8. All of the above information about the origins of the play and its various productions in Russia and abroad were gleaned from the excellent notes provided by the editors of Blok's *Sobranie sochineny*, IV, 567–73.

9. Meyerkhold, *Stati* ... p. 250.

10. *Ibid.*

11. *Ibid.*

12. The above information on the unsuccessful implantation of the Italian *commedia dell'arte* in Russia can be found in V. Vsevolodsky-Gerngross, *Istoria russkogo teatra* (A History of the Russian Theatre) (Leningrad–Moscow: Tea-Kino-Pechat, 1929), pp. 349–54. Specific mention of Pietro Miró is found on p. 354.

13. Robert F. Storey, *Pierrot. A Critical History of a Mask* (Princeton University Press, 1978), pp. 93–139.

14. G. Yu. Sternin, *Khudozhestvennaya zhizn Rossii nachala XX veka* (The Artistic Life of Russia at the Beginning of the Twentieth Century) (Moscow: Iskusstvo, 1976), p. 204.

15. *Ezhegodnik imperatorskikh teatrov* (The Annual of the Imperial Theatres), St Petersburg, VI–XVII (1896–1907).

16. *Ibid.*

17. *Aleksandr Blok – Andrey Bely. Perepiski* (Aleksandr Blok–Andrey Bely. Correspondence) (Munich: Wilhelm Fink, 1969), p. 199.

18. Camilla Gray, *The Russian Experiment in Art. 1863–1922* (New York: Abrams, 1970), p. 44.

19. Storey, *Pierrot*, pp. 109–10.

20. Robert F. Storey, 'Verlaine's Pierrots', *Romance Notes*, 20:2 (1979–80), 230.

21. Russian Symbolists' perceptions of drama and poetry were steeped in the ideas expressed by Friedrich Nietzsche in *The Birth of Tragedy*. Andrey Bely tells us that the impact of this book upon turn-of-the-century Russian intellectuals was enormous. (Andrey Bely, *Vospominania o A. A. Bloke* (Reminiscences of A. A. Blok), Munich: Wilhelm Fink, 1969, pp. 20–1.) There can be no doubt that Blok read or was aware of the numerous articles devoted to *The Birth of Tragedy* which was available in Russian from 1900. Certainly, his close association with Andrey Bely in the years just prior to the writing of *The Puppet Show* guaranteed his exposure to the elements of the Apollonian and Dionysian elements in drama and poetry. Bely wrote a number of articles on themes from *The Birth of Tragedy*, and Blok himself undertook a thorough study of this work at the time *The Puppet Show* was being staged. (Aleksandr Blok, *Zapisnye knizhki* (Notebooks), Moscow: Khudozhestvennaya Literatura, 1965, pp. 78–84).

22. Blok, *Sobranie sochineny*, IV, 434.

23. E. Anichkov, 'Komedia', *Entsiklopedichesky slovar* (Encyclopedic Dictionary) (St Petersburg: Brockhaus & Ephron, 1895), XVᵃ, 824.

24. Meyerkhold, p. 218.

25. See note 21 above.

26. Bely, *Vospominania*, p. 307.

27. Allardyce Nicoll, *Masks, Mimes and Miracles* (London: George Harrap & Co. 1931), pp. 218–19.

28. Bely, *Vospominania*, pp. 96, 380–2.

29. *Ibid.*, chapters entitled 'Nochnaya fialka', 'Nechayanaya radost', 'Trety – mesyats naverkhu – iskrivil svoy rot'.
30. *Ibid.*, p. 329.
31. *Ibid.*, pp. 396–97.
32. Bely, 'Okno v vechnost', *Vesy*, 12 (1904), 1–11.
33. *Ibid.*, p. 2
34. Bely, *Vospominania*, p. 373.
35. Bely, 'Okno v vechnost', p. 10.
36. Vsevolodsky-Gerngross, *Istoria russkogo teatra* pp. 450–451. Vsevolodsky-Gerngross's perceptions of the eighteenth century as an era of decadence were not unique for the Russian Symbolists as the following anonymous review of Ernest Dowson's *The Pierrot of the Minute* attests. 'Herein is also found his one-act fantasy in verse, *The Pierrot of the Minute*, where Dowson gives free rein to his love for the preciosity of the eighteenth century, and he brings to life daydreams about the former magnificence of Versailles and about a lovely lady in pale pink satin *à la Watteau*. It is a precious, graceful joke – a lesson in love for the poor *pagliaccio* – a nocturnal vision dispersing at the first rays of dawn. The malicious and whimsical drawings of Beardsley reveal that great irony of the world which Dowson sensed but for which there were no words in his fragile musical soul.' ('Ernest Dowson. Poems. *The Pierrot of the Minute*. Four Illustrations by Aubrey Beardsley. London. John Lane. 1905', *Vesy*, 8, 1905, 61.)
37. Blok, *Sobranie sochineny*, VIII, 130.
38. Bely, *Vospominania*, p. 150.
39. E. P. Ivanov, 'Zapiski ob Aleksandre Bloke' (Notes on Aleksandr Blok), *Blokovsky sbornik* (The Blok Collection) (Tartu State University, 1964), I, 420.
40. *Ibid.*, p. 418.
41. *Ibid.*, p. 397.
42. 'Okno v vechnost' p. 4.
43. *Ibid.*, p. 9.
44. *Ibid.*, p. 10.
45. *Ibid.*, p. 11.

THE PUPPET SHOW 1906
Dedicated to Vsevolod Emilevich Meyerkhold
Translated by Virginia H. Bennett

Characters

Columbine
Pierrot
Harlequin
Mystics of both sexes in frock-coats and fashionable dresses, and later in masks
    and masquerade costumes
The Chairman of the mystical seance
Three couples in love
A *pagliaccio*
The Author

An ordinary stage set with three walls, a window and a door.
 Mystics of both sexes in frock-coats and fashionable dresses are sitting with a con-
centrated air at a spotlighted table. A little distance away, Pierrot with no eyebrows or
moustache and wearing a white smock sits at a window. He is dreamy, downcast, pale, like
all Pierrots. The mystics are quiet for some time.
First Mystic. Are you listening?
Second Mystic.   Yes.
Third Mystic.   The event is starting.
Pierrot. O, eternal terror, eternal darkness!
First Mystic. Are you waiting?
Second Mystic.   I'm waiting.
Third Mystic.   The arrival is surely near:
   The wind has made us a signal outside the window.
Pierrot. Faithless One! Where are you? A long chain of
   Street lamps has extended through the sleepy
   Streets, and lovers warmed by the light of their
   Love walk, one couple after another. Where are
   You? Why can't we, too, enter the designated
   Circle after the last couple? I shall go strum
   My mournful guitar under the window where you
   Dance in chorus with your girlfriends!
   I shall rouge my pale moon-face,
   I shall paint on eyebrows and glue on a moustache.
   Can you hear, Columbine, how my poor heart
   Sustains, sustains its sad song?
  [Pierrot indulges in daydreams and becomes more lively. But the worried Author creeps
  out from behind the curtain.]
Author. What is he saying? Most esteemed audience! I hasten to assure you that
  this actor has made a cruel mockery of my rights as an author. The action
  takes place in Petersburg during the winter. Where did he come up with a
  window and a guitar? I did not write my play for a puppet show . . . I assure
  you . . .
  [Suddenly becoming embarrassed about his unexpected appearance, he hides himself
  back behind the curtain.]
Pierrot [*He had paid no attention to the author. He sits there and sighs dreamily*].
  Columbine!

First Mystic.   Are you listening?
Second Mystic.   Yes.
Third Mystic. A maiden from a distant land is approaching.
First Mystic. O, her features are like marble.
Second Mystic.   O, there is emptiness in her eyes!
Third Mystic. Oh, such purity – and such whiteness!
First Mystic. She will come towards us – and all voices will be instantly stilled.
Second Mystic. Yes. Silence will ensue.
Third Mystic.   For a long time?
First Mystic.   Yes.
Second Mystic. All white, like the snows.
Third Mystic.   Over her shoulder is a scythe.
First Mystic. Who, then, is she?
          [*The second leans over and whispers in the ear of the first.*]
Second Mystic.   You won't betray me?
First Mystic [*in unfeigned horror*]. Never!
          [*The Author again pops out from behind the curtain in a frightened way but quickly
          disappears as though someone had pulled him by the coat-tails.*]
Pierrot [*dreamily, as before*]. Columbine! Come!
First Mystic.   Quiet! Do you hear footsteps?
Second Mystic. I hear rustling and sighs.
Third Mystic.   O, who is among us?
First Mystic. Who is in the window?
Second Mystic.   Who is behind the door?
Third Mystic.   It is pitch dark.
First Mystic. Give some light. Is it not she who has come at this hour?
          [*The second mystic raises a candle.*
          *An uncommonly beautiful girl with a simple and quiet face of a dull white color
          completely unexpectedly appears at the table from no one knows where. She is dressed in
          white. The gaze of her calm eyes is dispassionate. Over her shoulders is a plaited braid.*
          *The girl stands motionless. Ecstatic Pierrot falls to his knees in a prayerful pose. It
          is evident that he chokes with tears. All for him is inexpressible.*
          *The terrified mystics cringe against the backs of their chairs. The foot of one of them
          dangles helplessly. Another makes strange movements of the hand. A third's eyes pop
          out. After a certain time, they whisper loudly:*]
                    – She has arrived!
                    – How white her clothes are!
                    – There is an emptiness in her eyes!
                    – Her features are as pale as marble!
                    – There is a scythe over her shoulders!
                    – It is – Death!
          [*Pierrot has overheard. Getting up slowly, he approaches the girl, takes her by the hand
          and leads her out to center stage. He speaks in a joyful ringing voice, like the first clang
          of a bell.*]
Pierrot. Gentlemen, you are mistaken! It is Columbine! It is my fiancée.
          [*General terror everywhere. Hands are thrown up in horror. The coat-tails of the
          frocks sway. The Chairman of the seance triumphally approaches Pierrot.*]
Chairman. You have gone mad. We have been awaiting the event all evening.
          She came to us, the silent Deliverer. Death has visited us.
Pierrot [*in a ringing child-like voice*]. I don't listen to fairy tales. I am a simple man.
          You won't fool me. This is Columbine. This is my fiancée.
Chairman. Gentlemen! Our poor friend has become crazed with fear. He has

never given a thought to that for which we have spent a whole lifetime preparing ourselves. He has not plumbed the depths and has not readied himself to submissively greet the Pale Friend at the final hour. We shall magnanimously forgive the simpleton. [*He turns to Pierrot.*] Brother, you must not remain here. You are hindering our final evening. But I beg you, glance one more time at her features: you see how white is her raiment and what pallor there is in her features; O, she is white like the snows on mountain peaks! Her eyes reflect a mirror-like emptiness. Can you not see the scythe over her shoulders? Don't you recognize Death?

Pierrot [*a perplexed smile wanders over his pale face*]. I'm leaving. Either you are right and I am a miserable lunatic. Or you have lost your minds and I am a lonely, misunderstood suitor. Blizzard, carry me off through the streets. O eternal terror, O eternal darkness!

Columbine [*goes to the exit after Pierrot*]. I won't abandon you.

[*Pierrot stops, confused. The Chairman places his hands in a prayerful gesture.*]

Chairman. Airy phantom! We have been awaiting you a lifetime. Don't abandon us!

[*A well-built youth in Harlequin's garb appears. The bells on him sing out in silvery voices.*]

Harlequin [*approaches Columbine*]. I await you my friend at the cross-roads,
    In the grey shadows of a winter's day!
    Overhead my blizzard will
    Sing out like ringing bells for you!

[*He places his hand on Pierrot's shoulder. Pierrot flops down flat on his back and lies motionless in his white smock. Harlequin leads Columbine off by the hand. She smiles at him. The mood is destroyed. Everyone slumps lifelessly on the chairs. The sleeves of the frock-coats have extended over the fingers, as though there were no hands. Heads have disappeared into collars. It seems as though empty frock-coats are hanging on the chairs. Suddenly Pierrot jumps up and runs off. The curtain moves. At that very moment the disheveled and agitated Author jumps out onto the stage in front of the curtain.*]

Author. Gracious ladies and gentlemen! I humbly excuse myself before you, but I decline all responsibility! They are ridiculing me! I wrote the most realistic of plays, the essence of which I consider it my duty to set forth in a few words: it is a story of reciprocal love between two young people! A third party impedes their way: but the obstacles finally fall away, and the lovers are united in lawful marriage for ever after! I never dressed my characters up in buffoon's dress. Unbeknown to me they re-enacted some kind of ancient legend. I acknowledge neither legends, nor myths, nor other such vulgarities. And especially, the allegorical playing upon words: it is unseemly to call a woman's braid the scythe of Death! This will corrupt the female estate. Gracious ladies and gentlemen ...

[*A hand poked out from behind the curtain grabs the Author by the scruff of the neck. With a yelp, he disappears into the wings. The curtain quickly draws apart. A ball. Masks are circling to the quiet sounds of a dance. Among them other masks, knights, ladies, and* pagliacci *stroll about.*

A sad Pierrot sits in the midst of the scene on the same bench where Venus and Tannhäuser usually embrace.]

Pierrot. I stood between two street lamps
    And listened to their voices,
    And to how they whispered, concealing themselves in cloaks,
    And night kissed them on the eyes.

And the silvery blizzard wound
A wedding band around them.
And I saw through the night how my fiancée
Smiled up at his face.

Ah, then he seated
My fiancée in a hired sleigh!
I wandered in the frozen mist
Following them from afar.

Ah! He enmeshed her in nets,
And laughing, jingled his bells!
But when he wrapped her up –
Ah, my love fell flat on her back!

He in no way offended her,
But my love fell into the snow!
She was unable to sit upright! ...
I couldn't restrain my laughter! ...

And to the accompaniment of frosty needles,
Round my cardboard love –
He jingled and leapt up high,
And I danced after him round the sleigh!

And we wended our way along the sleepy street:
'Ah! What a misfortune befell us!'
And up above – over my cardboard love –
High up a star shone green.

And all night we wandered – Harlequin
And Pierrot – through the snowy streets ...
He embraced me so tenderly,
And a feather tickled my nose!

He whispered to me: 'My brother, we are together,
Inseparable for many days ...
Let us sorrow together over your fiancée,
Over your cardboard fiancée!'
[*Pierrot sadly moves off. Shortly thereafter, a pair of lovers appears on the very same
bench. He is in blue, she in pink. Their masks are colored to match their clothes.
They pretend they are in a church and look up at the cupola.*]

She. Dearest, you whisper 'incline your head ...'
I with face upturned look up at the cupola.
He. I look at the overwhelming height
There, where the cupola has admitted the evening twilight.
She. The gilt up above is so old.
How the images glimmer up there.
He. Our dreamy tale is quiet.
You sinlessly closed your eyes.
[*A kiss.*]
She. ... Someone dark stands by a column
And winks a cunning eye!
I'm afraid of you, enamoured one!
Let me cover myself in your cloak!
[*Silence.*]

He. Look at how quiet the candles are,
How the dawn is breaking in the cupolas.

She. Yes, our meetings together are sweet.
As if I had abandoned myself to you.
[*She presses close to him. The quiet dance of masks and* pagliacci *conceals the first pair from the audience. In the midst of the dance, a second pair of lovers bursts forth. In front – she wearing a black mask and a billowing red cloak. Behind – he all in black, a supple body in a red mask and black cloak. His movements are impetuous. He chases after her, sometimes reaching her, sometimes outdistancing her. A whirlwind of cloaks.*]

He. Leave me alone! Don't torment me, don't persecute me!
Don't predict a dark fate for me!
You are gloating over your victory!
Will you remove your mask? Will you disappear in the night?

She. Follow me! Attain me!
I am more passionate and melancholy than your fiancée!
Embrace me in your supple arms!
Quaff my dark goblet to the dregs!

He I pledged passionate love – to another!
You flashed a fiery glance at me,
You led me off into a distant alley,
You poisoned me with deadly venom!

She. It was not I who lured you, – my cloak flew
In a whirlwind behind me – my fiery friend!
You yourself wanted to step
Into my enchanted circle!

He. Watch out, Sorceress! I shall snatch off my mask!
And you will learn that I am faceless!
You swept away my features and led me off into obscurity,
Where my black double nodded, nodded to me!

She. I – am a free and easy lady! My path leads to conquests!
Follow me whither I lead.
O, you shall follow in my fiery tracks
And shall be delirious with me!

He. I go submissive to my stern fate,
O swirl cloak, fiery guide!
But three tread the ominous path
Thou and I – and my double!
[*They disappear in a whirlwind of cloaks. It seems as though some third person has broken away from the crowd and follows them, someone exactly like the lover, entirely like a flickering tongue of black flame.*
   Amidst the dancers a third couple of lovers appears. They are sitting center stage.
   The Middle Ages. Pensively inclined she follows his movements, – he, in completely severe outlines, large and thoughtful, wearing a cardboard helmet, draws a huge circle on the floor in front of her with his wooden sword.]

He. Do you understand the play in which ours is not the final role?

She [*like a quiet and discernible echo*]. Role.

He. You know that the masks have made our meeting of today extraordinary?

She. Extraordinary.

He. Do you have such faith in me? O today you are more beautiful than ever.

She. Ever.

He. You know all that was and will be. You understood the significance of the here inscribed circle.

She. Of the circle.

He. O, how captivating are your words! Diviner of my soul! How much your words speak to my heart!

She. Heart.

He. O, Eternal Happiness! Eternal Happiness!

She. Happiness.

He [*with a sigh of relief and triumph*]. Day is near. On the wane is this evil night.

She. Night.

> [*At this moment one of the* pagliacci *has the bright idea of pulling off a joke. He runs up to the lover and sticks his long tongue out at him. Taking his heavy sword, the lover hits the* pagliaccio *on the head with all his might. The* pagliaccio *slumps over the ramp and hangs there. From his head spurts a stream of cranberry juice.*]

Pagliaccio [*screams piercingly*]. Help! I am bleeding cranberry juice!

> [*Having dangled there awhile, he goes off.*
> *Uproar. Confusion. Joyous cries: 'Torches! Torches! A torchlight parade!' A chorus with torches appears. The masks crowd around, laugh, jump up and down.*]

Chorus. Into the twilight drop after drop of pitch
> Falls with a faint crackling!
Faces overcast by shadows.
> Are illuminated by the dim luster!
> Drop after drop, spark after spark!
> Pure, tarry rain!
> Where are you twinkling, swift,
> Ardent leader?

> [*Harlequin steps out from the chorus as Master of Ceremonies.*]

Harlequin. Along the dreaming and snowy streets
> I dragged a simpleton behind me!
> The world revealed itself to rebellious eyes,
> The snowy wind sang overhead!
> Oh, how I wanted to breathe, expanding
> My youthful chest, and go out into the world!
> To conclude my joyful springtime feast
> In an empty uninhabited place!
> Here, no one dares to understand that
> Spring is floating up on high!
> Here no one is capable of loving,
> Here they live in a sad dream!
> Greetings world! You are with me once again!
> Your soul has long been near me!
> I am going through your golden window
> To breathe in your spring!

> [*He jumps through the window. The distance visible in the window turns out to be painted on paper. The paper breaks through. Harlequin flies off head first into emptiness.*
> *In the tear in the paper the only thing visible is the sky growing light. Night fades away, and morning dimly advances. Against the backdrop of the breaking dawn, barely rippling from the predawn breeze, stands – Death, in a long white shroud, with*

*a lustreless feminine face and with a scythe over her shoulder. The blade gives off a
silvery shine like an upended moon which is dying out in the morning.*

*Everyone rushes in terror in all directions. The knight trips over his wooden sword.
The ladies have dropped their flowers all over the stage. The masks, motionlessly
pressed together as though crucified to the walls, look like dolls from an ethnographical
museum. The female lovers have hidden their faces in their lovers' cloaks. The profile
of the blue mask is faintly outlined against the morning sky. At his feet, the frightened
kneeling pink mask has pressed her lips to his hand.*

*As though sprouted from the earth, Pierrot slowly walks across the whole stage, his
hands outstretched towards Death. As he approaches, her features begin to come alive.
A blush begins to kindle her dull cheeks. The silvery scythe disappears in the spreading
morning mist. Against the background of the dawn, in the window's alcove stands a
pretty girl with a quiet smile on her calm face – it is Columbine.*

*At the very minute that Pierrot draws near and wishes to touch her hand with his, –
the triumphal Author forces his head in between them.*]

Author. Esteemed audience! My cause is not lost! My rights have been established! You can see that the obstacles have collapsed! That gentleman
disappeared through the window! All that remains for you is to witness the
joyous meeting of two lovers after their long separation! If they lost a great
deal of strength in overcoming the obstacles, then now, to make up for it,
they are united forever!

[*The Author wants to join the hands of Columbine and Pierrot. But suddenly all the
scenery is raised and flies upwards. The masks scamper about.*

*The Author finds himself bent over only Pierrot, who lies helplessly on the empty
stage in his white smock with the red buttons.*

Noticing his position, the Author dashes off stage.]

Pierrot. [*raises himself up slightly and speaks sadly and dreamily*].
Where did you bring me? How can I guess?
You committed me to a perfidious destiny.
Poor Pierrot, you've lain long enough, Go on, go look for your fiancée.
[*He grows silent.*]
Ah, how bright was she who went away.
(My jingling comrade led her off.)
She fell down (she was made of cardboard).
And I came to laugh at her.

There she lay, on her back – white,
Ah, how gay was our dance.
But she was completely unable to get up.
She was a cardboard fiancée.
And look at me, pale of face, standing here,
But it is sinful for you to laugh at me.
It can't be helped! She fell on her back ...
I am very sad. And is it funny to you?
[*Pierrot pensively pulls a little flute out of his pocket and begins to play a song about
his white face, about a difficult life, and about his fiancée Columbine.*]

REVIEW SECTION

PRODUCTION

Theme and symbol in contemporary Australian drama:
Ray Lawler to Louis Nowra

DENNIS BARTHOLOMEUSZ

The symbol of the doll makes its first significant appearance in European drama in *A Doll's House* (1879); the woman as an ornamental possession, a precious toy, a prisoner. I cannot recall this notion appearing in poetry of any great significance before William Blake's *Song* (1783):

> With sweet May dews my wings were wet,
>   And Phoebus fir'd my vocal rage
> He caught me in his silken net,
>   And shut me in his golden cage.

Blake, as Ibsen was to do a century later, suggests that in the emotional life at any rate, property can be a form of theft. In his *Song* he suggests too, that it can be accompanied by sadism, which is the enjoyment of another's pain:

> He loves to sit and hear me sing
>   Then, laughing, sports and plays with me;
> Then stretches out my golden wing,
>   And mocks my loss of liberty.

These precious possessions, and here the comparison with mechanical toys must end, can feel and think. In *A Doll's House* and Blake's *Song* the case is pretty one-sided. 'The Prince of Love' in Blake's poem and Helmer in *A Doll's House* clearly have no case – they are the sole villains of the piece – though Blake's target conceivably may be wider. He may be attacking, as D. H. Lawrence does so often, the whole received idea of love itself.

In Patrick White's *Big Toys*, first staged at the Parade Theatre, Sydney, on 27 July 1977, by the Old Tote Theatre Company, directed by Jim Sharman, and set by White in the winter of 1976 in the Sydney he knows, the case against was not as one-sided as it is in Ibsen, nor was his ending as unconvincingly programmatic. While at the end of Ibsen's play Nora leaves the 'doll's house' with a declaration of independence that is not in a dramatic sense convincing, for it sounds really like a manifesto and might suit a liberation movement, Mag half seduced by the gift of a new Ferrari stays on in her penthouse, with its magnificent views of Sydney Harbour Bridge, and the Opera House – the lady in the high tower – as the room darkens and filaments of black cloud sail high and fast over the sea in the fading light.

Of course Mag's situation is in every way more elevated than Nora's. Nora's drawing room in which the action of the play takes place is on the ground floor, stolidly respectable, airless and petit-bourgeois, the furnishings dark, and heavy with a dull sheen; while Mag's bedroom, a single permanent set in which the play runs its course, is placed high over Sydney harbour exhibiting uncluttered contemporary luxury in bad taste mistaken for good, furnishings that were for the haut-bourgeoisie of Sydney, in the winter of 1976, doubtless in the latest fashion.

The difference between Mag Bosanquet and Nora Helmer, when the plays begin, is that Mag gives every appearance of being free and liberated; she is very chic, sophisticated, and takes to a 'star' of the trade union movement, who becomes her 'lover', and to anti-uranium politics, as a means of 'self-expression', while Nora's sole indulgence is the secret consumption of confectionery. Nora's husband is a narrow-minded small-town lawyer; Mag's husband, Ritchie Bosanquet, a QC with the wealth of the establishment behind him, and interests in uranium, accepts the principle that Mag must so express herself. Music from *The Marriage of Figaro*, 'Voi che sapete ... You ladies / Who know what love is ...', revealed Mag, when the curtain rose, lying in bed, in a 'bra and very brief panties' and a dressing gown which half-revealed them, conducting a telephone conversation, while she played with an enormous cerise balloon which she sent floating ceiling-wards with bare toes, or clutched against her side, deforming it when it descended. The theatrical images indicated from the start that Mag was a toy as well as a player of some sophistication and skill, who at first quite enjoyed the game.

Signs of the void within and outside her are gradually revealed. The toys have their special brilliance, and the view of Sydney harbour through the penthouse window, when it is first revealed, is as breathtaking as San Francisco and the Golden Gate Bridge at night, with its glittering poetry of the treasures of this world. As the trade union leader, Terry Legge, captured at first for her amusement, stands beside her, Mag draws the curtain in her bedroom to reveal one of the great cities of the world, and we smell the aroma not of love or sexuality, but of power. It is power that Ritchie Bosanquet is concerned with when he blesses the relationship after discovering his wife and Terry Legge in bed together. Terry Legge is a key witness for the prosecution in the case of the Crown versus Sir Douglas Stannard, a case in which Ritchie Bosanquet is the defending counsel. Ritchie finds the 'affair' excellent for softening up Legge, thus taking the teeth out of the Crown's case. For in the end Sir Douglas Stannard becomes Chairman of Intermond Mining which has 'a nice plot of uranium out there at Livermore', and Ritchie Bosanquet is made legal consultant for the company. Terry Legge has a few shreds of dignity left, when he refuses the Ferrari that is offered as a gift for his services in the witness-box. Patrick White's response to Sydney in the 1970s is more severe than D. H. Lawrence's in *Kangaroo* (1923), but there are some attitudes in common. Somers in *Kangaroo* calls Sydney

> One of the great cities of the world. But without a core ... The friendliest country in the world: in some ways, the gentlest. But without a core. There was no heart in it all, it seemed hollow.[1]

As Katherine Brisbane points out, 'the Bosanquets "live" nowhere ... Their sexuality has been honed into an instrument of domination. They have nowhere to rest their sense of self. Their apartment is a decorator's fantasy of modishness ... Only a stunted bonsai tree grows there. It is a void, like the void outside the window.'[2]

The penthouse from which Terry Legge flees is luxurious but empty of meaning. Presumably he has somewhere to go. But Mag we discover, born, unlike Nora, on the wrong side of the tracks, has fled into the penthouse, from horror into vacancy. Ritchie is by no means a father-substitute as Helmer was to Nora in *A Doll's House*, but only a means of escape:

> *Terry.* I thought they said you come off some grazing property up north.
> *Mag.* My Aunt Ella was married to a cow cockie at Casino. Let P. R. give it the right *nuances* – and that becomes the 'grazing property'. [*Advancing on him*] Are you so innocent my darling? (act II; p. 25)

During Mag's reminiscence she remained still, concentrating on the bonsai tree on the low table, and then moved off restlessly as she recalled the car ride with her father, a hawker by profession:

> *Mag.* Dadda and me, we went on jogging across those red dust-ridden plains. He tried to screw me on the floor of the truck one night outside Tibooburra. That's where I pulled out. I walked. I thumbed a lift ... I got here. I made it ... after a lot of rather murky ... experience ... down the wrong end of town. I made it, however. The fashion world liked what I had to offer ... what was called my 'cool attitudes'.
> *Terry.* You belong then on the right side of the fence – only you fell over on the wrong.
> *Mag.* I wasn't going to sit with the barbs eating into my bottom. When Ritchie proposed, I accepted. (act II; p. 26)

If the doll in *Big Toys* is manipulated, she is tough-minded and manipulative herself. Her sexuality becomes an instrument of power and is therefore sterile. The sexual symbolism of the opening scene, where Mag toys with the large cerise balloon, prefigures the sexual cycle in the play, which moves from light-hearted farce to disillusionment. Patrick White tells us in a stage direction that as the balloon lolls against Mag, she pricks it with a finger nail. The explosion provokes loud enquiries from the telephone and an explanation from Mag:

> That was a balloon. It burst ... Oh, it was only a fun thing Ritchie brought home – because he thought it amusing – as it was. But now it's horrid! Ugh! Like some ugly old wrinkled scrotum! ... (act II; p. 5)

This excellent black comedy ends on a tragic note, when black clouds have shrouded the glittering lights of Sydney harbour, and Mag looks out into an abyss of darkness:

> [... *Mag drags herself upstage towards the glass doors, as though cold and aching. She stands looking out a moment, then closes the doors. She stands silhouetted ... the palms of her hands pressed against the glass.*]
> *Mag* [*very softly*]. Christ ... oh, Christ ... [*soundlessly crying*] (act III; pp. 57–8)

The last line as Kate Fitzpatrick spoke it, when I saw the play staged at the Comedy Theatre in Melbourne in October 1977, was not as clichétic, or banal, or as conventionally religious as it might look on the page. It was a tragic cry without any carrion-comforting of despair, as she pressed her palms against the glass, while the stage darkened, and the room seemed to close round her. The actress, with extraordinary genius, saved it from being a sentimental conclusion, gave it even a certain dignity. Patrick White had attempted to protect his play from sentimentality, save it with irony, by letting Mag, a few seconds earlier, accept the Ferrari that Terry Legge had refused; making her even enjoy the prospect, in imagination, of driving it:

> *She puts on the fur hat of earlier that afternoon, at the angle at which someone who looks 'smashing at the wheel' might aspire to.*   (act III; p. 57)

The Nora of 1976, despite her tears, will, one suspects, stay on in her fashionable 'doll's house'. The despair and rebellion are strictly within (see plate 24).

Patrick White's concerns are wider than Ibsen's. He shows Mag to be the willing, despairing victim of a glittering, hollow, capitalist ethos, a free society without a centre ruled by immature, clever, grown-up children who play with bigger and more exciting toys and see life as a sophisticated game where the greatest pleasure lies in winning. The diagnosis that emerges, not didactically but dramatically, echoes Proudhon on the kind of logic inherent in the acquisition of toys, that property, not in a strictly material sense but on the profoundest emotional levels, can be a form of theft. White's art has affinities with Ben Jonson rather than with Shakespeare and future social historians might say that *Big Toys* offers an excellent introduction to the social history of the period, as Jonson's plays do for London in the early seventeenth century. A structuralist might say, on the other hand, that *Big Toys* is really *A Doll's House* rewritten, that a play is a play and not any other thing. White might admit the resemblances and insist on the differences, insist too that his play holds a mirror up to Sydney, that his actors were the abstracts and brief chronicles of the time. It would be useful at any rate to place *Big Toys* with its concrete particularities against the generalisations of the politicians, as they appear in the daily press, like the assertions made by the Prime Minister, Malcolm Fraser, quoted in *The Age* (12 December

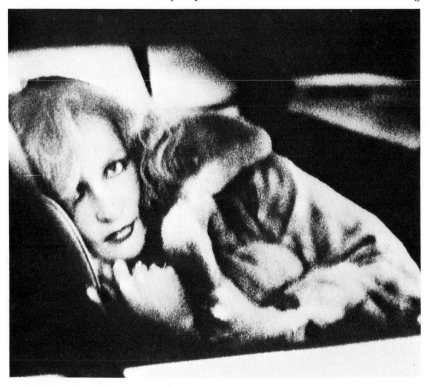

24   Kate Fitzpatrick as Mag in *Big Toys*, 1977

1980): 'From the beginning the private enterprise economy carried with it two promises. First it promised continued improvement in the material condition of the whole people . . . It has kept that promise . . . poverty and deprivation have become the exceptions rather than the rule . . . the private enterprise system carried with it a second promise, the promise of much greater freedom for those living under it. And this promise too has been kept . . .' *Big Toys* is a play which shows how these promises may have been kept.

There are no children to complicate Mag's predicament in *Big Toys*, and Nora's children in *A Doll's House* seem to be easily dispensable; they are heard but not seen. In *The Precious Woman* (see plate 25) by Louis Nowra, staged at the Sydney Opera House in December 1980 by the Sydney Theatre Company, directed by Richard Wherrett, the presence of a child added a new burden of complexity to the theme of the doll. The play offers significant variations on an old theme. It is set in Northern China between 1920 and 1923; when it opens, the precious woman and her maid look out across the garden for the return of Teng her husband, autocratic ruler, soldier and war-lord of the kingdom in which they live. 'Precious' because protected by Teng

25   Robyn Nevin as Su-Ling in *The Precious Woman*, 1980

and insulated against harsh realities, played at first with exactly the right degree of charming, cloying sweetness, by Robyn Nevin, Su-Ling is an exquisite doll-like creature existing more as an ornament than for use, twittering affectionately for Teng in her golden cage. Among the harsh realities from which the hard-headed, commonsensible, autocratic Teng protects Su-Ling is the rebellion in his kingdom and the fact that he has had an English mistress for several years. Teng is shot by his mistress when he attempts to leave her and survives for a time as a mindless vegetable, propped in a chair with his mouth open, eyes rolling, unseeing and veiled in forgetfulness, with lolling tongue and head like a Mongoloid child. Su-Ling's illusions are suddenly destroyed and her anguish excludes any forgiveness. Teng, who protected Su-Ling in life as something precious, is not forgiven for it even after he dies.

When she has to rule the kingdom in Teng's place we sense that the playwright intends Su-Ling to be precious in yet another sense. She is kinder, more humanitarian than Teng, though like him she seeks an alliance with western capitalist interests and becomes the mistress of the successful businessman who continues to supply her with the guns that kept Teng in power. She is less inclined to use them and the rebels grow stronger, until Bao, her son, returns from the west. Here the thematic pattern repeats itself, for Su-Ling has tried to shield Bao from harsh realities as she herself has been shielded. Born with a club-foot, he is now able to move without falling down, though he walks rather like a marionette dragging his left foot behind him. More cruel and ruthless than his father ever was, because more insecure, Bao sets fire to villages, to men, women and children, burning them alive, and is appointed by the Council to rule in Su-Ling's place, a move she passionately resists, paying for her resistance with the loss of her lover – whom Bao yanks from her bed at night – with blindness, and exile.

The connection between the theme of the protected doll and the atrocities of Bao becomes clear when we realise that Su-Ling has begun to reap what she herself has sown. She had protected Bao, instructing the children who played with him always to let him win. She had ignored his club-foot, pretending it did not exist. Suffocating him with affection, as Bao later remembers, she protects him with clinging desperation from the harshness of reality and earns his deep distrust. At the end of the play Su-Ling destroys what she has helped to create. She joins the rebels and, with the support of her name, the rebellion triumphs. She orders the execution of Bao, and it is when the body is being carried away by two raucously triumphant soldiers that she dismisses them and, in weeping horror, holds the corpse in her arms, clinging to it, suffocating it with kisses, asking the blind gods why it had to be so. The question is asked, but neither the corpse nor Su-Ling can answer it. The play is not a tragedy in the fullest sense because tragedy, I suggest, involves self-realisation, and there is only a shadow of self-realisation in the precious woman; only dimly aware of the steps that reach into the abyss, she is engulfed by a blind, overwhelming misery. There is no paradox here of physical blindness and inner vision. Su-Ling does not see. Tragedy, D. H. Lawrence once said, should be a great kick at misery, and I do not think that *The Precious Woman* has quite that kind of effect. It is sentimental rather than tragic at its close, for Louis Nowra does not really follow through his own insights. Being a precious woman is a matter of human choice after all. 'The female idea of love is suffocation', says Bao, who generalises from his experience of Su-Ling's love. Can we entirely blame the blind gods for the traps we make partly by and for ourselves? Security, as the first witch tells Macbeth, may after all be a mortal's 'chiefest enemy', because it so easily threatens the reality of full, complex, responsible living, making the colours of the spectrum narrow into black and white.

Louis Nowra and Patrick White expressed the central theme of the precious woman through a pattern of verbal and visual images which together created a symbolic core of significance. In *Summer of the Seventeenth Doll* (first staged by the Melbourne Theatre Company in 1955, later revived in 1977, directed on both occasions by John Sumner), Ray Lawler used a single image to dramatise a similar theme – the glittering visual image of the doll.

When the play opens in a terraced house in Carlton in the summer of 1953, the garden has been allowed to become a wilderness, and overgrown ferns and shrubs on the front and back verandahs enshroud the house in a tangle of plant life. The overall effect, when the play was staged, was not one of gloom, but of a glowing interior luminosity, of light filtered through subterranean greenery, as if one were in Queensland and not in Melbourne. Here Lawler's stage directions were carried out with great fidelity.[3] The main decorative items in the room were the sixteen kewpie dolls on walking sticks, glowing in the luminous interior with a curious radiance, stuck behind pictures on the walls, flowering from vases in twos and threes, and clustered in a pattern over the mantelpiece.

The cane-cutters Roo and Barnie have brought them down every summer holiday from Queensland for the barmaids Olive and Nancy, their summer mistresses for sixteen years. But in the December of 1953, when the seventeenth doll will arrive, Nancy has left, opting for marriage and sober domesticity with Harry Allaway. Allaway, who works in a bookshop, has seduced Nancy with books smuggled into the pub – a style of courting which makes Olive scornfully call him 'the book bloke'; his conquest of Nancy bears no resemblance to Barney's. Barney, all the evidence suggests, has never read a book in his life.

The pronounced anti-intellectual strain in Australian life, the admiration for pure physical athleticism, is given an undeniable glamour. As Peter Fitzpatrick points out, 'Olive's ecstatic vision of the cane-cutters includes Barney quite as fully as Roo: they are "two eagles flyin' down out of the sun", even if the incongruity is greater in relation to the smaller man; Barney is presented as sharing equally an easy wordless authority over the "soft city blokes" when he and Roo walk into the bar, like "a coupla kings." [4] Olive tells Pearl, the barmaid, who is being tried out as a replacement for Nancy:

> Listen, lovey, you better make up your mind. These are a coupla sugarcane-cutters fresh from the tropics, not two professors from the university.
>
> (act I; p. 211)

In their cultural context – Australian society is not classless but has more social mobility than one finds in most other cultures – the words are plausible: cane-cutters and university professors may not be as remote from each other as they are elsewhere; there is no good reason why Olive should not speak of them in the same breath, or why she should not see the cane-cutters as infinitely more glamorous.

The tragedy in the play is that eagles age like anyone else, and Roo for sixteen years the fastest of the cane-cutters has lost his place in the cane-fields during this seventeenth summer. A new king of the cane-cutters has succeeded him. The play is contemporary and Australian but contains as well a ritualistic pattern which goes back to the earliest drama. The King is dead. Long live the King. Roo seems prepared to accept his fate, to settle for a stable domesticity, marriage to Olive and a drab factory job in Melbourne.

It is here that Lawler presents us with his greatest surprise. The alternative of living in harmony with the drab necessities of urban employment after the visionary glories of the high summers of the past is an alternative that Olive finds unthinkable for Roo:

> 'Seven months they spend up there killin' themselves in the cane season, and then they come down here to live a little. That's what the lay-off is. Not just playing around and spending a lot of money, but a time for livin'. You think I haven't sized that up against what other women have ... Even waiting for Roo to come back is more exciting than anything they've got. (I, i; p. 216)

She rejects the whole notion of suburban marriage, but not without the most terrible anguish.

Olive at thirty-nine, Lawler tells us in a stage direction (I, i; p. 209), has an eagerness that properly belongs to extreme youth despite her surface cynicism. It is in relation to Olive that the doll symbol becomes most telling, most awesomely powerful. At several points in the play she cuddles the kewpie doll with an affection that suggests it is a child surrogate (see plate 26). The seventeenth doll is particularly beautiful in her eyes as the conversation with Roo shows:

> [*She moves away to pick up the seventeenth doll from the rocking chair, and stands stroking it tenderly.*]
> Prettier than ever. You know, I think they take more trouble with them than they used to. There's more tinsel and – they're dressed better. (I, i; p. 231)

26 June Jago as the first Olive in *Summer of the Seventeenth Doll*, 1955

It is essential to the reality of Lawler's art that Olive cannot be aware of any irony that the word 'tinsel' inevitably must carry:

> *Olive.* . . . this one's beautiful. You can see . . .
> [*She holds the doll almost as if it were a baby, and speaks suddenly.*]
> You know why I like the dolls more than anything else you've brought down
> . . . they're something you thought of by yourself. So they're special!
> [*He looks at her questioningly, and then grunts, embarrassed. She fluffs out the doll's skirts.*]
> And don't make noises at me, they are. Where'll I put her?
> *Roo.* Gettin' a bit crowded, maybe you should start upstairs.
> *Olive* [*crossing to vase*]. No, I won't, she's staying right here with the others.
> [*Places doll in vase*] Look at her now, she just dazzles yer.
> *Roo* [*touched but gruffly*]. She's all right.
> *Olive.* Beautiful. (I, ii; pp. 231–2)

The symbol of the doll attains by a process of accretion, and suggestion, an imaginative presence, not merely for Olive and Roo, but for the audience, growing slowly, becoming more distinct and clear, until it sits perched on that ridge in the mind which rises between conscious and unconscious awareness.

The first rending shock comes at the end of the quarrel between Roo and Barney (II; ii; p. 277) when, angry beyond measure, Barney seizes the object closest to him, the vase containing the seventeenth doll, and swings it at Roo's head. Roo rips it from his hands and throws it away into the centre of the room. Olive sinks to her knees with a strangled cry and holds the doll close. This piece of stage business had more than an emotional force; when I saw the production in 1976 it was felt not in the heart only, it had the impact of a physical blow. There was no difficulty in understanding why Olive came down in the middle of the night, as her mother tells Roo, and sat on the floor, hugging the doll and howling.

The destruction of the doll summons in a single moment the awesome power of devouring time. Olive has to confront the fact that the glories of the high summers are over and will not return. When she clears the room of the dolls, the brilliantly plumaged, stuffed North Queensland birds, the tinted coral pieces, and shells from the Great Barrier Reef, we experience the sense of finality with her.

Indeed the doll is a richly ambiguous symbol. A kewpie doll in particular is bodiless and legless, the seventeenth doll had 'more tinsel' and was 'dressed better'. It is associated with the glamour of seventeen summers, which Olive has looked forward to with an excitement that is in some ways like that of a child looking forward to the feast of Christmas, when tinsel and frills announce that Christ is born among the barbarous hills. When Roo at the end of the play beats the doll 'down and down again on the piano, smashing and tearing it until it is nothing but a litter of broken cane, tinsel and celluloid', the dream itself is torn to shreds and appears to have no reality any longer. But as Emma, the moralist in the play, confesses, it was, when it existed, more than tinsel. It was a richer, intenser life, not, as Pearl suspects, a mere indulgence in self-deception and delusion. The doll clearly has immense reality for Olive.

In the world to which she is confined she will not accept the dreary materialism of a suburban marriage with Roo, the depressing alternative to the romantic radiances of the high summer, or permit her eagle from the north to be imprisoned in a factory. The cage she refused to accept for herself is not even golden, and perhaps she does well to refuse it. The action she finally takes in refusing a dull marriage, freeing Roo to return to the cane-fields, keeping her own dream intact, is more dramatically convincing than Nora's in *A Doll's House*, and shows more fine courage than Mag's sad acceptance of her penthouse in Sydney, though it is less realistic: for behind the illiterate surface of the barmaid lives an exceptional spirit, a spirit both more childlike and more mature than we suspect. Her refusal to accept anything less than a special kind of 'livin'', both sensational and visionary (a barmaid is as entitled to visions as a peasant girl from Domremy) despite the immense anguish that the rejection of marriage brings, is in its own way a kind of affirmation. In the end she reveals an unsuspected strength. Because the choice she makes goes against the grain of many of our comfortable preconceptions it has been imperfectly understood. She refuses certainly to be a doll herself. Like some of the great and stubborn heroines of drama she will have her eagle or nothing; though it must be said that Ray Lawler, through his imaginative deployment of the symbol of the kewpie doll, surrounds the whole proposition with the profoundest ironies.

Lawler's own comments on his play give no idea of its organic complexity; they are helpful in a very general way.

> I deliberately avoided laying stress on a manufactured plot line, determined that the play should stand on the merits of its characterization. There is a central theme to hold the pieces together, that of the unbearable nostalgia and bewilderment felt by a group of people when an enchanted private world, built almost entirely on a physical basis, crumbles away under the stress of years and changing circumstances. It is meant to be the tragedy of the inarticulate who feel more than they rationalize or express.[5]

The play is inarticulate in a masterly kind of way. Peter Fitzpatrick draws our attention to the dramatic power Lawler achieves through what cannot be said when Roo, his overalls stained with red paint after a day in a factory, meets Johnnie Dowd, the new king of the cane-cutters:[6]

Dowd. 'Lo Roo.
Roo. 'Lo.
Dowd. Y' look like you been paintin' the town.
Roo. Yeah.   (II, ii; p. 262)

Roo's ''Lo' and 'Yeah' are the brief, brusque signs of the turbulence within, before he can bring himself to shake Dowd's hand. The words succeed in being both convincingly laconic and thoroughly dramatic, with emotion intensely understated.

Lawler has succeeded in conveying the tragedy of those who are made inarticulate by words. Tragedy, however, requires a more powerful expression than this laconic language can give, and the characters express themselves ultimately through silent symbols which are immensely expressive. Communication in *Summer of the Seventeenth Doll* is accomplished through the currents and whirlpools of feeling that move beneath language and find expression in complex, visual symbols. Lawler's play is firmly established within a naturalistic tradition, but its deeper tragic life has its roots in a central symbol, which is organic, and convincing on a naturalistic plane. The doll has, to begin with, a believable, literal existence. Louis Nowra's play *The Precious Woman* is set on the other hand in a non-naturalistic tradition, but its symbols are not as powerful or as organic. Nowra's symbols, like the blindness of Su-Ling, do not grow as naturally out of the play's inner-life. One is tempted to remark that, in the art of drama, symbols should come as naturally as the leaves of a tree, or they better not come at all. If one were to have any reservations about the powerful, visual symbols in Patrick White's *Big Toys*, it would lie here. They seem to have too deliberate a design upon us.

A poem, Paul Valéry once said, is 'une sorte de machine'. The machine Valéry had in mind was the reverse of mechanical. And it seems to me that *Summer of the Seventeenth Doll* is still the most perfect machine devised for the Australian stage. It is the least mechanical of our dramatic machines, and it has a group of realised characters, Olive, Roo, Barney, Pearl, Emma, Bubba and Johnnie Dowd. It is a genuine ensemble play, whereas *Big Toys* and *The Precious Woman* each have only one developed character, Mag and Su-Ling. The other characters are really allegorical types, cleverly disguised as characters, but used in fact as satirical objects to make points about culture and society. The successful QC, Ritchie Bosanquet, is a target for satire, one of the rich on whom assurance sits like a silk hat on a Bradford millionaire. He has no centre, and echoes D. H. Lawrence's criticism of Australian society, for one is made aware of the big, empty spaces in Ritchie's consciousness 'like his country, a vast empty "desert" at the centre of him'.[7]

Some of the most popular successes on the stage in the 1970s have been satires like David Williamson's *The Club*, which presents allegorical types, and is a satiric–comic treatment of football – the opium of the people of Victoria; its didactic purpose was evidently to show that football was neither a sport nor a religion but a form of capitalist enterprise in which all ends have been lost. Allegorical drama in the tradition of the moralities, though a

limiting form, dealing with types, didactic or satiric in intention, has at
certain times in history performed a serious function, and has had its great
use. In recent years the form has spawned a series of most astonishing
grotesques in the plays of Alexander Buzo, David Williamson, Steve J.
Spears, Jack Hibberd and Barry Oakley. Benjamin Franklin in *The
Elocution of Benjamin Franklin* by Spears, and Monk O'Neill in *A Stretch of the
Imagination* are the most human of these grotesques. They are both, of course,
monologues, plays for a single actor, and demand no ensemble work. Monk
O'Neill is an antipodean *Krapp's Last Tape*. Though the ironic pun on
'Monk' is not as telling as Beckett's pun on Krapp.

Allegory though useful is a dangerous form because it has the capacity to
freeze up drama, and when a playwright succeeds in converting D. H.
Lawrence and Frieda into allegorical types in a play based on *Kangaroo* called
Upside Down at the Bottom of the World, the spirit rebels. Frieda emerged as a
German baroness with an enormous sexual appetite and Lawrence as an
archetype of the arrogant Englishman with a Nottingham accent, fastid-
iously withdrawing from the flies as well as the natives. The play was acted
and directed with great verve and a lively sense of the comic at the Playbox
Theatre in Melbourne; and the production in Sydney by the Nimrod
Theatre Company, though less strong on the comedy, managed to convey
some of Lawrence's more sombre criticism of the paradox of the passion for
equality co-existing with the nostalgia for Fascist authoritarianism in
Australian life.

Yet symbolism conceived in the right way, and the exploration of character are probably healthier for drama than allegory. There is a great danger
that Australian playwrights, taking D. H. Lawrence's strictures on the
Australian character as always true, will believe that it is not possible to be
faithful to the Australian reality and create character at all. Recently a
programme note to Barry Oakley's play *Marsupials* quoted the celebrated
passage on character in *Kangaroo*:

> But there is this difference in Australia. Each individual seems to feel himself
> pledged to put himself aside, to keep himself at least half out of count. The
> whole geniality is based on a sort of code of: 'You put yourself aside, and I'll put
> myself aside.' This is done with a watchful will: a sort of duel. And above this, a
> great geniality. But the continual holding most of himself aside, out of count,
> makes a man go blank in his withheld self. And that too is puzzling.[8]

The characters in *Marsupials* were uncannily like this. As long as Lawrence's
observation remains true for the playwrights there appears to be no alternative to satire and allegory in contemporary drama.

There is a myth assiduously proclaimed, to which I do not subscribe, that
Australian drama has improved since the 1950s. If we believed in the
quantitative heresy this would be true, for an incredible number of new plays
have been written between 1950 and 1980. Believers in myths of progress will

say that the movement from naturalistic to non-naturalistic modes is progressive, and suitably avant-garde. Histories of drama tell us that the art of drama does not necessarily proceed in simple evolutionary ways; the theory that Australian drama has actually 'progressed' from Lawler to Nowra is a theory that one has to approach with the greatest caution.

NOTES

1. Penguin edition, p. 336.
2. Preface to *Big Toys* (Sydney, 1978), p. xi.
3. All references to the Currency Press edition of *The Doll Trilogy* (Woollahra, NSW, 1978).
4. *After the Doll* (Melbourne, 1979), p. 24.
5. Letter to Leslie Rees in *The Making of Australian Drama* by Rees (Sydney, 1978), 2 vols. 1, 266.
6. *After the Doll*, p. 22.
7. *Kangaroo*, p. 48.
8. *Ibid.*, p. 43.

BOOKS

Nietzsche on Tragedy by M. S. Silk and J. P. Stern

reviewed by GEOFFREY ARNOTT

When Friedrich Nietzsche published *The Birth of Tragedy*[1] in January 1872, he was a 27-year-old fledgling Professor of Greek at the University of Basle. In the same year reviews began to appear. The most impassioned of these came from the pens of two Hellenists who (like Nietzsche) were still in their twenties, but (unlike Nietzsche) went on to earn high distinction as teachers and researchers in the world of traditional classical scholarship. Erwin Rohde was an intimate friend of Nietzsche's[2] from their student days at Leipzig, and the two then shared scholarly interests and inclinations. Not surprisingly, Rohde's review[3] of 'this most highly remarkable book' was adulatory, praising its insight and its aims from a shared Wagnerian idolatry. The other review was a complete contrast in everything except its emotional base. Its author, Ulrich von Wilamowitz-Moellendorf,[4] had been educated at the same boarding-school as Nietzsche, and was to become the most influential Hellenist in Germany of his generation. It is now difficult to calculate precisely how far Wilamowitz's antipathy to Nietzsche's book was fired by personal factors,[5] and how far by hostility to a triad of general features in *The Birth of Tragedy* – Nietzsche's tone of dogmatic assertiveness, his rejection of traditional classical scholarship, and his obsession with alleged irrelevancies such as the works of Schopenhauer and Wagner – but Wilamowitz's review damned *The Birth of Tragedy* as totally worthless in tones of savage sarcasm and vituperative hysteria. It was not difficult for Wilamowitz to condemn the important factual errors in Nietzsche's discussion of the ancient world (for example, Apollo was not the Greek god of dreams; the role of music in fifth-century-BC Greek tragedy was not equal, but subordinate, to that of the words; no such genre as 'tragic dithyramb' ever existed outside Nietzsche's imagination; 'tragic avatars' of Dionysus could not be postulated in at least half of Aeschylus's extant plays – *Persae*, *Supplices, Eumenides*), and thus to destroy significant parts of the foundations of Nietzsche's theoretical edifice. Yet what offended Wilamowitz even more than these errors was the book's 'tone and bias' (*Ton und Tendenz*), which rejected the language and methodological argumentation of traditional scholarship, replaced logic by intuition, and introduced classical scholars to the style of the pulpit with its evangelical fervour. Wilamowitz would 'have nothing to do with the metaphysical and apostolic Nietzsche'.

Wilamowitz's review could have been – perhaps ought to have been – devastating. Few Hellenists since the Renaissance have combined the flair, range and acumen of Wilamowitz.[6] If he had presented his criticisms in logical sequence, avoided errors himself, and written with the cold, dry analytical language of *Wissenschaft*, he might well have been taken more seriously by Nietzsche and Nietzscheans. But in attacking the *Ton und Tendenz* of *The Birth of Tragedy* he himself screamed and ranted, answering dogmatic assertion with hysteria, and aesthetical philosophising with sarcasm.[7] Yet whatever feelings modern scholars may wish to parade about the rights and wrongs of that sad critical brawling, they must remember that Wilamowitz went on to contribute rather more to our present-day understanding of Greek tragedy than did Nietzsche with his more explosive theories. Students who wish to learn about Euripides's relation to Socrates, about the connections between choral lyric and the origins of Greek tragedy, or about Aeschylus's originality, find Wilamowitz's classic account, written first in 1895 and dedicated to his and Nietzsche's old school,[8] altogether more coherent and less dated than Nietzsche's.

In fact, the general modern reaction to *The Birth of Tragedy* has been conditioned less by the remarks of hostile philologists such as Wilamowitz, and more by Nietzsche's own later disparagement of what he considered to be a youthful indiscretion. In his *Attempt at a Self-Criticism*, which he prefixed to a re-publication of *The Birth of Tragedy* in 1886, he called 'this strange and almost inaccessible book' incautious and intrepid, alleged that it was marred by 'every defect of youth', and described it as 'image-mad and confused, sentimental, logically unclear, disdainful of proof, arrogant and rhapsodic'. Nevertheless, partly in that same essay, and partly in his later autobiographical *Ecce Homo*, he reiterated the importance of *The Birth of Tragedy*'s Dionysiac and Socratic concepts.

Ecce Homo was written in 1888. Since then, informed attitudes to *The Birth of Tragedy* have tended to vary according to the nationality or special interest of the writer. Nietzscheans do not place it at or even near the pinnacle of his achievements, but they maintain none the less that it is 'one of the most suggestive and influential studies of tragedy ever written. Perhaps only Aristotle's *Poetics* excels it.'[9] Creative writers and literary critics have been particularly beguiled by its seminal polarisation of the Dionysiac and Apolline elements in art, religion and life, although this enthralment has often been accompanied by the mistranslation of *das Apollinische* and *das Dionysische* as the 'Apollonian' and 'Dionysian', forms more properly applied to the various Apollonii and Dionysii of Greek history and literature.[10]

And what about the response of classical scholars? H. Lloyd-Jones has given an excellent account of Nietzsche's influence on classical studies both in his native Germany and in the English-speaking world.[11] Generally speaking, German scholars have appreciated, English and American scholars have neglected or repudiated, his contributions. It is, for instance, striking that in one of the most influential works published in Britain this century about the origins of Greek tragedy, Sir Arthur Pickard-Cambridge's *Dithyramb, Tragedy and Comedy* (Oxford University Press, first edition 1928), Nietzsche's name is never mentioned (Wilamowitz's is).

The present situation resembles rather a smoke-laden battlefield, where desultory sniping continues and the overview is uncertain. I hope, however, that the air will be cleared considerably by the very welcome publication of the first major study devoted solely to *The Birth of Tragedy*, by M. S. Silk and J. P. Stern, working in happy collaboration.[12] Much previous discussion of *The Birth of Tragedy* has been distorted by the prejudiced outlook of the critic, from Wilamowitz onwards; a fair critique can emerge only when the critic is both immersed in the works of Nietzsche (as Germanist and philosopher) and professionally competent in the study of ancient Greek literature and culture. Few critics (apart from H. J. Mette) have shown expertise in both areas, and it is one of the many strengths of this new study that it is the product of a collaboration between Germanist and classicist which shows no sign of generative strain or discordancy.

It can be said at once that Silk and Stern are splendidly successful in their aim of producing an exhaustive, objective (to the limit of what is humanly possible) and sensitively judicious study of *The Birth of Tragedy* from the relevant standpoints: historical, biographical, cultural, classical, philosophical and rhetorical. The study is deliberately limited; it does not investigate Nietzsche's philosophy as a whole, or indeed *The Birth of Tragedy* in its relation to his later philosophy; it is concerned with *The Birth of Tragedy*, *tout court*.

They commence their task by setting *The Birth of Tragedy* against a series of backgrounds which they fully probe and illuminate. There is the background of German theoretical enquiries into the nature of tragedy and the tragic, going back to Herder and Lessing in the eighteenth century; the background of that German admiration for the allegedly superior (but in some respects homologous) culture of ancient Greece, with the 'noble simplicity and serene grandeur' of its classical art, its ideal of liberty, and its prestigious drama; and thirdly, the background of classical scholarship as it had developed in Nietzsche's Germany, *Altertumswissenschaft* as a single but comprehensive scientific study divorced from the excitements of creative art.

With parallel thoroughness Silk and Stern examine the relevant details of Nietzsche's personal life, going back to his schooldays at Schulpforte near Naumburg (now in the GDR, and still an *Internatschule* but without Latin and Greek). Nietzsche's three major conversions in his twenties are clearly outlined: to Schopenhauer, to Hellenism (but with a rejection of academic

philology), and to the ideas and music of Wagner. The germinating seeds of
the ideas which flowered in *The Birth of Tragedy* are systematically uncovered. Nietzsche's 1870 Basle lecture on 'Socrates and Tragedy' introduced the idea that Greek tragedy died in the second half of the fifth century
BC under the onslaught of Socratic and Euripidean rationalism. Nietzsche's
lecture notes on the *Oedipus Rex*, from about the same time, made an initial
reference to the Apolline and Dionysiac antithesis, which was developed
further in his essay on 'The Dionysiac Philosophy'.

Silk and Stern's analysis of these and other important precursors of *The
Birth of Tragedy* reveals no new source materials, but it does enable them to
counter the view about the work's genesis circulated by Nietzsche's sister
Elisabeth, who played here (as so often elsewhere) her Mephistophelean
role, unreliable, anamorphic and distortive, as evangelist for the Nietzschean
philosophy. Silk and Stern argue plausibly that there was never any long-
standing or deep commitment on Nietzsche's part to a large-scale work on
Greek culture. *The Birth of Tragedy* was largely a reworking of ideas that had
already been adumbrated in 1870 (§1–10 from 'The Dionysiac Philosophy',
but 5–6 partly too from the *Oedipus Rex* notes; 11–14 from 'Socrates and
Tragedy'; 15–25 from other prefigurations). There is no evidence that
the final sections (20–5) were added as a hasty afterthought. *The Birth of
Tragedy* was Wagnerian in its approach right from its conception, reflecting
the composer's glorification of Aeschylean tragedy as the complete art-
form.

The Birth of Tragedy is a difficult work, 'condensed, elliptical and im-
patient' in its style, as Silk and Stern neatly sum it up, labyrinthine and
allusive in its argument,[13] and reminiscent more often of a diatribe or sermon
than of a controlled, organised dialectic. Many of its assertions are based on
premises that are not merely unproven or unverifiable, but often unstated or
relegated to other sections of the work. The normal scholarly apparatus of
footnotes, exact citation of primary and secondary sources, and cross-
references, is totally lacking. Dazzling illuminations of intuition replace the
colder lights of logic. These factors in combination create all manner of
problems and uncertainties for those readers of *The Birth of Tragedy* who are
not equally informed about (1) the cultural history, philosophy and music of
Germany, (2) the literature, art, religion and philosophy of ancient Greece,
and (3) the traditional methodology of classical scholarship – and that
means most of us. For this reason the authors of this new study are most
warmly to be thanked and congratulated for including a logically structured, cross-referenced and clearly intelligible summary of the argument of
The Birth of Tragedy – a summary which clarifies some of Nietzsche's ideas by
presenting them in a more logical order, incorporates (within brackets)
many of his unstated premises, and substitutes the drier tone of the study for
the imbricated and at times opaque frenzy of the rostrum. This summary is

inevitably denser, more compact than Nietzsche's original, but not exces-sively so (it fills some twenty-six pages of text), and it presents accurately the kernel of Nietzsche's ideas even when it loses the flavour of his style.

Précis-writing, however, involves subjectivity, and no summary of so convoluted a work as *The Birth of Tragedy* could satisfy the varied require-ments of every reader. Silk and Stern are never careless or slipshod, rarely wilful, and most of their work is refreshingly free from the bias of emotional and unresearched commitment. Yet occasionally they seem to me guilty of two kinds of misinterpretation or distortion in their summary of Nietzsche's arguments. Once or twice Nietzsche's intentions are not conveyed exactly. In §7, for instance, Nietzsche rejects A. W. Schlegel's familiar interpretation of the Greek tragic chorus as 'the ideal spectator' (*der idealische Zuschauer* in Nietzsche, though Schlegel himself says *idealisierte*),[14] because (according to Silk and Stern) there was 'originally no spectacle for it to be spectator of'. Here they appear to be garbling a sentence of Nietzsche's that comes later in §7 ('The spectator without the spectacle is an absurd notion'), and at the same time misrepresenting it as his reason for rejecting Schlegel's interpre-tation. In this section of *The Birth of Tragedy* admittedly, the thread of Nietzsche's argument is rather snarled and hard to disentangle, but accord-ing to my reading of it the two reasons there advanced by Nietzsche for his opposition to Schlegel are very different from the one stated by Silk and Stern in their summary. These two reasons are (1), the typical theatre audiences of Nietzsche's own time lacked refinement and insight. Could the ancient Greek audiences have been so very different? And if they were not, how could it 'ever be possible to idealise from such a public something analogous to the Greek tragic chorus'? And (2), the Greek tragic chorus 'is forced to recognise real beings in the figures on the stage', and so is part of the tragic action, involved in it. The second of these reasons, if I have rightly understood Nietzsche's words here, is the effective rebuttal of the Schlegelian view, prefiguring with characteristic divinatory insight the more balanced twentieth-century interpretations of the chorus's function.[15] Schlegel's theory fails because it is too simplistic; it illumines some (but by no means all) of the choral *stasima*, but is blind to the complexity of the relationship between the lyric utterance of the chorus in these *stasima* and their role as participants or involved onlookers in the *epeisodia*.

The other type of misrepresentation or distortion which can be detected on at least one occasion in their summary of *The Birth of Tragedy*'s argument is equally serious, although it will arouse the sympathy of all who have wrestled with the ineluctable problems of translation from a foreign lan-guage. Translations are always lies, and in this context the lie, *pace* Nietzsche, is not divine. The context here is §15, in which Nietzsche begins his onslaught on the *Wissenschaft* of his contemporary Germany. The word *Wissenschaft* cannot be simply translated by any single English all-purpose word; Silk and

Stern at least do not fall into the trap of using the nearest, but still danger-ously misleading, English equivalent of 'science', as Walter Kaufmann does in the most accessible modern English translation of *The Birth of Tragedy*. In fact they wisely retain the German word in their summary whenever the concept needs to be mentioned; but on its first occurrence, in the second half of §15, they gloss it as 'science, learning and philosophy', and thereby stand accused of distortion. I am no Germanist, but it seems to me that any commentator on *The Birth of Tragedy* at this point needs first and foremost to point out two basic facts about the use and meaning of this word *Wissenschaft*. It subsumes not only the physical and biological sciences, but also those arts subjects (such as classics, in German *Altertumswissenschaft*) which have adopted 'scientific' methods. Secondly, *Wissenschaft* is not only the subject, but also the methodology and its results. It was, after all, the application *in* and *to* ancient Greece of something which purported to be 'scientific reason-ing' that Nietzsche considered an indication of degeneracy and inadequacy.

These criticisms must be made; they refer, however, to only a few passages in one small but important section of an excellent book. They impair only marginally the usefulness of the summary of Nietzsche's argument, and I doubt indeed whether a more serviceable summary of it could be put together.

The next section of Silk and Stern's study is devoted to an examination of the impact made by *The Birth of Tragedy* subsequently both on the world of scholarship in general, and in particular on the closed ranks of German philologists in the 1870s. The analysis is thorough, basically unopinionated, and judicious. They deal fairly with Wilamowitz's blinkered but academi-cally crippling assault. It epitomised, as they rightly point out, the alienation between academic scholarship and those who, like Nietzsche, advocated an interplay between learning, the creative arts, and life. But are Silk and Stern also right to allege that Wilamowitz's attack was entirely or mostly inspired by petty jealousy of Nietzsche's early success in gaining the Basle chair without the customary preliminaries of Ph.D. and *Habilitation*? I have already referred to the complexity of the reasons underlying Wilamowitz's hostility to Nietzsche,[16] but Silk and Stern note that in his autobiography Wilamowitz himself claimed that Nietzsche had aroused his 'moral indig-nation' mainly by the 'impudent attack' in §19 of *The Birth of Tragedy* on Otto Jahn, Wilamowitz's own mentor.[17] Silk and Stern rather airily dismiss this allegation as 'bizarre'; I am not so sure. In the German university system, relations between teacher and student could be very close, and the resultant ties of personal loyalty quite strong enough to inspire vitriolic attacks and defences.

In fact Nietzsche's own precocious elevation to the Basle chair was partly at least the result of a similarly warm pupil–teacher relationship between himself and Friedrich Ritschl, successively professor at Bonn and Leipzig.

The portrait of Ritschl offered by Silk and Stern is less satisfactory, because less complete, than their comparable cameos of the other classical scholars with whom Nietzsche came into contact. When Ritschl's embarrassed silence after the publication of *The Birth of Tragedy* is discussed – and well discussed – the plausible suggestion is made that Ritschl may have interpreted Nietzsche's characterisation of the contemporary classical professor (an 'Alexandrian man ... a critic without joy or strength ... at bottom a librarian and proof-corrector', §18) as a caricature of Ritschl himself. Perhaps so: but it would have been helpful for non-classicist readers of this book if the authors had informed them that Ritschl was no run-of-the-mill pedant but a great Latinist whose work on the early Latin language, metre and the plays of Plautus was in itself fundamental and an inspiration to the school of students who gathered round him. The man whose brilliant identification of the Greek original of Plautus's *Bacchides* in an 1836 lecture has been triumphantly confirmed by new discoveries first published in 1968 deserves at least this measure of tribute to his talents.[18]

The Birth of Tragedy takes a knowledge of ancient Greek literature, art and culture, as disseminated in the early 1870s, for granted, but it is never, in method or presentation, a traditional work of classical scholarship. Its parentage is mixed – a century of Greek studies in Germany, native philosophy, aesthetics, cultural and musical criticism. It mixes insight with error, untidiness with profundity, originality with perverse distortion. It is composed emotively like a sermon, not as a structured and argued thesis. The arrangement is unsystematic. Its provocative statements are unsupported by argument and often based on false hypotheses. A modern classicist will inevitably judge it by the canons of scholarship today, and so to some extent unfairly. In 1872 Schliemann was only just beginning to uncover the remains of bronze-age civilisation at Troy; the Egyptian desert still concealed its vast stores of Hellenistic and Imperial documents and lost literature; the relevance of such disciplines as anthropology to classical studies was not yet appreciated. The critic who wishes to play Zoilus to *The Birth of Tragedy* needs to understand all this.

All this, fortunately, and much more that is pertinent can be found in those sections of this book which follow the authors' analysis of the scholarly reception of *The Birth of Tragedy* in Germany and elsewhere. Here they introduce the longest and perhaps the most important part of their study, beginning with a structured discussion (rather than a textual commentary) of those areas of classical Greek culture subsumed, taken for granted, or openly treated in *The Birth of Tragedy*. The discussion is wide-ranging and well-informed, taking full account of the scholarly discoveries and controversies of the last hundred years. It is evaluative, but although in consequence it must lack something in objectivity, the knowledge and the judgement of the two authors make it difficult for any conversant critic to

disagree with most of their general assessments and detailed analyses. It is
perhaps an indication of the excellence and success of their achievement that,
when I started to work on this review, I imagined that this section of the book
would call for most comment, both critical and illustrative; but in fact
virtually all my remarks, after the initial blanket approval and praise of their
work here, will be confined to the superficial flea-bites of criticised detail,
and to a more general disagreement with the tone and shading – not with the
factual accuracy – of a few, mainly interlinked, areas of the discussion.

Silk and Stern structure their analysis of the Hellenic ingredients of *The
Birth of Tragedy* under five sub-headings: music, the origins of tragedy,
literary history, *mores* and religion, the Dionysiac and Apolline antithesis.
Few will object to the authors' opinions that Nietzsche is at his best on
religion, at his worst on Greek music; and that his many infuriating factual
blunders and distortions are counterbalanced by the flashes of insight and
inspiration which blaze out on page after page: Nietzsche's ideas, for example, on the ecstatic loss of individuality felt by worshippers of Dionysus (§1),
on the amorality of the Olympian religion and the popular understanding of
the horror of existence (§2), on the artificiality of dramatic illusion and
language, along with the brilliant interpretation of the tragic effect (§7), on
the Oedipus myth (§9), on the enigmatic depth beneath the deceptive
distinctness of Aeschylean tragedy (§11, 12), or on the enjoyment of dissonance (§24).

Lists, however, are likely to prove boring, even where the approbatory
comment is linked to analysis or evaluation, and it will do little useful service
either to Nietzsche or to Silk and Stern merely to compile a catalogue of good
points and acceptable arguments in those sections of the book devoted to the
investigation of *The Birth of Tragedy*'s Hellenic background, or in the subsequent chapters which discuss its mode and originality, its concepts about
tragedy, music and aesthetics, its debts to earlier German theories of tragedy, and the relationship between style and content. The three major
influences on Nietzsche at the time of *The Birth of Tragedy*'s gestation
(Wagner, Schopenhauer, and his own Hellenic schooling) always require,
and in this study receive, a sensitively balanced assessment of counterweight-
ings. Nietzsche's obsession with archetypes, which reduced individual men
(Archilochus and Socrates, for instance) and individual gods(such as Apollo
and Dionysus) to unhistorical symbols, is here demonstrated with exemplary
clearness. Classicists will learn a good deal from this detailed critique of
Nietzsche's views on the aesthetics of tragedy; Nietzscheans will learn much
from a trenchant discussion which reveals some important deficiencies in
Nietzsche's portrayal of Greek religion; classicists and Nietzscheans alike will
benefit from the splendid analysis of *The Birth of Tragedy*'s most fruitful
concept, the Apolline and Dionysiac polarity. Particularly illuminating is
the full and delicately weighted account of the antecedents of this last

concept, not merely the more familiar precursors in German thought (Hölderlin's antithesis between the Apolline and Junonian, for instance, and Bachofen's pioneering work on Dionysus), but also some embryonic intimations in ancient Greek culture, exemplified best in some aspects of religious cult, Orphic reinterpretations, and the writings of Plutarch.

In these sections of their book Silk and Stern can rarely be criticised for errors of fact (but on p. 137, the reference should be to *auloi*, 'pipes' in the plural, for the individual player played double pipes), omission (but on p. 142, there is a failure to mention the presence of tragedies at the Dionysiac festival of the Lenaea in Athens), or distortion (but again on p. 142, Aristotle does not say in chapter 4 of the *Poetics* that tragedy developed *ek saturikou*, 'from a satyric element', but rather that it developed 'from those leading the dithyrambic chorus', and 'gained seriousness' late because it had suffered a transformation *ek saturikou*; Aristotle's words are not easy to interpret here,[19] but the offered version is garbled). There are perhaps four passages, however, in these sections where the tone and shading in otherwise meritorious discussions seem to me unacceptable. All four concern Greek literature, and although the facts are presented accurately, their subjective slanting must be challenged.

The first passage occurs in an otherwise balanced and sensitive treatment of a very dark subject, the origins of Greek tragedy. Like Nietzsche, most modern theorists derive Greek tragedy from the worship of Dionysus, but against Nietzsche they tend to reject the hypothesis of a primitive ritual enacting the sufferings of Dionysus. Silk and Stern duly praise Pickard-Cambridge's 'sober and scrupulous evaluation' of the evidence and of earlier theories in his still authoritative *Dithyramb, Tragedy and Comedy*, but later they abandon Pickard-Cambridge's wise scepticism for T. B. L. Webster's unsuccessful attempt[20] to reactivate the neo-Aristotelian theory (which conflated some ideas in the *Poetics* with the idea of a satyric dithyramb, on Nietzschean lines) together with that of Gilbert Murray (based on the putative *eniautos daimon*, or 'year spirit'). Webster's arguments (together with those of Nietzsche and Murray) are effectively demolished by Brian Vickers in the opening chapter of his stimulating if uneven book, *Towards Greek Tragedy* (London: Longman, 1973, pp. 33ff.). Unfortunately, Vickers's book appears to have escaped Silk and Stern's wide bibliographical net.

The second bone of contention concerns Euripides. Nietzsche's assault on him in *The Birth of Tragedy* was not original (he took many of the details of his criticism from Aristophanes's *Frogs*, much of its tone from Schlegel's lectures), but it is, as Silk and Stern point out, in many respects 'grossly unfair'.[21] However, in their attempt to assess Nietzsche's strictures on Euripides with unprejudiced minds, they are themselves grossly unfair to Euripides at several crucial points. They recognise his genius, of course, and few will quarrel with the main outlines of their picture of the dramatist as a man of wide range, rationalistic (*pace* Dodds![22]) and naturalistic, a de-glamoriser of myth who was discontented with tradition and engrossed by the psychology of individual characters under stress. At the same time, however, they allege certain 'indefensible characteristics' in Euripides's plays, such as the 'futility' and rebarbative rhetoric of numerous debates, just as earlier (in their summary of *The Birth of Tragedy*'s argument, §14) they accuse the playwright of introducing choral odes that are irrelevant to the plot. Both allegations have a superficial speciousness that has won them an uncritical hearing from most opponents and a few advocates of Euripides, but nevertheless both allegations can be successfully countered. The best general defence of the rhetoric and dialectic of Euripidean debates can be found in a paragraph of Brian Vickers's book on Greek tragedy;[23] these debates are dramatically gripping partly because the life of a character often depends on their outcome, partly because the audience is not impartial but as a rule committed emotionally in favour of one of the antagonists. As for the choral odes, accusations of irrelevance are usually limited to one or two allegedly flagrant examples of gratuitous pictorialisation, such as the 'Arms of Achilles' *stasimon* in the *Electra* (ll. 432ff.) and the 'Wandering Goddess' ode of the *Helen* (ll. 1301ff.). New studies of these odes, however, have revealed a subtle and purposed nexus of relationships between ode and play, in mood and image, comprehensively and in pointed detail.[24]

The other two topics of Nietzschean literary criticism where the stance seems to me uncertain or insecure are of much less importance. Nietzsche's own remarks here are peripheral, Silk and Stern's comments correspond-ingly brief (perhaps to the extreme of inadequacy), and criticism accord-ingly ought to be proportionate. The topics are Greek New Comedy (§§11, 17) and the literature generated by Alexandrian culture (§§17, 18). Nietzsche attacks New Comedy for its dependence on Euripidean tragedy and its preoccupation with the 'perpetual triumphs' of the cunning slave. Silk and Stern are here guilty of dereliction, since they fail to observe that the important papyrus discoveries of Menandrean comedy in the last eighty years, while confirming New Comedy's debt to Euripides,[25] have also shown that servile 'triumphs of cunning and craftiness' are much less a feature of Menander's drama than of the Roman adaptations of New Comedy by Plautus. Nietzsche's views on Alexandrian culture, on the other hand, are neither outdated nor wholly distorted. His picture of Alexandrian scholars labouring in the service of *Wissenschaft* on soluble problems cannot be faulted for what it portrays – only for what it leaves out. Silk and Stern could have provided the necessary corrective, but instead they accept Nietzsche's evalu-ation a little too readily. And yet Alexandrian science and scholarship did not entirely stifle literary genius, and any account of its culture that neglects the fresh vivacity and lyricism of Theocritus's idylls, or the bittersweet crispness of the best epigrammatists, to take just two examples of its literary peaks, must be incomplete.

It would be ungenerous, however, to end this discussion of so masterly and serviceable a book with such minor cavils. Errors and omissions are rare in any section of the book, which is sure to become the standard critique of *The Birth of Tragedy* for many years to come. It clarifies, but does not oversimplify, the difficulties of a work that will always be contentious. It shares with *The Birth of Tragedy* – necessarily maybe – the limitations of a dual viewpoint, surveying the culture of the early 1870s from the vantages of ancient Greece and modern Germany. Such limitations may evoke a sigh of regret. If only Nietzsche had not cramped himself by nationalistic preoccupations ... but unprofitable speculation is often marked by unfulfilled conditionals.[26]

NOTES

1. *Die Geburt der Tragödie aus dem Geiste der Musik*, reprinted as *Die Geburt der Tragödie, oder Griechenthum und Pessimismus*.

2. They were on *Duzfuss* terms, and at Leipzig so inseparable that Friedrich Ritschl nicknamed them the 'Heavenly Twins' (*Dioskuren*).

3. *Norddeutsche allgemeine Zeitung*, 26 May 1872, reprinted in *Der Streit um Nietzsches 'Geburt der Tragödie'*, ed. K. Gründer (Hildesheim, 1969), pp. 15ff.

4. *Zukunftsphilologie* (Berlin, 1872), reprinted in Gründer, *Der Streit*, pp. 27ff.

5. For example, personal hostility dating from their schooldays (see W. M. Calder's edition of Wilamowitz's *In wieweit befriedigen die Schlüsse der erhaltenen griechischen Trauerspiele*, Leiden, 1974, pp. 4f, and n.22). For Wilamowitz's resentment of Nietzsche's strictures on Otto Jahn, see p. 202, and n.16.

6. M. S. Silk and J. P. Stern (*Nietzsche on Tragedy*, Cambridge University Press, 1980, pp. 100f.) assemble some contemporary and later acknowledgements of Wilamowitz's primacy in scholarship. For evidence of his confident assurance at about the time of *The Birth of Tragedy*'s appearance the curious reader should turn to the delightful anecdote of the window and the piles of slips told by Ed. Fraenkel in the introduction to his edition of F. Leo's *Ausgewählte kleine Schriften* (Rome, 1960), xviii.

7. For a sensible view of this academic brawl, see H. Lloyd-Jones's paper in *Studies in Nietzsche and the Classical Tradition*, ed. J. C. O'Flaherty *et al.* (Chapel Hill: University of North Carolina Press, 1976), pp. 7f.

8. In the introduction to his edition of Euripides's *Heracles* (Berlin, 1895; second edn, 1909), I, 1ff.

9. So W. Kaufmann, in the preface to his translation of *The Birth of Tragedy* (New York: Random House, 1967), p. 3.

10. It is good to see that Silk and Stern employ the terms Apolline and Dionysiac (cf. their pp. 38 and 384 n. 22), here following the example of A. H. J. Knight's *Some Asects of the Life and Work of Nietzsche* (Cambridge University Press, 1933).

11. See n.7 above.

12. See n. 6 above.

13. Cf. W. Kaufmann, *Nietzsche: Philosopher, Psychologist, Antichrist* (Princeton, third edn, 1968), p. 72: 'As soon as one attempts to penetrate behind the clever

epigrams and well-turned insults to grasp their consequences and to co-ordinate them, one is troubled.'

14. In Schlegel's *Vorlesungen über dramatische Kunst und Literatur*; the most accessible text is that edited by G. V. Amoretti (Bonn and Leipzig, 1923; repr. Turin: Einaudi, 1960), 1, 54f. An English translation was produced by J. Black (London, 1846; repr. New York: AMS Press Inc. 1965, 1973), p. 70.

15. For example, A. M. Dale, 'The Chorus in the Action of Greek Tragedy' in *Classical Drama and its Influence, essays presented to H. D. F. Kitto*, ed. M. J. Anderson (London: Methuen, 1965), pp. 17ff., and reprinted in the authoress's *Collected Papers* (Cambridge University Press, 1969), pp. 210ff.; Brian Vickers, *Towards Greek Tragedy* (London: Longman, 1973), pp. 10ff.; and R. P. Winnington-Ingram, *Sophocles: An Interpretation* (Cambridge University Press, 1980), pp. 200ff.

16. See above, p. ■■■, and Calder's remarks (*loc. cit.* in n.5 above).

17. *Erinnerungen* (Leipzig, 1928), pp. 128ff., translated by G. C. Richards as *My Recollections* (London, 1930), pp. 150ff.

18. Cf. E. W. Handley, *Menander and Plautus: A Study in Comparison* (London, 1968), pp. 6 and 19 n.3.

19. *Poetics*, 1449^a10f., 19ff. Cf. A. Pickard-Cambridge, *Dithyramb, Tragedy and Comedy* (first edn, Oxford, 1928), pp. 121ff., and the commentaries of D. W. Lucas (Oxford University Press, 1968) and G. F. Else (Cambridge, Mass.: Harvard University Press, 1967), *ad loc.*

20. In the second edition of Pickard-Cambridge's book (Oxford University Press, 1962).

21. Cf. B. Snell, *The Discovery of the Mind*, trans. T. G. Rosenmeyer (Oxford: Basil Blackwell, 1953), pp. 119ff.; and W. Kaufmann, 'Nietzsche and the Death of Tragedy: A Critique', in O'Flaherty, *Studies in Nietzsche*, pp. 247ff.

22. See his paper 'Euripides the Irrationalist', *Classical Review*, IV (1920), 97ff.; and cf. Kaufmann, 'Nietzsche and the Death of Tragedy', pp. 251ff.

23. *Towards Greek Tragedy*, pp. 48f., n.38.

24. See especially (1) on the *Electra* ode, M. J. O'Brien, *American Journal of Philology*, LXXXV (1964), 13ff., and G. R. Walsh, *Yale Classical Studies*, XXV (1977), 277ff.; (2) on the *Helen* ode, A. N. Pippin, *Classical Philology*, LV (1960), 155ff., A. J. Podlecki, *Transactions of the American Philological Association*, CI (1970), 411f., and C. Wolff, *Harvard Studies in Classical Philology*, LXXVII (1973), 70ff.

25. Cf. my own *Menander, Plautus, Terence, Greece and Rome, New Surveys in the Classics*, no. 9 (Oxford, 1975), pp. 10ff.

26. I should like to thank most warmly two of my colleagues in the University of Leeds, Dr H. B. Gottschalk and Mr R. Hargreaves, for their helpful comments, particularly on those matters outside my professional competence as a teacher of ancient Greek language and literature.

David Daniell's *'Coriolanus' in Europe*

reviewed by JOHN RIPLEY

It is frequently asserted that Shakespeare's *Coriolanus* has been an unpopular play in the theatre; but such claims are at variance with the evidence. A rough count of English and American performances in all versions over the past three centuries reveals that *Coriolanus* has received about two-thirds as many professional airings as *Julius Caesar*, a perennial box-office favourite. Eighteenth- and nineteenth-century tragic stars – with the exception of Garrick and the Booths – found the title role irresistible. Kemble made his reputation in it; and Quin, Sheridan, Macready, Phelps, Forrest, and Benson enjoyed gratifying, if rather more modest, successes. Only Edmund Kean and Henry Irving met with outright failure.

If in this century Caius Martius has seldom evinced the incandescent grandeur captured by Kemble, Macready, and Forrest, productions have featured fuller texts, apter staging, and better interpretations of the play itself, as distinct from the title role, than at any time since the Restoration. Terry Hands's *Coriolanus*, which opened at the Royal Shakespeare Theatre in October 1977, with Alan Howard as the arrogant patrician, is not only the latest major revival, but one of the best in recent memory. Its Stratford run was followed by an Aldwych season in 1978; and in the spring of 1979, to mark the centenary of the birth of Stratford's first Memorial Theatre, the production toured a series of European cities. Between 3 April and 13 May the Company played for a week in Paris and made briefer stops in Vienna, Amsterdam, Brussels, Hamburg, Berlin, Munich, and Zurich. David Daniell, Lecturer in English at University College, London, went along as an observer and records his impressions in a handsomely-produced volume.[1]

Despite its ambitious title, *'Coriolanus' in Europe* is almost exclusively an account of the RSC tour. Previous continental productions of the play receive but scant and whimsical attention. 'There have been many adaptations of this play in Europe', Daniell notes in parentheses. 'I refer only in this book to those which in some way impinged on the Company and the tour in 1979' (p. 78). Daniell offers no proof that any European adaptation of *Coriolanus* impinged on the RSC at any time. The Company, it appears, had all it could do to mount its own *Coriolanus* adequately, bedevilled as it was by communications foul-ups, unco-operative managements, intractable stages, and other hazards common to strollers. The author, however, had leisure to be impinged upon by several relatively recent French and German productions and notes them superficially. In Paris he was reminded of the riotous political ambience which accompanied the staging of the Piachaud version at the Comédie Française in the 1933–4 season. In Berlin he journeyed east to the archives of the Berliner Ensemble where he consulted documents related to Brecht's *Coriolan*. In Hamburg he relaxed over coffee and mineral water with Boy Gobert, Intendant of the Thalia-Theater, while the latter reminisced about Hans Hollman's adaptation. Staged at the Thalia in 1977, with Gobert as the star, it was arguably the most tasteless mutilation of the play since Nahum Tate's time. Unfortunately Daniell fails to endow these revivals with either intrinsic interest or manifest relevance to the RSC tour; and their inclusion tends to interrupt rather than illuminate the narrative.

As a personal and somewhat impressionistic account of one man's experience of an RSC tour, Daniell's study is both enjoyable and enlightening. His purpose is clearly two-fold: to document the complex system of professional skills required to create and transport a production by a major company, and to map the fresh features revealed by *Coriolanus* as it is reborn on a succession of stages before audiences with varied cultural backgrounds and theatrical expectations. The exercise leads author and reader to a heightened appreciation of both the RSC and *Coriolanus*.

Daniell is not a man of the theatre; and that circumstance, although the source of certain weaknesses in the study, is not entirely a liability. A more experienced theatre hand, one suspects, might have judged the tour not worth recording. The cities visited were, after all, hardly exotic; and the junket itself, as such affairs go, turned out to be relatively uneventful. To Daniell's unjaded theatrical palate, however, the trek was a rare adventure. He notes with rueful surprise at his initial rehearsal in Paris, 'My first experience of a working theatre, and disconcerting. No-one had told me that it would be pitch dark' (p. 5). This discovery proved to be but prologue to a succession of revelations, both pleasant and unpleasant, which the author communicates with an unforced charm irresistible to theatre veteran and tyro alike. The traditional bugbears of touring projects – recalcitrant officials, time constraints, equipment breakdowns, and personality clashes – stalk his pages with lively menace. Commonplace rehearsal practices, when looked at freshly, assume the quality of religious ritual. The stage manager, he remarks at one point, 'goes unhurriedly off-stage to an illuminated alcove, like an aumbry in an ancient church, which holds a copy of The Book, a small lamp, and a microphone. His quietly pastoral voice goes out over the back-stage tannoy "Company on stage, please. Scene fourteen. Scene fourteen on stage, please"' (p. 8). A technical rehearsal, for most theatre people a necessary evil, acquires a sensuous fascination:

Philip Hoare, the unflappable Stage Manager, has just announced, from the stage, 'We're going to run through all the battle-cues.' I stand in the wings, tucked into a corner by a large sound control-board, hoping I'm invisible. In front of me John Moore, kneeling and wearing headphones, looks large and comfortable. There is a faint smell of soldering-resin on a hot iron, and a bench littered with tools and meters and plugs and wire . . . .

Behind John it is very dark. There is a gleam of helmets, a faint flash of spears amid the black drapes . . . . There is a heavy sawing and banging near me, as the underspoken, muttered run-through goes on. Some-one shouts 'One, two, three, go!', and again a quiet voice says 'Let's try again, shall we . . . .'

(pp. 6–7)

The book is structured, to good effect, around the cities visited. Paris gets two chapters, and Vienna one. Amsterdam and Brussels share a chapter, while Hamburg, Berlin, Munich, and Zurich are allotted a chapter each. At every port of call Daniell chronicles, with growing technical ease, the features which make or mar a touring venture: the arrival (or non-arrival) of the Company and its stage gear, the set-up, rehearsals, the performance, the reactions of audience and press, and the get-out. Mechanical and aesthetic considerations, however, never obscure the author's awareness that tours are made by, and for, people. From the outset he lures us into relaxed contact with the Company – during rehearsals, at social functions, on buses and planes, even in a Turkish bath. Now and again he amuses us with mischievous verbal portraits of audience-members or administrative officials. Throughout the study he subtly and tellingly juxtaposes the frigid grandeur of Coriolanus's tragedy with the down-to-earth delights and dismays of those who act it: Young Martius celebrates a birthday; the Fifth Roman Citizen writes a book; the Second Roman Citizen oversleeps and misses his flight; and Caius Martius, himself, develops laryngitis.

Daniell's alertness to the humanity of others does not preclude a lively awareness of his own. Sometimes he chafes at the role he has chosen, and finds himself alienated and resentful. 'I take my paranoia for a walk, having disguised it from myself long enough', he confides to his journal with engaging frankness.

This company is young, happy, lively and very friendly: I am quite remarkably accepted everywhere. But I am *not* a member. I am always an outsider, observing, noting. In a group like this there are sensitivities, irritations, a network of feelings, and at times I feel many of these pointing at me in a way that is hard to take. (p. 83)

Social discomfort proves to be both an impetus and an impediment to Daniell's enterprise. Most of the time it simply intensifies his perceptiveness and enhances his objectivity. Occasionally, and less productively, however, it prompts him to seek escape – in private jaunts to museums and churches, an evening with Parisian friends, a pilgrimage to the Berliner Ensemble to view *Mother Courage*, or a nostalgic side-trip to Tübingen. None of this would signify much had not the author committed these outings to his journal and injected liberal selections into his tour coverage. Such interventions contribute little to the book's main subject, and blur the narrative clarity of the memoir to a degree. Yet so absorbing are some of these vignettes (Daniell's frightening brush with totalitarian officialdom at the Berlin Wall, for example) that one is disinclined to censure the author very severely.

However casually diverting Daniell's tale of theatrical nomadism may be, it is his eyewitness description of Hands's *Coriolanus* to which the book will owe any permanent interest it achieves. And it is disappointing to find that record, if undeniably valuable, something short of ideal. Tours are notoriously unapt occasions on which to view performances; and the RSC tour, the last gasp of the production's eighteen-month stage career, was no exception. One could wish that the account had been prepared in the comparative peace of Stratford, and that it had begun with the earliest rehearsals. Equally regrettable is a want of coherence in the author's reconstruction. Chapter 2, appropriately enough, provides a scene-by-scene summary of the play's action, with vivid re-creations of settings, costumes, blocking, lighting, music, and business. One is then obliged, quite inexplicably, to wait until chapter 10 for an analysis of Howard's *Coriolanus* and an interview with the performer. Strewn throughout the intervening chapters, and organized only by the cities in which they occur, are the author's further remarks on particular stage effects and background interviews with the principal players. The reader is left to fuse these discrete elements into whatever semblance of unity he can. Perseverance will elicit a fair picture of *what* was done on stage, but no amount of tenacity will discover *why* the production assumed the shape it did. The question can be answered definitively only by the director, and Daniell never has Hands address the subject. His failure to do so defies explanation. The two men were apparently on familiar terms; and, although Hands did not travel full-time with the company, he dropped by on several occasions. During the Brussels stop he and the author spent some time together; and the opportunity for Daniell to secure at least a brief statement seems to have been ample. 'I hauled Terry off for tea and sandwiches', he recalls, 'amid the gilt and mirrors of the Palace Hotel. We had a lot of talk to catch up, including all the strong feelings surrounding his Covent Garden *Parsifal*, and experiences on this tour so far' (p. 79). Yet, if Daniell and Hands talked then, or at any other time, of the latter's artistic intentions, we hear nothing about it. In lieu of directorial comment we are offered only actors' recollections that during rehearsals Terry 'worried' about something, or 'reminded' someone, or 'set his face against' this or that. The rest is silence; and the consequences for the study are more than unfortunate.

To read through Daniell's performance memoir, whatever its deficiencies, and to savour his splendid collection of production photographs, is to understand why Bernard Levin described Hands's *Coriolanus* as 'the strong-est, clearest and most consistent Shakespeare I have seen anywhere for years' (*The Sunday Times*, 23 October 1977). It is also to be reminded of how much more justice has been done to *Coriolanus* by Hands and other twentieth-century directors than by their predecessors. A glance at the stage history of the play reveals that until fairly recently, actors, managers, and critics have found themselves distinctly uneasy with it. Its bleak, craggy features, hacked as it were out of granite, were ill-calculated to charm neo-classical pro-ponents of regularity and high finish. Nor was its want of rich colour, lush imagery, or rousing rhetoric apt to tickle romantic or Victorian sensibilities. Its protagonist, a creature of blind passion, almost a war machine, offered scant uplift to societies which demanded some evidence of mental and spiritual capacity as a concomitant to the physical prowess of their tragic heroes. Nevertheless, the theatrical potential of the play's characters and situations could hardly escape the most jaundiced actor-managerial eye; and attempts to fit the play to box-office tastes were as legion as they were inventive. Several times the drama was rewritten; more often, however, Shakespeare's text, savagely blue-pencilled, was retained. Flamboyant stage effects were conjured up to compensate for the play's alleged lack of visual glamour. And by an ingenious combination of textual tampering, astute stagecraft, and subtle interpretation, the character of Coriolanus was rendered palatable if not downright savoury.

Our century has proved more willing than earlier ones to accept *Coriolanus* warts and all. Its bleak style bothers us not a whit; after all, visual starkness, poetic dissonance, and realistic crudity are commonplaces of contemporary aesthetics. Coriolanus's unbridled individualism, too, seems more com-prehensible, if not necessarily more attractive, to us than to our forefathers. His defiant 'Would you have me/False to my nature? Rather say I play/The man I am' (III, ii, 14–16) holds no terrors for an audience schooled in the virtues of 'doing your own thing'. It comes then as no surprise to learn that within roughly the past two decades English audiences have witnessed eight major *Coriolanus* revivals. Such popularity is unmatched in the play's stage history.

Hands's production, like those of Barton (RSC, 1967) and Nunn (RSC, 1972), was virtually a full-text affair. Only about two hundred lines were cut, according to the promptbook, and most of these were excised on the grounds of obscure expression or over-complex syntax. One would be glad to know why, though, Hands chose to remove a clutch of speeches which tend to soften, subtly but crucially, Coriolanus's grim severity. The loss of the Messenger's assertion

> I have seen the dumb men throng to see him, and
> The blind to hear him speak. . . .
> I never saw the like. (II, i, 260–6)

is particularly regrettable, for the observation suggests that Caius Martius possesses considerable natural charisma. That he chooses deliberately to stifle it is a contributing factor to his tragedy. One also misses the general's somewhat rueful admission that for Menenius's sake he has re-offered the Romans his original peace terms (v, iii, 12–17), and his remarkably gracious appeal to the Volscian lords (v, vi, 105–10) just before his death.

To have been battered breathless by the RSC's three-and-a-half-hour hurricane is to recognize both the cumulative force of Shakespeare's tragedy and the unique good fortune which has permitted contemporary audiences to experience it whole. Theatregoers at the first recorded performances in the winter of 1681/2 no doubt found their encounter with the play – in Nahum Tate's lurid adaptation titled *The Ingratitude of a Common-Wealth* –[2] small cause for rejoicing. Not content with reducing Shakespeare's five acts of dense dramatic interplay to four brief episodes of barebones action, Tate appended a new final act of chemically-pure melodrama. In a busy quarter-hour Coriolanus and Aufidius mortally wound each other, and the latter, before he expires, attempts to ravish Virgilia, who thwarts him by taking her own life. Meanwhile, Nigridius, a monstrous kinsman of Shakespeare's Lieutenant, breaks the arms and legs of Young Martius and drives Volumnia mad. At curtain-fall Volumnia slays Nigridius with a partisan, and Coriolanus and his son die in each other's arms. There is no evidence to suggest that the play enjoyed any success.

Tate's failure in no way deterred John Dennis from trying his hand. *The Invader of His Country*,[3] which premièred at Drury Lane in 1719, featured, in addition to an abridged Shakespearian text, unified action, and emasculated dialogue, a touching concern for poetic justice. In the final act, the Roman people hurled their tribunes from the Tarpeian rock; Aufidius was dispatched by Coriolanus; and the hero found himself run through the back by a Volscian tribune. The version, much to its author's dismay, lasted but three nights.

In 1747 James Thomson, author of *The Seasons*, fabricated an entirely new *Coriolanus*, using as his sources Livy and Dionysius of Halicarnassus rather than Plutarch. The script, a soulless exercise in neo-classical dramaturgy, takes up the action with Coriolanus's defection to the Volscians and concludes it with his death. Aufidius, rechristened Attius Tullus, is more credibly motivated and altogether better-bred than Shakespeare's general. Volumnia, now dubbed Veturia as in Livy, appears only in the final act, but makes a brave affair of her pleading episode. Pressing a dagger to her breast, she climaxes her harangue with the challenge:

> Go! barbarous son! go! double parricide!
> Rush o'er my corse to thy belov'd revenge!
> Tread on the bleeding breast of her, to whom
> Thou ow'st thy life! – Lo, thy first victim![4]

At the last Coriolanus received his quietus, not from Tullus, but from a group of conspirators led by Volusius, a near relation of Tate's Nigridius. The play made its début at Covent Garden in 1749, not long after the author's death, and enjoyed a ten-night run with James Quin in the title role and an artfully-wrinkled Peg Woffington as Veturia. The only other recorded performance took place at the Southwark Theatre in Philadelphia on 8 June 1767.

Actor–manager Thomas Sheridan considered both the Shakespeare and Thomson dramas to some degree defective, but was persuaded that if the two could be judiciously combined 'they might mutually assist one another and each supply the other's wants'.[5] In 1752, at Dublin's Smock Alley Theatre, he premièred his attempt at a merger, and titled it *Coriolanus: or, The Roman Matron*. The first four acts of Shakespeare's text were compressed into two, and followed by three acts of Thomson's play with certain Shakespearian interpolations. The adaptation proved a hit with Dublin audiences, and in 1754 Covent Garden playgoers were treated to the London première of the script. Its success was sufficient to warrant six Covent Garden revivals over the next fourteen years.

Performances of Shakespeare's version in unalloyed, if much-cut, form were staged at intervals throughout the eighteenth century. Garrick's revival in 1754, with Mossop as Caius Martius, is probably the most celebrated.[6] Such experiments, however, failed to convince either audiences or actors that Shakespeare's script was patently beyond improvement. When John Philip Kemble revived *Coriolanus* at Drury Lane in 1789, and later at Covent Garden, he took his inspiration from Sheridan rather than Garrick.[7] Although he relied less upon Thomson than Sheridan had done, he retained several significant sequences: a scene between Volusius and Aufidius (Thomson's Attius Tullus) in which the latter confesses the threat Coriolanus poses to his self-esteem; another in which Volusius whips Aufidius's insecurity into jealousy of his rival; the greater part of the pleading scene, including Volumnia's (formerly Veturia's) dagger speech; and a series of exchanges between Coriolanus and Aufidius just before the former's death. Kemble's cuts are drastic. Aufidius is not permitted to appear prior to Coriolanus's banishment. Most of the battle sequences are excised, as are the Belly fable and a number of scenes between minor characters. Kemble's version remained in regular use on British stages for several decades after his death, while in America it was regarded as the standard acting edition throughout the nineteenth century.

Edmund Kean, in his 1820 Drury Lane revival, made a valiant effort to purify and restore Shakespeare's text, but received small thanks for his pains. 'It does not follow', sniffed a representative critic, 'that because Shakespear's scenes contain deeper beauties than those of any other poet, that they are calculated to produce greater effects in a theatre.... The alterations in

Coriolanus, which were made by JOHN KEMBLE with the aid of Thomson's Play, seem to us singularly felicitous' (*The Champion*, 29 January 1820). Macready in his turn showed little inclination to flout the Kemble tradition. His first appearances as Caius Martius in 1819 featured Kemble's adaptation; and, even as late as 1838, although he staged more of Shakespeare's text than in his youth, he continued to cling to certain Kemble–Thomson corruptions. Samuel Phelps, in his Sadler's Wells revivals of 1848, 1850, and 1860, finally rid the play of Thomson's ghost, but somewhat mitigated his achievement by an acute abridgement of Shakespeare's script. Phelps's curtailments seem relatively mild, however, when compared with the mutilations effected by Henry Irving, who played the briefest *Coriolanus* text on record. Suffering from ill-health during rehearsals for his 1901 Lyceum revival, and never a very convincing soldier at the best of times, he opted to pare away most of the play's military action in favour of a static three-act display of aristocratic ill-temper artfully framed by Laurence Alma-Tadema's lavish reconstructions of ancient Roman architecture.

With the neo-Elizabethan productions of Robert Atkins (Old Vic, 1920, 1926) and William Bridges-Adams (Memorial Theatre, 1926, 1933), the integrity and theatricality of Shakespeare's text were finally vindicated. Throughout the past half-century flexible stagecraft has been *de rigueur* for *Coriolanus* productions and drastic cutting has been frowned upon.[8] To keep the playing-time within a three-hour limit, internal cuts have been made within speeches and dramatic sequences; but whole scenes are rarely omitted. And from Bridges-Adams's time onwards, in Stratford productions at least, the overall trend has been toward ever-fuller texts. Bridges-Adams cut the play by close to 700 lines; Glen Byam Shaw (1952) eliminated about 650; Peter Hall (1959) removed about 800; John Barton (1967) excised approximately 600; Trevor Nunn (1972) blue-pencilled only about 300; and Hands dropped just a minimal 200. It is even more noteworthy, perhaps, that in Hands's production the text was not only virtually full, but paramount. Settings, costumes, lighting, music, and special effects were all firmly subordinated to the spoken word. Under such conditions, the play wonderfully demonstrated its capacity to hold an audience by its rugged characterization, its harsh musicality, its raw directness. Even now my recollections of the production remain more auditory than visual; and apparently that rarest of theatre experiences was not confined to native English-speakers. The splendour of the verse was magically accessible to all. The critic of Hamburg's *Die Welt*, for example, delightedly informed his readers, 'The mimetic and gesticulatory expression of this simple yet fascinating performance is derived from language alone.... The Hamburg audience, spellbound till almost midnight, applauded thunderously – and rightly' (p. 105).

Farrah's designs, appropriately enough, provided simply flexible sites for word-wielding. Two sets of massive walls, opening inwards and outwards like doors, fluidly met and parted at various angles to shape acting areas. Costumes were predominantly black. Directional lighting, devoid of both colour and emotional tonality, served solely to define and illuminate. Groupings were severe, often frieze-like; and business was minimal. Incidental sound and music were omnipresent, but never intrusive. Future theatre historians will bless Mr Daniell for his scene-by-scene reconstructions of the unique environment within which Shakespeare's text revealed a structural harmony almost symphonic. Act I, scene iv was particularly memorable, and is memorably re-created by the author:

> A great noise of tympani and short, heavy brass chords and calls made Roman music. In sudden glows of light in the darkness, the upstage walls moved inwards to form the leaves of giant gates. Roman soldiers in round, visored helmets faced their leader Caius Martius as he swung downstage with Titus Lartius.... The Volscian army issued from the parting of the great gates before, to full brass and percussion, battle was joined upstage, Caius Martius pressing from behind. The Romans, defeated by Volscian spears, fell back downstage in some disorder.... Martius, breaking through his own men, follows the fleeing Volscians and goes through the gates into Corioles. They close behind him.... One suddenly cries 'Look, sir.' To braying brass in a tremendous tune of victory the big walls parted a little to show, spotlit high up inside the very top of the opening gates, Caius Martius, blood on his face and arms, smoke about his feet, bowing forward with his bloody sword. His troops below rushed into the city, the walls closing after them (pp. 25–6).

The theatrical impact of that great, black-leather-clad figure, spreadeagled between the gates like an avenging angel, was devastating. Here, and frequently elsewhere during the performance, I wondered why managers have so often neglected the play's intrinsic opportunities for sensational effects in favour of extraneous pageantry.

As early as 1718 the play was performed at Lincoln's Inn Fields 'With Scenes, Machines, Triumphal Arches, and other Decorations after the Custom of the Romans' (*Daily Courant*, 13 December 1718). Kemble invested a remarkable £3000 on his 1789 production, a Roman cultural panorama on a scale hitherto unimagined by theatre audiences. Macready's breathtaking land and sea vistas for his 1838 revival at Covent Garden very nearly eclipsed his own performance. 'The first scene', a contemporary reports, 'presents Rome from the skirt of Mount Apennine across a bend of the Tiber ... taking in a view of the Capitoline hill, a glimpse of the porticos of the forum, the temple of Vesta, the Cloaca Maxima, and the palatine covered with its patrician dwellings. It is by an exquisite arrangement of art that throughout the play ... the Capitol is kept in view, and ... the three temples of Jupiter, Juno, and Minerva.' Coriolanus's first appearance after his banishment found him silhouetted against 'a view of the city of Antium, by starlight'. Immediately behind were 'moles running out into the sea, and at the back of the scene the horizon drawn beyond the sea in one long level line, interrupted only by a tall solitary tower, the pharos or watch-tower of Antium' (*The Examiner*, 18 March 1838). Henry Irving's decision to portray Rome during its Etruscan, as distinct from its classical, era inspired Alma-Tadema to create the most elaborate and archaeologically-correct décor in the play's history. Painters, designers, historians, and archaeologists, however slight their interest in Shakespeare, thronged the Lyceum to marvel at the artist's expertise. Even the *Architectural Review* honoured Alma-Tadema's research, design, and construction with a lengthy essay.[9]

Living scenery – civil and military parades, colourful mobs of plebeians, and artfully-posed Senates – has been almost as prized by spectacle-loving managers as picturesque locales. Sheridan probably initiated the trend with his introduction of an ovation (an inferior form of triumph) to celebrate Coriolanus's victorious return from the wars (II, i). In the 1754 production at Covent Garden some 118 persons marched in military gear, preceded by substantial numbers of civil functionaries. For more than a century thereafter, ovations were a fixture of *Coriolanus* revivals on both sides of the Atlantic. Not infrequently trudging supers found themselves cheek by jowl with livestock. In Boston in 1805 'a Ram adorned for the sacrifice' was featured (*Boston Gazette*, 30 December 1805), while Philadelphia audiences six years later watched Coriolanus enter in 'a Superb Car drawn by real HORSES' (*The Tickler*, 6 March 1811). As late as 1893 at Stratford, a 'votive lamb' graced Frank Benson's train. In addition to a splendid ovation, Kemble contrived generous quantities of military ritual to enhance his battle episodes; and managed in the process to employ a total of 240 supers. Macready, by emulating Kemble's pageantry and increasing the size of the civilian crowds, raised to 300 the number of supers in his 1838 production. Henry Irving, in keeping with the non-military mood of his revival, gave the Senate scene (II, ii) particular attention. 'Against grey stone walls, with little ornamentation', recalls Frederick Harker, 'tier upon tier of seats filled the whole back of the scene, on which were seated the white-robed, grey-bearded senators, whose interest in the proceedings was intense.'[10] In bizarre contrast to Irving's severe pageantry stands Edwin Forrest's (Broadway Theatre, New York, 1855) garish cremation of Coriolanus during which troops of priests and vestal virgins warbled a dirge round the blazing funeral pyre, and a phoenix launched itself heavenward from the flames.

Throughout the past half-century a new-found respect for *Coriolanus*'s text has led directors to forego sensational décor and effects in favour of flexible stagecraft. Bridges-Adams's *mise en scène* for his 1933 Memorial Theatre *Coriolanus*, with its flights of steps, platforms, and freestanding arches set against a colourful cyclorama, strikingly demonstrated that theatricality and fluidity are by no means mutually exclusive concepts. And designers took the lesson to heart. Since the 1960s, however, partly due to the malign influence of Brecht, settings, costumes, and lighting have shown a distressing proneness to visual monotony; and, with supers now a luxury, processions have all but vanished and plebeian mobs have dwindled markedly. Nevertheless, even in an era of austere production values, I wonder if Hands's harshly-lit spaces, monochromatic costumes, and aggregation of nine supers were not a trifle too ostentatiously ascetic, almost a *reductio ad absurdum* of the cult of drabness. On the positive side, it must be admitted, the actors were healthily challenged to transcend the décor, and invited to lend colour, movement, and grandeur to the text by their own unassisted resources. It is no small tribute to the skill of the ensemble that visual interest was seldom lacking. The principal players were, I suspect, as thoughtful and creative as most who have tackled the play; and that they also proved to be articulate about their craft is an unlooked-for boon. Daniell's interviews with the interpreters of Coriolanus, Volumnia, Menenius, and the Tribunes are one of the book's most stimulating and engaging features.

Alan Howard's remarks on his interpretation of Caius Martius are worth special attention, since his performance was not only the key to the success of Hands's revival, but probably the most original and effective reading of the part since Olivier's in 1959. The role, although not particularly complex, is one of the most difficult in the tragic repertory; for the actor is called upon to elicit an audience's sympathy for a character ill-calculated, on the surface of things, to deserve it. If the drama is to have its tragic effect, the modern playgoer must be persuaded at least to respect, and ideally to empathize with, a personality he views as compounded primarily of aristocratic arrogance, ruthless militarism, and mother-dependency.

Eighteenth- and nineteenth-century audiences tended to view Martius's character in a more charitable light. His military prowess, it goes without saying, was highly prized in an era when warmongering was an international pastime. And to our pre-Freudian forebears, a hero's attachment to his mother was more a matter for dewy-eyed approbation than psychoanalytic concern. The patrician's disdain for the lower orders might well have cost him considerable audience-sympathy, however, had not alert actor–managers ensured that Martius's scorn was directed at targets as unlike the conscientious working man as possible. Played invariably by the company's low comedians, Shakespeare's citizens assumed the character of ludicrous street ruffians, greedy for gain, heedless of lawful authority, and as much an object of the spectator's scorn as of the hero's wrath. Coriolanus's contempt was the wholly-admirable response of a civilized leader to barbarian behaviour.

John Philip Kemble's legendary Coriolanus was primarily remembered for its statuesque grandeur. 'His person', John Howard Payne recalls, 'derived a majesty from a scarlet robe which he managed with inimitable dignity. The Roman energy of his deportment, the seraphic grace of his gesture, and the movements of his perfect self-possession displayed the great mind, daring to command, and disdaining to solicit, admiration.'[11] The godlike remoteness sustained by Kemble throughout the rest of the play disintegrated with telling effect in the pleading episode. 'How touching was the scene', marvelled Alexander Dyce, 'where he sat, with heaving breast and averted face, listening to the supplications of his wife and mother, till nature's holiest feelings overcame the thirst for vengeance on his ungrateful country!'[12] If Kemble's Coriolanus awed by his sculptured stillness, Macready's Roman thrilled with his frenetic vitality. For Macready Caius Martius was a military noble savage, dedicated from birth to the ideals of heroic conquest proper to an infant state. 'In the earlier scenes of the Tragedy he gave all the enthusiasm of a Roman soldier, in its youthful bloom', noted a contemporary. 'His hurried impatience in rushing from battle to battle, while a foe remained to be conquered, was as energetic, as his modesty in declining praise after victory was beautiful' (*The Champion*, 5 December 1819). With Rome's emergence into national adolescence, political skills came to be valued as highly as military ones. Macready's Coriolanus, champion of a frontier code, found himself unable to comprehend, much less adapt to, a more complex social order. 'The vices of a state of semi-civilisation, where pride and baseness, ferocity and hypocrisy, blend together, perpetually jar with his nature', concluded another eyewitness. 'They excite his contempt, mar his course of life, falsify his position, and co-operate with his own best feelings to work his destruction' (*Morning Chronicle*, 22 March 1838). Edwin Forrest's interpretation, in its turn, was quite as idealized as those of his predecessors, but out of deference to the egalitarian sentiments of American audiences his Martius seemed 'not so much a patrician by status as by mind'. He showed 'the Roman to shrink', one reviewer maintained, 'with all the acute sensibility of a superior mind, from too familiar contact with natures that are vulgar' (*Sunday Mercury*, New York, 8 November 1863). All interpreters of Coriolanus from the late eighteenth century onward took their direction from one or another of the compass points fixed by Kemble, Macready, and Forrest.

Martius's *beau idéal* image died with the century which fostered it. Frank Benson's 1898 revival, featuring a protagonist with 'no patriotism, but a mere selfish love of glory' (*Stratford-upon-Avon Herald*, 22 April 1898) signalled the anti-heroic shape of things to come. Three years later, Henry Irving's Roman, shorn even of Bensonian military splendour, struck the *Athenaeum* critic as 'a turbulent, haughty, exacting, and wholly unmanageable being, such as subsequent history has scarcely given us, except perhaps in Charles the Bold' (20 April 1901). Anew McMaster's Martius, in Bridges-Adams's Memorial Theatre production of 1933, climaxed a chilling study in anti-democratic arrogance with a peal of sardonic laughter which left theatre-goers agape. Laurence Olivier's interpretations at the Old Vic in 1938 and the Memorial Theatre in 1959 fairly reeked of tainted genius. His portrait of the spoiled man-child and overweening militarist, whose egotism inexorably corrodes all honourable impulse, was probably the deftest essay in psychological realism in *Coriolanus*'s stage history.

Throughout the past two decades, the nature and scale of Martius's passions have dwindled sadly. John Neville's reading (Nottingham, 1963) endowed the character with homosexual proclivities and attributed their origin to Volumnia's dominance. Ian Richardson (RSC, 1967) played him almost as a neurotic machine, programmed to do a job. Ian Hogg's Martius (RSC, 1972) proved so diminutive and unauthoritative as to be wellnigh anonymous. Nicol Williamson, who replaced Hogg when the production transferred to the Aldwych in 1973, created a hollow man, a weakling who over-compensates for his fear by feats of epic bravery. The final disintegration of this whistler-in-the-dark was moving, but could hardly be said to be tragic. And that, of course, has been the weakness of *Coriolanus* productions throughout this century. As naturalism has barged through the door, tragic grandeur has slipped out the window.

The significance of Hands's revival derives primarily from his attempt to restore to the play some degree of tragic scale, without sacrifice of contemporary credibility and relevance. Each force in the play was given its due importance, and Coriolanus assumed in turn his focal position. The patricians were represented not as acquisitive overlords or benign sages, but as strong men confident of their innate right to rule. The plebeians, for their part, were no comic street-rabble, but a group of honest tradesmen organized, not always to best effect, by self-serving officialdom. Martius, much to his chagrin, found himself the fulcrum of a power-struggle. In conversation with Daniell, Howard suggested that 'the man is a metaphor for Rome. Everyone has an attitude to him. They all want him to be *their* Coriolanus. . . . Virgilia is the only one who keeps her silence. For the rest, he is the battleground for all their problems' (pp. 163–4).

Where Macready found in Shakespeare's Martius a military noble savage, Howard discovered a war-deity incarnate. 'No father is ever mentioned –' he reminded Daniell; 'it is as if his mother bore him alone, almost like the virgin birth of a god: and Coriolanus is attended by three women everywhere, making a sort of *pietà*' (p. 167). Straddling the gates of Corioles, hoisted aloft on the weapons of an ecstatic soldiery, hurling defiance at Rome's ungrateful populace, and finally flinging himself on the sword even as Aufidius raised it, he remained an alien, impelled by his own drives and governed by his own code. Accommodation and compromise were beyond his comprehension. His death, far from being an act of retribution, was a release from the toils of his would-be exploiters. 'Coriolanus dies in a kind of exhilaration', Howard told Daniell, 'as a creature from a different sphere . . . . His trip has ended, and he has to return. . . . leaving the mayhem behind that the others have created' (p. 167).

Howard's epic interpretation, however much one might admire the art which informed it, fell as far short of tragic effect as the soap-opera readings which preceded it. His grandeur commanded awe but left the heart untouched. No hint of human warmth invited empathy. Nevertheless, his achievement was by no means negligible. As an antidote to the anti-heroic indulgence of his immediate predecessors, his reading was both timely and apt. And its long-term influence has yet to be measured.

Howard's deification of Martius inevitably diminished the stature of Volumnia. This hero was transparently a creature of his own making, not his mother's; he yielded to the maternal will neither from unconscious habit nor Oedipal urges, but solely because he chose to do so. Never in the history of the play can Volumnia have seemed so dispensable. Such an effect would have mystified Sarah Siddons, whose Roman matron vied for pride of place with the Coriolanus of her brother. Her entrance in the act II ovation, 'marching and beating time to the music; rolling ... from side to side, swelling with the triumph of her son',[13] was for Charles Young the highlight of Kemble's production. Her 'tones of familiar elegance' and 'artful persuasions' in Rome, powerfully counterpointed by the 'pathetic and chilling accents' of her pleas in the Volscian camp (*The World*, 9 February 1789), set the standard of interpretation for generations thereafter. Although many nineteenth-century actresses essayed the role, few approached the distinction of Siddons's prototype. Ellen Terry, described by one critic as 'a Christmas-tree decorated by a Pre-Raphaelite' (*Saturday Review*, 27 April 1901) was a particular failure.

Twentieth-century audiences have probably enjoyed, thanks to Genevieve Ward, Sybil Thorndike, and Edith Evans, the best performances of the character since the Kemble era. Miss Ward, who frequently partnered Frank Benson, wonderfully revealed Volumnia's passionate heart. In the pleading scene, the *Pall Mall Gazette* (29 February 1908) critic tells us,

> The reasoned appeal, the poignant, bitter warning, the broken supplication and the scorn, sounding all the gamut of such emotions as are proper to the situation and the character, are spoken with a very touching dignity of realism. The long speech utterly convinces; and one looks on at the picture, the watching Volscian chiefs and Coriolanus, with his back turned, grasping, motionless, the arm of the stool, as if at a scene of real life in which great destinies were in the balance. She prevails, but wins no show of affection, and there is much pathos in her stumbling, quiet exit.

Without abating a jot of Volumnia's heroic strength or maternal tenderness, Sybil Thorndike (Old Vic, 1938) endowed her matron with a vein of satirical humour. Edith Evans's Volumnia (Memorial Theatre, 1959), noble in spirit and indomitable of will, breathed, even at seventy, an ageless charm which rendered Coriolanus's filial devotion as plausible as it was fatal.

All three interpretations were remarkable explorations of the outer limits of human potential. In Hands's revival, however, Maxine Audley's Volumnia seemed small, cold, and stiff by comparison. Howard's Coriolanus, it is true, was not calculated to bring out the best in Volumnia; but Miss Audley's conception of the character was primarily to blame. 'One key to Volumnia, she felt,' according to Daniell, 'was her possessiveness; this child was hers' (p. 100). If theatre history teaches us anything about Volumnia, it is that her uniqueness reveals itself, not in isolated moments of pettiness, but in her consistent acts of affirmation. Siddons found greatness in her patriotism and maternal pride; Ward located it in her emotional range and intensity; and Evans celebrated her eternal femininity. To attempt to motivate Volumnia Victrix, as Swinburne called her, by negative drives is to paralyze her utterly.

If Volumnia rather cheated expectation, the Tribunes of John Burgess (Sicinius) and Oliver Ford Davies (Brutus) considerably exceeded it. Throughout *Coriolanus*'s stage history, Sicinius and Brutus have been played as a pair of unscrupulous demagogues who neatly manipulate to their base ends a rag-tag mob unable to resist their wiles. Contrary to theatrical tradition, Burgess and Ford Davies concluded that 'far from leading a Popular Front, the Tribunes are usually in difficulties, are often undecided, and at the end have achieved nothing' (p. 148). In Hands's production both characters were somewhat uneasy in their new roles; and, despite a certain amount of native craftiness, they frequently found themselves out of their depth. 'At various times,' Ford Davies remarks, 'they announce what they're going to do and then you don't see them doing it. Shakespeare ... constantly keeps the balance between their being shrewd operators who appear to have a plan and stick to it, and being swept along by events, changing their minds, not operating their plan' (p. 150). It might be argued that two such bumbling souls constitute a poor foil for Coriolanus; yet it is precisely the militarist's inability to counter their feeble machinations with even the most elementary diplomatic gestures which lends an almost Greek inevitability to his tragedy. It is high time that both study and stage took a fresh look at the character and function of the Tribunes; and the lengthy and insightful discussion of these figures by Burgess and Ford Davies offers as good a starting-point as any.

The informative and provocative features of *'Coriolanus' in Europe* cannot fail to be appreciated by the contemporary reader; but Daniell's most enthusiastic fans, I suspect, will be grateful theatre historians a century or so hence.

NOTES

1. *'Coriolanus' in Europe* (London: The Athlone Press, 1980).

2. *The Ingratitude of a Common-Wealth: Or, the Fall of Caius Martius Coriolanus,* 1682 (Cornmarket Press Facsimile, London, 1969).

3. *The Invader of His Country: or, The Fatal Resentment,* 1720 (Cornmarket Press Facsimile, London, 1969).

4. *The Works of James Thomson* (London: 1773), IV, 277.

5. Advertisement to *Coriolanus: or, The Roman Matron,* 1755 (Cornmarket Press Facsimile, London, 1969). This version is traditionally attributed to Sheridan, although his name does not appear on the title page. For a useful study of this adaptation, see Esther K. Sheldon, 'Sheridan's *Coriolanus*: An 18th-Century Compromise', *Shakespeare Quarterly,* XIV (Spring, 1963), 153–61.

6. This is probably the version published in Bell's edition (1773).

7. Kemble published his acting edition in 1789 under the title *Coriolanus; or, The Roman Matron.* A somewhat revised version appeared in 1806. Both editions have been issued as Cornmarket Press facsimiles (London, 1970) with introductions by Inga-Stina Ewbank. Kemble's promptbook appears in *John Philip Kemble Promptbooks,* ed. Charles H. Shattuck (Charlottesville: University Press of Virginia, 1974), vol. 2. Professor Shattuck's introductory essay is invaluable.

8. *Coriolanus*'s 3,410 lines make it the fourth longest of Shakespeare's plays. While *Hamlet, Richard III,* and *Troilus and Cressida* are longer, *Othello, Lear, Henry V,* and *Cymbeline* are within a hundred lines of its length.

9. R. Phéné Spiers, 'The Architecture of *Coriolanus*', *Architectural Review,* X (July 1901), 3–21. See also Sybil Rosenfeld, 'Alma-Tadema's Designs for Henry Irving's *Coriolanus*', *Deutsche Shakespeare-Gesellschaft West Jahrbuch* (1974), ed. Hermann Heuer, pp. 84–95.

10. 'Irving as Coriolanus', *We Saw Him Act: A Symposium on the Art of Sir Henry Irving,* ed. H. A. Saintsbury and Cecil Palmer (London: Hurst & Blackett, 1939), p. 382.

11. *Actors and Actresses of Great Britain and the United States,* ed. Brandor Matthews and Laurence Hutton (Boston: L. C. Page, 1900), II, 85–6.

12. *The Reminiscences of Alexander Dyce,* ed. Richard J. Schrader (Ohio State University Press, 1972), pp. 73–4.

13. Thomas Campbell, *Life of Mrs Siddons,* 1839 (reissued New York: Benjamin Blom Inc., 1972), p. 250.

FORUM: SYMBOLISM IN CHEKHOV

Chekhov and the resistant symbol

PETER HOLLAND

In act II of *The Seagull* the bird makes the first of its two appearances on stage. Treplev enters 'carrying a sporting gun and a dead seagull' and lays the bird at Nina's feet. Nina is bemused.

> *Nina.* What does that signify?
> *Treplev.* I meanly killed that seagull this morning. I lay it at your feet.
> *Nina.* What's wrong with you? [*Picks up the seagull and looks at it.*]
> *Treplev.* [*after a pause*]. I shall soon kill myself in the same way.
> *Nina.* You've changed so much.
> *Treplev.* Yes, but who changed first? You did. You're so different to me now, you look at me coldly and you find me in the way.
> *Nina.* You're touchy lately and you always talk so mysteriously, in symbols or something. This seagull's a symbol too, I suppose, but it makes no sense to me, sorry. [*Lays the seagull on the bench.*] I'm too simple to understand you.[1]

Over the years, critics have been reluctant to side with Nina. Instead, they have assumed that she is wrong and that Chekhov is some sort of symbolist. Critics then divide neatly into two groups: those who see the symbolism as successful and achieved and those who damn Chekhov for the failure of the same symbolist language.

The first group is the more numerous. Donald Rayfield, for instance, sees Chekhov as 'not the first Symbolist *malgré lui*' and finds in *Three Sisters* 'an elaborate system of images that operates with the symmetry and self-sufficiency of a set of symbols'.[2] But this desire to see the 'system of images' as a separable entity is a dangerous undermining of the play. That 'self-sufficiency' implies a diffusion and separation of the play's own means of achieving its unity. By making the symbols a virtue in themselves, Rayfield and others deny here what elsewhere they clearly recognise: that our primary focus of attention in Chekhov's plays is the actions of people. Chekhov's dramaturgy demands a continual testing of each aspect of the play against the actions of the characters. The meaning of the symbols is given by the characters themselves and we are entitled and even encouraged to question the process by which certain natural objects are given such artificial symbolic values. We need not take the characters' word for it; Nina may be right.

However, seeing the symbolic pattern as one open to question and seeing that questioning as possibly deliberate are two different matters. For some, the failure of the symbolic discourse of the plays is a serious error of judgement on Chekhov's part. Raymond Williams is undoubtedly the most influential of the critics in this group:

> The seagull emphasizes, as a visual symbol – a piece of stage property – the action and the atmosphere. It is a device for emotional pressure, for inflating the significance of the related representational incidents ... But this very characteristic naturalist device is clearly a substitute for adequate expression of the central experience of the play in language. It is a *hint* at profundity ... any serious analysis must put it down as mainly a lyrical gesture.[3]

For Williams the seagull as a symbol is a mark of a failure in naturalism. It is Chekhov's way of avoiding the problems posed by the attempt to represent everyday experience and, being unsatisfactorily carried through, its failure points at the crisis of naturalism. There is little in Williams's analysis that I would want to disagree with, except for the confidence with which the failure of the symbolic convention is ascribed to Chekhov, rather than his characters. Treating the symbolic as a failure on Chekhov's part makes him a far more traditional writer than we have tended to believe. Our instinctual awareness that Chekhov's plays marked a radical change in Russian drama seems to me worth trusting.

The tradition at its best can be seen in Ostrovsky's *The Storm* (1859), one of the greatest of all Russian plays before Chekhov. In *The Storm*, the title-motif functions within the play as a direct and accepted symbol. Ostrovsky gives the storm two meanings, making of it a symbol which, in its ambiguity, points directly at the conflict at the centre of the play. At the end of the first act, Catherine admits to Barbara, her sister-in-law, that she is in love not with her husband, Tikhon, but with another man. Barbara's announcement of the impending storm is plainly naturalistic: 'Why doesn't Brother come? That looks like a thunderstorm getting up over there.'[4] But Catherine's reaction and the subsequent dialogue immediately undercut any meteorological force that the storm might have, giving it instead a meaning only too plainly and conventionally emblematic:

> *Catherine* [*in horror*]. Thunder? Let's run home! Quick....
> *Barbara.* I never knew you were so frightened of thunder. I'm not.
> *Catherine.* What, girl! Not frightened? Everybody ought to be frightened. The dreadful thing is not that it can kill you, but that death can come upon you so suddenly, just as you are, with all your sins, with all your wicked thoughts. I've no dread of dying, but when I think that there I'd suddenly be, in the presence of God, just as I am here with you, after that talk we had – that's what's dreadful! What have I got on my mind? What a sin! I'm terrified to mention it.   (p.339)

Catherine's speech is closed by the sound of thunder and her husband's entrance summons up another thunderclap. We are no longer interested in the storm as a storm at all but as a symbol of sin and its consequences, divine justice and punishment. For any English reader or spectator, this is closely analogous to the thunder of Jacobean drama; in both the thunder marks a divine system that responds on cue to man's actions. The dramatic coincidence of language and sound effect would be painfully weak, were it not that the ethical system makes the divine echo acceptably pat. However, in *The Storm*, the thunder is not accepted solely in this way; as the play develops, this meaning of thunder, as a divine comment on sin, is marked as the product of provincial stupidity, the narrowmindedness that, in the end, causes the suicide of Catherine.

Act IV is dominated by the thunder. Catherine has been meeting her lover, Boris Dikoy, every evening while her husband has been away. By the start of act IV, ten days after the events at the end of act III, Tikhon has returned and a confrontation is inevitable. The act opens with another simple use of the thunder-motif, this time as an indication of the inevitably approaching climax:

> *First Man.* Those are spots of rain; there'll be a thunderstorm brewing, eh?
> *Second Man.* Any minute now.
> *First Man.* It's lucky we've somewhere to take shelter.   (p.371)

By this stage, the sophisticated spectator would be forgiven for seeing in Ostrovsky's use of the thunder as symbol nothing but a succession of dramatic clichés. Thunder as sin and thunder as imminent catastrophe are both over-used parts of theatre's traditional vocabulary. But, in the conversation between Dikoy, Boris's father, and Kuligin, the strange clockmaker and eccentric inventor, Ostrovsky redefines the symbol of the thunder in the gap between the announcement of the impending climax and the climax itself. Throughout the play Kuligin functions as an oddly peripheral figure; his rationalism is contrasted with his comic obsession with finding a perpetual motion machine. He maintains a choric position in relation to the central tragedy. For Kuligin, thunder is nothing more than itself: 'we have frequent thunderstorms, but we don't put up lightning conductors' (p. 374). Dikoy cannot accept a scientific explanation of thunder:

> *Dikoy.* And what is thunder, in your opinion? Eh? Come on, tell us?
> *Kuligin.* Electricity.
> *Dikoy* [*stamping his foot*]. What has ellistrixity to do with it? ... Thunder is sent
> to punish us, to make us think what we're doing, and you, Lord forgive you,
> want to protect yourself with a lot of rods and stakes.   (p.374)

Kuligin responds with a quotation from Derzhavin: 'Dust unto dust moulders my earthly form / Yet with my mind I rule the thunderstorm' (p. 375). For Dikoy, as for Catherine earlier, thunder is a symbol of the power before which man must abase himself, aware of his humble position in God's universe. For Kuligin, thunder can be controlled, can be diverted and ought to be wondered at, rather than feared. As he says a little later in the scene,

Come, what are you afraid of, for goodness' sake! Now every blade of grass and
every flower is rejoicing, and we hide ourselves, as if fearful of some disaster
hanging over us! Thunder's a sign of wrath; it kills! It is not a sign of wrath, it's
God's Grace! Yes, Grace! Everything is a sign of wrath to you ... You have
made bogies for yourselves out of everything.   (p. 378)

Science, even pseudo-science like Kuligin's, makes of thunder a sign of
beneficence and optimism. This progressive optimism is contrasted with the
symbol-ridden myopia of the townsmen:

Second Man. Mark my words; that storm isn't coming this way for nothing. It's
the truth I'm telling you, because I know. Either someone will be killed, or
there'll be a house burnt down.   (p. 379)

It is this latter interpretation of the meaning of the thunder, rather than
Kuligin's reformulation of its significance, that Catherine accepts: 'I'm the
one who'll be killed' (p. 379). As a mad-woman threatens Catherine, the
traditionalist meaning is re-emphasised by the return of the thunder as
sound effect: 'Where are you hiding, you silly creature? You can't get away
from God! [*Clap of thunder*]' (p. 380). Confronted by her husband and his
terrifying, dominating mother, Catherine admits she has been seeing another man and, as the thunder sounds for the last time in the act, she reveals
his name:

With Boris Dikoy! [*Thunderclap.*] Oh! [*She falls fainting into her husband's arms.*]

Ostrovsky's technique at moments like this is a full-throated and unashamed melodrama; the theatrical power of Catherine's admission and the
echo of the thunder are undeniable. Yet *The Storm*, as a whole, is rescued from
melodrama by the intervention of Kuligin in the symbolic discourse of the
play. The very strangeness of Kuligin, with the difficulty of placing him
easily within the social system of the play, allows him to make of the thunder
a much richer and more satisfying symbol than it could otherwise be. The
link of scientific progress and divine grace, added to the daring which allows
the meaning of the thunder to be redefined at all, opens out a new focus on
the closed provincialism of the play's world, the town on the Volga. Even if
the play does depend to a considerable extent on the self-satisfaction of a
metropolitan audience at the spectacle of the consequences of provincial
stupidity, it still manages to create a new doubleness out of a hackneyed
symbol. The thunderclap which sounds after the revelation of the name is as
much an echo of the happiness and joy that Catherine found with Boris, a
happiness that in its heterodoxy is aligned with Kuligin's scientific optimism,
as it is a final imposition of thunder as a mark of punishment. Kuligin's speech
has denied an unquestioned acceptance of that meaning for the audience.
Nonetheless, Kuligin's response to the thunder is still the imposition of a
new meaning. Even though he mentions the effect of the storm on 'every

blade of grass and every flower', even though the whole act is played against the naturalistic background of the real storm, it is the symbolic meaning that really matters. Ostrovsky's naturalism is willingly submerged within the symbolic discourse. In this storm no one cares about getting wet.

Chekhov uses the motif of the storm in *The Wood Demon*, the early play out of which *Uncle Vanya* eventually emerged. In act II, George Voinitsky (Vanya in the later play) announces 'There's going to be a storm' (III, 225) and the statement is followed by a stage effect to ram it home to the audience, in this case a flash of lightning rather than a rumble of thunder. Later, left alone with Helen, Serebryakov's wife, Voinitsky uses the storm in order to express his sense of frustration, making it into an unashamed emblem of his condition: 'Soon the rain will be over. All living things will revive and breathe more freely. Except me. The storm won't revive me. Day and night my thoughts choke me, haunt me with the spectre of a life hopelessly wasted' (III, 227). But, as he develops his theme, Helen stops him with 'George, you're drunk.' For Helen, as for the audience, George's drunkenness frees his tongue but does nothing to guarantee the sense or truth of what he is saying. Instead it has the opposite effect. We distrust Voinitsky's language as drunken meanderings and melancholia, particularly when Voinitsky returns to the emblem of the storm, when left alone, in a fantasy of having married Helen, all the while distrusting his own thinking. It is not simply that the symbolic language is in itself demonstrated to be untrustworthy – that would be too great an assumption – but that its association with drunkenness and maunderings leads us to see it as a means chosen by Voinitsky to view himself at a distance. It is that attempt to achieve a distance from the direct experience of the self which allows him to evade the truth of his own ineffectuality. No one would assume from this that Voinitsky is somehow capable of achieving and maintaining an understanding of his own position when sober. The symbol is immediately defined as a limited and limiting language, the choice of a man who is able to choose little else, except suicide.

But Chekhov does not leave the storm at that. When Sonya appears, she makes the audience see the storm for what it is, as a storm and nothing else: 'We haven't got the hay in yet. Gerasim told me today it would all rot in the rain, and you spend your time on illusions' (III, 230). That is the real indictment of Voinitsky's use of the storm as symbol. Sonya shows us its true significance, a direct and concrete manifestation of Voinitsky's abandonment of the work of running the estate. His choice of the storm as a symbol for his own suffocation ignores the fact that the storm is an example of his idleness since the arrival of Serebryakov and Helen. The choice he makes is defined as self-indulgent.

In rewriting this part of *The Wood Demon* for *Uncle Vanya*, Chekhov chose to emphasise precisely this aspect of the storm's significance. Vanya's conversation with Helen and his soliloquy make use of the storm in a manner that is

very little changed from *The Wood Demon*. But Sonya's attack on Vanya's
indolence is made both longer and more precise in its criticisms: 'The hay's
all cut, there's rain every day, and it's all rotting. And you spend your time
on illusions. You've completely abandoned the farm. I do all the work myself
and I'm about at the end of my tether' (III, 37). The waste is no longer a
possibility for the future as in *The Wood Demon*, 'would all rot', but a fact for
the present, 'it's all rotting'. Vanya's course of action is spelt out plainly in its
consequential strain on Sonya. His retreat into taking the storm as a symbol
has an effect that can no longer be limited only to himself; in *Uncle Vanya* his
choice also rebounds directly on others. The imposition of meaning onto the
storm, a meaning other than itself, is a distortion of its true significance
within the society of the play and, almost in itself, this distortion constitutes a
criticism of the character who chooses to make it.

Sonya's speech, taken in isolation, strikes the spectator as slightly heavy-
handed, with an obviousness and deliberateness that is not characteristic of
Chekhov at his best. But, by an alteration earlier in the act, Chekhov
prepares for Sonya's outburst, delicately indicating the importance of the
storm at its first mention. In both *The Wood Demon* and *Uncle Vanya*,
Voinitsky's first announcement of the storm is his first line on entering. But in
Uncle Vanya, Chekhov changes Sonya's lines to Serebryakov immediately
before Voinitsky's entrance:

> Of course you're happy. And even if you do have gout you know perfectly well
> it will be gone by morning. So why all the groans? What a lot of fuss about
> nothing!   (*The Wood Demon*, III, 225)

> Please stop behaving like a child. It may appeal to some people, but don't treat
> me that way, thank you very much. I dislike that sort of thing. Besides I'm too
> busy, I must be up early tomorrow. There's haymaking to see to.
>   (*Uncle Vanya*, III, 32)

The added reference to the haymaking is now immediately juxtaposed with
Voinitsky's announcement of the imminent storm, hinting at precisely the
significance that Sonya ascribes to the storm later. Through the juxtaposition the audience can see the storm as a threat to the running of the estate,
the work that Vanya has abandoned to Sonya. Vanya's use of the storm as a
symbol for what suffocates him is already undercut by our awareness of the
storm's meaning in itself.

This is coming close to the heart of the problem of the symbolic language
in Chekhov. In speaking of Sonya's understanding of the significance of the
storm, I have described it as a 'manifestation' or an 'example' of Vanya's
idleness. I have deliberately not spoken of it as a 'symbol' of that apathy. Of
course, I do not want to delimit too narrowly and ruthlessly the use of the
word 'symbol', but cases like this involve a use of the significance of stage
object or naturalistic phenomena and hence of dramatic reference that is of a

different order from Vanya's or Ostrovsky's language. As a symbolic discourse approaches the emblematic it increasingly denies the natural meaning and significance of the object that underlies the symbol. If a tree is given a symbolic meaning of 'strength', it loses its significance as a tree; the pelican feeding its young with its own blood signifies Christ much more than it signifies a pelican. At this level of discourse the arbitrary and conventional nature of the sign is particularly plainly apparent. If we replace the tree by a bar of iron or the pelican by an elephant it makes little difference. The symbol means exactly what we choose to make it mean and accept as a conventionally determined meaning. But when Sonya speaks of the storm, her language accepts the object in and of itself. The storm is, for her, a real storm. What matters is the effect of the rain. The meaning is direct and concrete, not a culturally imposed or consciously literary meaning dependent on a shared convention of meaning. Rain ruins hay and that is what upsets Sonya. That Voinitsky's laziness is apparent in many other ways does not make the significance of the effect of the storm any the less concrete. It can perhaps be taken as a sort of naturalised symbol, a symbol still attached to its natural meaning, but the strength of the link between the object and its meaning seems to me to go against the conventional theatrical practice of symbolic discourse. As a sign the storm need not be arbitrary at all; Vanya chooses to make it so. The directness of the meaning of the storm in relation to the haymaking militates against Vanya's attempts at a fully-fledged symbolic language. Vanya's illusions are rejected and undercut by the reality of the storm. The storm simply refuses to work as a conventional symbol with any degree of ease. It resists being treated as a symbol.

While Ostrovsky chooses to advance a new symbolic meaning for the storm through Kuligin, Chekhov denies the symbolic reading altogether. It is no longer a matter of using the right explanation of a symbol; now, the choice to create any fully symbolic explanation is in doubt. Along the continuum of the symbolic mode, any move away from the natural and non-symbolic towards the emblematic risks being perceived as a failure on the part of the character. From this perspective, the question of symbols in Chekhov is now firmly reconnected to the actions of characters.

Of course, the storm in *Uncle Vanya* is only a small and comparatively unimportant moment. The seagull in *The Seagull* is quite another matter. One of the problems is the vexing relationship of *The Seagull* to Ibsen's *The Wild Duck*. When Chekhov's play was first submitted to the Theatrical Literary Committee in 1896, their report attacked the 'Ibsenism' in the play,

To begin with, the 'symbolism', or rather 'Ibsenism' (in this case Ibsen's influence seems to be particularly in evidence, if we keep in mind the Norwegian dramatist's *Wild Duck*), which runs like a red thread through the whole of the play, creates a painful impression, all the more so since there is no real need for it ...[5]

The confidence of the Theatrical Literary Committee runs up against the fact that Chekhov did not see *The Wild Duck* until 1901 and did not like the play even then.[6] We must be wary of seeing in Chekhov's use of the motif of the bird anything as straightforward as 'a parody of Ibsen'.[7]

However, the Theatrical Literary Committee goes on, in its report, to perceive something crucial about the use of the seagull as symbol in the play: 'there is no real need for it (except, perhaps, to show that Konstantin, being a literary decadent, was partial to symbolism)'.[8] Seeing the seagull as a product of the character's own choice of symbol, rather than as a symbolic choice imposed by Chekhov, changes our whole attitude to its function as symbol at all. As a choice of the character, it reflects Nina's comment: 'you always talk so mysteriously, in symbols or something' (II, 253).

If, then, the first reaction of the audience may be to ask what the character wants to make of his chosen symbol, a response to the character's being 'partial to symbolism', the audience can also respond to the odd tension between the way the seagull is spoken about and the way it is manifest on stage. Early in the play Nina uses the image of the seagull as a dreamily lyrical evocation of her feelings: 'But something seems to lure me to this lake like a seagull' (II, 237). That seems to me successful but it is much more difficult to achieve the same language when the seagull is actually present on stage. A dead bird is a peculiarly awkward prop. When the bird is presented as a gift-offering, as an action as well as in the dialogue, its actual presence is too concrete to make Treplev's idea work as a fully serious, almost tragic moment. Gielgud found this out to his cost when he played Treplev in 1925. Setting out to play Treplev as 'a very romantic character, a sort of miniature Hamlet', he found that he

> resented the laughter of the audience when I came on in the second act holding the dead seagull, but on a very small stage it did look rather like a stuffed Christmas goose, however carefully I arranged its wings and legs beforehand.[9]

As the Theatrical Literary Committee recognised, Treplev 'is sometimes represented as a comic character'[10] and this moment, the presentation of the seagull, has always seemed to me to be irresistibly comic.

Stanislavsky's response to the problem of the seagull is to naturalise it as far as possible. Nina 'bends down to pick up the seagull', 'puts down the seagull at the end of the bench'; she stands 'stroking the dead seagull pensively' and strokes it again later in her conversation with Trigorin.[11] This sequence of actions is an attempt to make Chekhov fit into the naturalistic theatre's 'never-ending search for the fourth wall which has led it into a whole series of absurdities', a search that Meyerkhold believed Chekhov to have disliked.[12] In any case, Stanislavsky's choice of moves associates Nina directly with the seagull, going against Treplev's definition of the seagull as a symbol of his own death, not Nina's. Though we are encouraged later in the act to see the seagull as an emblem of Nina in Trigorin's eyes, Stanislavsky's staging undercuts the dramatic surprise that must accompany Trigorin's noticing the seagull, a surprise that Stanislavsky's notes make particularly clear: 'Trigorin picks up the seagull with two fingers by a wing and immediately throws it down squeamishly.'[13]

As if to reinforce the awkwardness of the seagull as a stage property amenable to a symbolic meaning, Chekhov transmutes it later in the play. The floppy dead bird becomes the stuffed bird that Shamrayev takes out of the cupboard and presents to Trigorin with 'Your order, sir' (II, 281). The stuffed bird is too comically and concretely there for it to function effectively as a deep and sentimental symbol of 'innocent life destroyed by human indifference'.[14] The blatancy of the seagull, the very thing that Williams and Styan variously find fault with, seems to me to be its strength. The symbol is imposed onto the natural object as a means of denying the responsibility of the individual. Treplev would rather talk in symbols than face up to the reality of his life, a childish egocentricity that culminates in his suicide.

Shortly before Shamrayev, like a magician, produces the stuffed bird comes the brilliant scene between Treplev and Nina. Nina now has a maturity that has not been shown on stage before and her ability to comprehend her experiences, even if she cannot yet fully come to terms with them, highlights the ineffectuality of Treplev. Treplev's mawkishness in act II had made of the seagull an easy way out, a choice to make the bird a symbol and thus to deny the reality of his actions. By act IV, Nina has earned the right to use a fully-fledged symbolic language to express her experiences, if anyone has.

Treplev has already told Dorn of Nina's use of the seagull as symbol of herself: 'She used to sign herself "Seagull". Like the miller who calls himself a raven in Pushkin's *Mermaid*, she kept calling herself a seagull in her letters' (II, 272). But Treplev prefaces this comment with a hint of Nina's nearmadness: 'She didn't complain, but I sensed that she was deeply unhappy. Every line seemed sick, like a frayed nerve, and her mind was slightly unhinged.'

When Nina appears, her speeches are dominated by a continuous attempt to maintain a balance between reason and madness. Her precarious hold on rationality and with it an ability to survive her experiences is the focus of an extraordinarily moving scene. Three times in the course of the scene she refers to herself as a seagull and the temptation to see this as an achieved symbol is strongest here. But, in exactly the same way as I accept her distrust of the symbolic seagull in act II, I accept her distrust of her own use of the symbol here. Each time that she announces 'I'm a seagull' she immediately retracts the statement: 'No, that's wrong' (II, 278, 279, 280). As her brain attempts to hold on to sense and resist the temptation of emotional self-indulgence and consequent collapse, so she resists the symbol of the seagull.

The symbol is a diversion from the confrontation with the self that she must attempt, a confrontation that Treplev cannot begin to achieve.

Viewed in this light, the seagull becomes one, the most important, of a group of techniques in the play to place the characters, to show up their actions and enable us to judge them. The symbol can be an excuse for one's own inadequacies analogous to the use of *Hamlet* in the play. Treplev would dearly love to be a Hamlet with his mother as Gertrude and Nina as Ophelia but he has no effective justification for his actions. As Chekhov complained in a letter to Suvorin about *Ivanov*, Ivanov does not choose to find an excuse in an external substitutive pattern,

> When narrow, unreliable people get in a mess like this, they usually put it all down to their environment or join the ranks of Hamlets and men at odds with society [superfluous men], and that comforts them.   (II, 292)

Treplev is, in the course of *The Seagull*, shown to be one of this class, while Ivanov 'is a very straight person. He tells the doctor and the audience quite frankly that he can't make himself out, keeps saying he doesn't understand' (II, 292). The desire to be Hamlet is a desire to participate in a tragic or quasi-tragic mode of existence. Hamletism, fully developed in Turgenev's essay 'Hamlet and Don Quixote' (1860), is a doctrine of inaction and lazy intellectual indulgence, precisely the sort of attitude that Chekhov consistently attacks, in the short story 'In Moscow', for instance, and in the one-act play *A Tragic Role*. Placed within the focus of a play like *The Seagull*, Hamletism, like the desire for symbols, is a desire to shirk individual responsibility by ascribing the fault to the arbitrary causality of the universe. Chekhov's demand is always that characters should face up to the reality of their position.

We can see the problem in little in the very first lines of *The Seagull*:

> *Medevedenko.* Why do you wear black all the time?
> *Masha.* I'm in mourning for my life, I'm unhappy.   (II, 233)

Taken seriously, the black dress becomes the first mark of the tragedy of the play, a symbol of tragedy. But it is difficult for the dialogue to have such force at the opening of the play. Audiences find it hard to accept so self-conscious a tragic tone placed awkwardly early in the play. The conflict between setting and tone makes of the black something rather self-indulgent and slightly ridiculous. As Georgina Hale proved so brilliantly when she played Masha in a BBC television production in 1979, Masha is wryly aware of her own pseudo-tragic pose. Indeed, the text makes that clear in act IV when Masha rejects her mother's tragic view of her predicament:

> *Polina.* My heart aches for you. I see everything, you know, I understand.
> *Masha.* Don't be so silly. Unhappy love affairs are only found in novels.
>   (II, 269)

The desire for tragedy, to be Hamlet, to be like a seagull, is an affectation that the play condemns. That desire is part of a comic illusion of the self, one of the reasons why Chekhov could call the play a comedy. The disjunction is inevitable between Gielgud's serious approach to Treplev as Hamlet and the comic dead bird.

My argument has emphasised Chekhov's distrust here of the symbolic, seeing it as a tactic to divert attention away from a true perception of the object and of reality. Even if we accept unequivocally Meyerkhold's picture of Chekhov as a dramatist who disdained naturalism in its fullest sense, that does not contradict a Chekhov whose aim is to make society clear, to analyse society directly. It is all to the good that such a view cuts across the traditional English view of a Chekhov whose plays languidly and sentimentally portray a nostalgic Russia. Certainly that view of Chekhov as social critic, rather than romantic dreamer, is echoed by two of the best recent attempts to produce English versions of Chekhov, Edward Bond's version of *Three Sisters*, directed by William Gaskill at the Royal Court in 1967, and Trevor Griffiths's 'version' of *The Cherry Orchard*, produced at Nottingham Playhouse in 1977. Both dramatists' own work has been fiercely political in a way that would imply a lack of sympathy for Chekhov, at least as traditionally seen in this country. Both work to strip away the cosiness of that traditional view. As Griffiths complains in his preface, 'for theatregoers ... Chekhov's tough, bright-eyed complexity was dulced into swallowable sacs of sentimental morality'.[15] Griffiths refuses to see *The Cherry Orchard* as elegiac, finding in the English tradition that

> the play's specific historicity and precise sociological imagination had been bleached of all meanings beyond those required to convey the necessary 'natural' sense that the fine will always be undermined by the crude and that the 'human condition' can for all essential purposes be equated with 'the plight of the middle classes'.[16]

As he found, critics complained that he had 'substituted, for an elegy, a cheerful and cheering march'.[17] That response is intriguingly and satisfyingly similar to Chekhov's own problems with the original production. Writing to Nemirovich-Danchenko, Chekhov was worried about the treatment of act II,

> What's this in your telegram about the play being full of people crying? Where are they? Varya's the only one, but that's because Varya's a cry-baby by nature, and her tears shouldn't depress the audience. You'll often find the stage-direction 'through tears' in my text, but that only shows the mood of the characters and not their tears. There isn't a cemetery in Act Two.

> (III, 326–7)

After the first performance Chekhov complained to Olga Knipper that Stanislavsky 'drags things out most painfully. This is really dreadful! An act which ought to last for a maximum of twelve minutes – you're dragging it out for forty' (III, 330), Stanislavsky summed it up later,

> The thing which struck him most, a thing he couldn't put up with until his
> dying day, was the fact that his *Three Sisters* – and after that *The Cherry Orchard* –
> was a tragedy of Russian life. He was sincerely convinced that it was a gay
> comedy, almost a farce.   (III, 315)

The debate on the precise genre of Chekhov's plays has been long and
tortured. Nonetheless, Chekhov's own response points to a refusal to take the
simply nostalgic line in *The Cherry Orchard*. To view the orchard as an
exquisite symbol of the decay of childhood pleasures – the elegiac view –
makes Lopakhin's attitude towards the orchard and its future irredeemably
foolish. Chekhov was sure that such a view was wrong: 'he's a decent person
in the full sense of the words . . . Lopakhin was loved by Varya, a serious and
religious girl. She wouldn't love some wretched money-grubbing peasant'
(III, 327).

What Griffiths has responded to in the play can be best pinpointed by
emphasising the date of the play. *The Cherry Orchard* was first performed in
January 1904, a month before the outbreak of the disastrous Russo-Japanese
war and a year before the first Russian Revolution. No one could have failed
to see the extent to which substantial change to Russian society was inevitable, whatever their preferences for the form of that change. The centrality of Trofimov, the prophet of change, is far more marked in Griffiths's
version than in others, displacing the backward-looking Mrs Ranevsky.
Even though Trofimov's actions are frequently comic, he voices the fact of
change. In *The Cherry Orchard* any character who fails to face up to the
present (Gayev and Mrs Ranevsky in particular) comes perilously close to
being aligned with Firs who ridiculously sees true happiness as the time of
serfdom, before the emancipation of the serfs by Tsar Alexander II in 1861,
forty-three years earlier:

> *Firs.* The same thing happened before the troubles, the owl hooting and the
>   samovar humming all the time.
> *Gayev.* What 'troubles' were those?
> *Firs.* When the serfs were given their freedom.   (III, 171)

The connection between this contrast of pose, facing the future or the past,
and the cherry orchard itself seems clear. As in the other examples I have
looked at, Chekhov sees those who use the cherry orchard as a symbol as
evading the reality, however painful that may be. I do not want to suggest
that Chekhov was either a revolutionary or an unremittingly cold-hearted
realist. Of course, he understands and has some sympathy with the nostalgia
and illusions of Gayev and Mrs Ranevsky but he also depicts them as both
comic and culpable in their refusal to see and face up to what is happening.
Mrs Ranevsky's wayward generosity with money is almost a parody of the
proper reciprocity of the estate-owner to the poor; she is so concerned about

the public image of generosity that she cannot feed her near family. Her deafness to the logic of Lopakhin's repeated reminders about the fate of the estate is exacerbated by Chekhov's emphasis that the family need not lose the estate in the first place. She can only believe, frustratingly, that it is all or nothing and that the lowering of social *ton* that the holiday-makers would bring is unbearable: 'Cottages, summer visitors. Forgive me, but all that's so frightfully vulgar' (III, 166). In fact, Mrs Ranevsky does not care about the cherry orchard at all. It is not the physical concreteness of the forest that appeals – for it has been neglected – but a romantic aura of childhood: 'Look; Mother's walking in the orchard. In a white dress. [*Laughs happily.*] It's Mother' (III, 157). Such self-indulgence is maddening and bound to fail in the harshness of the society. Mrs Ranevsky's continual yearning for the symbolic value of the orchard fails to take account of the trees as trees at all. Again, reality resists the imposed symbol. Lopakhin can see the trees as wood – hence the sound of the axe – and, if his materialism in action seems brutal, it is conscious of a process of history, the inevitability of change: 'I've bought the estate where my father and grandfather were slaves, where they weren't even allowed inside the kitchen' (III, 186). The Ranevskys cannot begin to come to terms with the reality of a change of that magnitude.

In his directness Lopakhin is oddly parallel to Astrov in *Uncle Vanya*. Astrov's great dreams of reafforestation combine the beauty of the tree and the reality of planting. He can see woods for what they are, a source of timber, and at the same time as an example of continuity and grandeur. If Lopakhin is not capable of setting his ideals so high, both are visionaries who see no point in visions unless they can be carried out. Both respond directly to the reality of society and social change. Both have a pragmatism that, in its seriousness of purpose, makes of the weak-willed visionaries and romantics, like Mrs Ranevsky or Vershinin in *Three Sisters*, something increasingly stupid and comic.

In the end, then, we must accept the cherry orchard as a cherry orchard and not try to make of it something more. But the play contains another 'symbol' that seems to be treated by Chekhov in a radically different way. While the orchard is only as symbolic as individual characters choose to try to make it, the breaking string is far more open-ended. At the end of his life Chekhov contemplated a play about arctic explorers, complete with ghosts of dead girls. Insofar as there are any real hints about what the play would have been like, it does seem to have been closer to a symbolist mode. It is tempting to read back and see the breaking string in the same way. More significant is the way that the characters try to explain the sound, attempting to establish the real nature and cause according to their own individual predispositions:

> [*Suddenly a distant sound is heard. It seems to come from the sky and is the sound of a breaking string. It dies away sadly.*

> *Mrs Ranevsky.* What was that?
> *Lopakhin.* I don't know. A cable must have broken somewhere away in the mines. But it must be a long, long way off.
> *Gayev.* Or perhaps it was a bird, a heron or something.
> *Trofimov.* Or an owl.   (III, 171)

The sound is deliberately imprecise, deliberately open-ended. We cannot be sure what causes it nor what it signifies. Its power is an emotional one; its effect resists the precision that the symbolic, even lyrical symbolism, usually demands. Treplev's seagull or Mrs Ranevsky's orchard are precisely defined by them, in their own terms and for their own purposes. The breaking string is not defined at all; it is nothing like the culturally determined signs towards which the emblematic symbol tends. Instead, it positively invites a plural response. Its openness gives it an honesty that contrasts with the manipulation of the natural into symbol practised by the self-deceivers in Chekhov. The play moves from the dishonesty and distortion of Mrs Ranevsky's response to the cherry orchard to the straightforwardly emotive force of the breaking string. It is almost as if the sound effect constitutes a withdrawal from the materialistic social analysis of most of the play into an empathetic response that is now justified.

In the conventionally defined group of symbols in Chekhov there is nothing else like the breaking string. But its status outside the control of the characters and beyond their comprehension makes it analogous to Chekhov's use of the sets in his plays. In *Three Sisters* in particular, the movement from set to set provides a dynamic in the play, a quasi-symbolic commentary on the action. The play opens in the sisters' house, in the drawing-room and in daylight; as the stage direction indicates, 'outside the sun is shining cheerfully' (III, 73). By act II, though the set is the same, the transition to a darker tone in the play is echoed by the darkness on stage, illuminated at first only by Natasha's candle. In act III Natasha's displacement of the sisters from the control of their own house is marked by the move to Olga's bedroom, now shared by Olga and Irina. When the last act moves outside the house into the 'old garden' (III, 124), the movement again mirrors the sisters' complete abandonment of their house. None of them now lives there: Olga lives at the school; Irina is just about to leave for the brickworks; even Andrey is left to push the pram round the garden. The house is now the preserve of Natasha and her lover, Protopopov. The victory of Natasha over the weakness of the sisters is now complete.

Tempting though it is to see this movement as a different mode of dramatic symbolism, the pattern seems to be as resistant to that mode as the storm, the seagull or the cherry orchard. It is, like them, a direct and concrete expression. It shows the displacement that the sisters undergo without providing a substitutive object to express it. It is a real manifestation of the consequences of their lack of control and apathy. Compared with the vague dream of

Moscow, an obviously woolly symbol of the sisters' ill-focussed yearnings, the shifting sets resist symbolic status.

In the endless battles between Stanislavsky and Chekhov, there is a recurrent note, even more frequent than the argued definition of the plays as comedies and tragedies: Chekhov could never accept Stanislavsky's passion for cluttering the production with sound effects. Writing to Olga Knipper during rehearsals for *The Cherry Orchard*, Chekhov complained that Stanislavsky 'wants to bring on a train in Act Two, but I think he must be restrained. He also wants frogs and corncrakes' (III, 329). To Stanislavsky he wrote on the same day,

> Haymaking usually takes place between 20 and 25 June, at which time I think the corncrake no longer cries, and frogs also are silent at this time of year . . . If you can show a train without any noise, without a single sound, then carry on.
>
> (III, 329)

Stanislavsky's endless passion for clutter was for Chekhov a quick way of obscuring the action of his plays. The clarity of presentation that he sought was designed to make the audience understand, simply and directly. Within the plays themselves, the characters' endless desires for an illusion propped up by symbols constitute an analogous form of clutter. The pragmatism that is at the heart of Chekhov's attitude sees the symbol-hunting as a manipulation and an escapism. Yet the manipulation cannot be entirely successful. The inherent toughness of reality prevents the search for illusion from being fully convincing. Even if the characters succumb, the audience is allowed, indeed enabled, to see that resistance of the real. The failure of imposed symbolism is, in the end, a cause for optimism.

NOTES

1. A. Chekhov, *The Oxford Chekhov* trans. and ed. R. Hingley, 9 vols (London: Oxford University Press, 1964-), II, 253. All quotations from Chekhov are from this edition.
2. D. Rayfield, *Chekhov: the Evolution of his Art* (London: Paul Elek, 1975), pp. 224 and 217.
3. R. Williams, *Drama from Ibsen to Brecht* (London: Chatto & Windus, 1968), pp. 103–4.
4. A. Ostrovsky, *Thunder* (= *The Storm*) in J. Cooper, *Four Russian Plays* (Harmondsworth: Penguin Books, 1972), p. 339.
5. Quoted in S. D. Balukhaty (ed.), *The Seagull Produced by Stanislavsky* (London: Denis Dobson, 1952), p. 13.
6. A. Chekhov, *The Seagull*, ed. P. Henry (Letchworth: Bradda Books, 1965), p. 29.
7. Rayfield, *Chekhov*, p. 205.
8. Balukhaty, *Seagull*, p. 13.

9. J. Gielgud, *Early Stages* (rev. edn, London: The Falcon Press, 1948), p. 84.
10. Balukhaty, *Seagull*, p. 13.
11. *Ibid.*, pp. 193, 195, 205.
12. E. Braun (ed.), *Meyerhold on Theatre* (London: Eyre Methuen, 1969), p. 30.
13. Balukhaty, *Seagull*, p. 205.
14. J. L. Styan, *Chekhov in Performance* (Cambridge University Press, 1971), p. 18.
15. A. Chekhov, *The Cherry Orchard*, trans. T. Griffiths (London: Pluto Press, 1978), p. v. Edward Bond's version, less radical in its treatment of the text than Griffiths's, is marked by a hard, colloquial style of dialogue. It has never been 'published' but was printed as the programme for the Royal Court production. Thomas Kilroy's brilliant version of *The Seagull*, which was performed at the Royal Court in the spring of 1981, is part of the same move to emphasise Chekhov's analysis of his society.
16. *Ibid.*
17. *Ibid.*, p. vi.

Chekhov and the irresistible symbol: a response to Peter Holland

LAURENCE SENELICK

When Noël Coward was asked his opinion of the Lunts' revival of *The Seagull* in New York in 1938, he is said to have replied, 'I *hate* plays that have a stuffed bird sitting on the bookcase screaming, "I'm the title, I'm the title, I'm the title!"'[1] Peter Holland's attempt to shift the responsibility of the symbols in Chekhov's plays from the author to his characters may arise from a similar discomfort in the presence of seemingly clumsy dramatic devices employed by a revered playwright. Useful and astute as his perceptions often are in observing the touches Chekhov uses to contrast his characters, Peter Holland nevertheless is rather narrow in his interpretation of a 'symbol' and, in my opinion, misses the truly symbolic (in places even 'Symbolist') qualities of Chekhov's major plays.

Drama is, by its nature, a symbolic form of art. Mounted upon a stage, set in view of an audience, any human action takes on an emblematic meaning. A man thus raised above his fellow-men or framed by a proscenium begins involuntarily to signify more than himself. The playwright, whether he will or no, conveys great import to anything that appears in his drama merely by including it. In this regard, Chekhov may be more than the 'unconscious Symbolist' Andrey Bely claimed he was, for his technique is very consciously worked-out. Every element in his last four plays is there for good reason, and this includes his symbols which are operative on two levels. There is the symbol-making activity of his characters, which, as Peter Holland points out, is usually footling; and Chekhov's own symbol-making beyond the sphere of the characters' actions, thereby endowing them with significance over and above the plane of realistic activity.

Perceptive critics of Chekhov's own time, even when they had no vested interest in associating him with the Symbolist dramatists, noted the dual nature of his plays, observing that they made sense only when the secondary meaning was apprehended. Sergey Glagol, a proponent of stage naturalism, noted that *Uncle Vanya* was totally devoid of everything normally thought to be dramatic, at the same time it rivetted the attention. The only explanation he could offer was that the drama's inner action was covert and greater than what could be seen and heard, or, in his words, the play 'has a symbolic character'.[2] It is not enough to isolate a seagull or an enchanted lake, a storm or a cherry orchard as a play's symbols; Chekhov interweaves them as strands in the intricate fabric of his dramatic pattern. After they have been identified, they must be reintegrated to show what the pattern is. In this respect, an approach to Chekhov which has not been widely taken but which might yield valuable results is that which G. Wilson Knight took to Shakespeare. Wary we may be of the dangers of symbol-hunting, but we must still try to find the all-encompassing meaning that emerges from the recurrent motifs, repeated phrases and symbolic discourse. It has been a long time since Chekhov was taken solely as a realist, even in the Soviet Union, and the larger meaning of what happens in his plays cannot be dismissed vaguely as the 'universality' of the characters' plights.

Let us take, for example, the storm in *Uncle Vanya* which Peter Holland uses as a touchstone to illustrate Vanya's pretentious self-dramatization and Sonya's forthright acceptance of things as they are. He is right to see the storm as a dramatic means of contrasting their characters. But the technique is not consistent. On stage, Vanya's flat entrance line in act II, 'Outside there's a storm brewing', gets a laugh, because it comes after a scene of tantrum and bickering, and seems an inadequate comment on what has gone before. The storm without is irrelevant compared to the storm within. The character is not referring to it to make a symbolic or even thematic statement, but the playwright *is* using it for ironic shading, and the audience, making the connection the character fails to make, takes the playwright's meaning and laughs.

Peter Holland accuses Vanya of being pretentious when he ascribes symbolic meaning to the storm, but Chekhov himself is guilty of such 'pretension' from the rise of the curtain. The verbal cement of *Uncle Vanya* is a recurrent imagery of suffocation and oppression. The play almost begins with Astrov's remark 'K tomu zhe dushno' – 'Besides, it's stifling'.[3] Translators who render this as 'It's muggy', 'It's sultry', 'It's close', or even 'The weather is stifling' miss both the ambivalence and the regular recurrence of the phrase and its cognates which culminate in Sonya's final *my otdokhnyom* ('We shall rest') which is etymologically related to *dushno* and suggests 'breathing easily'. The symbolism, therefore, is not conveyed by the characters' references to it or by the soundman's rain effects, but by a tightly-knit weave of verbal echoes, on a par with the symbolism of Sophocles in *Oedipus the King*, where the blind Teiresias and the self-blinded Oedipus are physical emblems concomitant with the language fashioned out of puns on *eidō*, meaning both to see and to know.

The storm in the action of *Uncle Vanya*, imminent in act I raging in act II, is both the time-honored dramatic metaphor which Peter Holland explicates in Ostrovsky's *The Storm*, and an all-encompassing authorial symbol like Shakespeare's *Tempest*, where, as Wilson Knight demonstrated, it not only emblematizes the state of the characters' souls but permeates the poetic diction of the play. *Vanya*'s storm is not an allegory standing for precise equivalents in the characters' natures, but works as a symbol in the true sense, open to multiple meanings and subject to interpretation. It is a real storm in nature, capable of ruining the hay crop; it is also Vanya's chosen simile for his frustration; but it is, moreover (and this is the level that Peter Holland neglects), Chekhov's tool as a creative artist for heightening the images of suffocation that run through the play. Chekhov does not, as Peter Holland claims, 'deny the symbolic reading altogether'; he stands aloof from his characters' interpretations of it to provide a more Olympian, less simplistic one of his own. In fact, a storm is Chekhov's not uncommon narrative device in such stories as 'The Steppe' and 'A Dreary Story', where it prefigures the protagonist's crisis at a new stage in life. Lacking the narrative voice when composing a play, Chekhov had to find a subtler but equally effective means of conveying his own ironic attitude towards the actions of his characters. What he came up with was the duplex nature of the stage action.

Chekhov's characteristic genius as a dramatist, the very element that has enabled him to survive even when the precisely-observed social ambience of his plays has become obsolete, is the balancing of these two levels. Reality can always be interpreted as reality, a storm as a storm; but simultaneously he hints at a more profound reality behind the everyday events. Unlike Maeterlinck, whom he greatly admired, he never flies off into legendary, metaphysical realms. He is always solidly grounded in the psychological and social data one would expect of a physician. But what makes him the first dramatist of the twentieth century and not the last of the nineteenth is his interpenetration of this physical reality by the subtly suggested reality of symbolic meaning.

One of the first and still among the best of Chekhov's English critics, George Calderon, noted as early as 1912 that the Russian 'did not often use symbols in the old-fashioned sense, material objects adumbrating immaterial meanings, designed to catch attention by their superficial irrelevance, like the lambs and lilies of pictured saints'. Instead, he practised 'a more beautiful and recondite Symbolism, one that harmonises better with the realistic method, and that is the Symbolism by which the events of the Drama are not merely represented for their own sake but stand also as emblems and generalisations about life at large'.[4] The only way in which such generalizations can be made is through the presence of a dominating intelligence which tacitly suggests an interpretation of events and objects superior to those of the characters. This superior signifier is what Peter Holland would deny by implying that Chekhov himself lent no relevance to symbols, abandoning them to his more self-deluded characters. But this takes us back to the sterile conception of Chekhov as a photographic realist, 'objectively' exhibiting his observed data, an approach which is a dead end in analyzing Chekhov's art.[5]

Of all of Chekhov's plays, *The Seagull* fits Peter Holland's thesis most exactly because the symbol of the bird is perhaps the most obtrusive and least integrated of any. In Ibsen's *The Wild Duck*, the title symbol is of essential importance: all the major characters are defined by their attitude to the bird, and it exists only as they re-create it in their imaginations. The seagull, however, is known only to three characters: Treplyov who establishes it as a symbol, Trigorin who reshapes its symbolic meaning, and Nina who adopts and then rejects the symbolism. (We can exclude Shamrayev who has it stuffed but is unaware of any hidden meaning.) Peter Holland's comments on Treplyov and Nina are just, but he neglects to mention Trigorin who turns the seagull into grist for his fiction mill: 'On the shores of a lake there lives from childhood a young girl, just like you; loves the lake, like a gull, and is happy and free, like a gull. But by chance a man comes along, sees her and having nothing to do, ruins her, just like this gull here.' Nina, who has rejected Treplyov's symbolic meaning for the bird, avidly adopts Trigorin's, even though the notion that she is happy and free and loves the lake is wholly inaccurate, nor is the man who ruined the bird the one who ruins the girl. More irony is added when Treplyov associates Nina's signing herself 'The Seagull' with the mad miller in Pushkin's dramatic poem 'The Nixie': the miller's daughter had been 'ruined' by a prince but drowned herself, leaving her father in Treplyov's position to mourn. In other words, both Treplyov and Trigorin are incorrect in their literary casting of Nina as the seagull. When, in act IV, she repudiates the sobriquet, 'I'm a seagull. No, not that', she rejects not only Treplyov's martyr-bird, but Trigorin's fictitious happy-free-and-then-ruined creature. Nina, having found her calling, is not ruined but survives, if only in an anti-romantic, workaday world.

Here, despite this wider application of the symbol, I grant Peter Holland's point that Chekhov does not invest it with his own overriding significance. But *The Seagull* is a transitional work, leading from such awkward attempts as *Ivanov* and *The Wood Demon*, compromises of Chekhov's vision with the conventions of the late nineteenth-century stage. It is in his interpretation of *The Cherry Orchard*, which I believe to be Chekhov's masterpiece, a play in which his vision is realized without compromise, that Peter Holland is least adequate in his response to the symbolism.

True, Stanislavsky did render the play maudlin because he preferred to identify with the aristocrats rather than with Lopakhin, the role Chekhov wanted him to play. He, the son of a textile manufacturer, turned down the part of an enriched serf for that of the feckless *barin* Gayev. Emigrés, fleeing the Revolution, identified so closely with Ranevskaya and Gayev that they disseminated a nostalgic view of the gentry's plight throughout Europe and America. But, by endorsing Trevor Griffiths's contrary positivist viewpoint and emphasizing the 'centrality' of Trofimov and Lopakhin, Peter Holland stumbles into two pitfalls: that of echoing, unwittingly, an outdated Soviet interpretation no longer current even there, and that of taking sides with

Chekhov's characters. Peter Holland seems to prefer characters who are clear-sighted enough to call a spade a spade and not amplify it into a symbol. (The example is apt, for Lopakhin's name recalls *lopat'*, to shovel, and is of the earth earthy.) He refers, for instance, to Ranevskaya's 'dishonest' response to the cherry orchard. However, neither Lopakhin nor Trofimov is more genuine in his attitude to the orchard than are Ranevskaya and Gayev. Trofimov, in particular, is consistently undercut by farce devices – he falls downstairs after a melodramatic exit line or is too absent-minded to find his own galoshes. Lopakhin, who shares Chekhov's background as a man of peasant origin who worked his way up in a closed society, is immensely attractive as a character, but for all his pragmatism, he too is comic and ineffectual when he proposes to Varya. Moreover, his dreams of giants and vast horizons are themselves effectively pricked by Ranevskaya's surprisingly matter-of-fact attitude. She may be an incorrigible romantic about the orchard but on such matters as sex she is far more hard-headed than either Lopakhin or Trofimov. Any attempt to grade Chekhov's characters as 'right-thinking' or 'wrong-headed' ends up simplifying and diminishing his achievement in creation.

'In the end, then', says Peter Holland, 'we must accept the cherry orchard as a cherry orchard and not try to make of it something more.' By which he means that we must accept Lopakhin's view of it as trees to be hewn, a view which is not only 'level-headed' but socially responsible. Yet Chekhov's close friend, the writer Ivan Bunin, pointed out that there were no such cherry orchards to be found in Russia and that Chekhov had invented an imaginary landscape for his play.[6] By 1904 there were any number of works about uprooted gentlefolk and estates taken over by wealthy peasants (Ostrovsky's *The Forest* is a very early example), and Chekhov would not have been raking over the old theme if he did not have something new to say.[7] And here his protests that the play is a farce comedy (and not the social-purpose drama Peter Holland would like to make it) is an important clue.

As the textbooks tell us, the standard theme of New Comedy or Roman Comedy, from which most modern comedy and melodrama derive, is that of the social misfit – miser or crank or misanthrope or lecher – creating a series of problems for the young lovers and, once baffled by the aid of a crafty servant who, for the sake of comedy's holiday spirit, often oversteps his rank, the misfit is re-integrated into society or expelled from it. The result is an affirmation of society's ideals and conventions. *The Cherry Orchard* is a fascinating variation on this formula. All the characters are misfits, from Lopakhin who dresses like a millionaire but still feels out of place at the tea table, to Yasha and Dunyasha, servants who ape their masters, to outdated Firs, to Ranevskaya and Gayev, arrested in their childhoods, to the expelled student Trofimov ('Fate simply hustles me from place to place'), to Yepikhodov who puts simple ideas into inflated language he barely understands, to the most obvious example, the governess Charlotta who has no notion who her parents were. If there is a norm, it exists off stage, in town, at the bank, in the restaurant full of soap-smelling waiters. No one really belongs on the estate. As in a Symbolist drama, it is a wasteland in which characters drift, filling in their lives with trivia while expecting something dire or important to occur. As in Maeterlinck, the play begins with waiting in the barely illumined dark, and it ends with the possible death of a character abandoned in emptiness. Chekhov was fond of the misfit device: the estate in *The Seagull* is similarly inhabited by characters who hate being in the country and feel out of place; and Uncle Vanya's estate is invaded by Petersburg sophisticates who turn everything upside-down. He was also fond of the New Comedy aura of holiday, the occasion on which licence reigns, ordinary routines are interrupted and unusual things can happen: the characters in *The Seagull* are on vacation, those in *Uncle Vanya* exist in wilful indolence, and *Three Sisters* progresses through a nameday party, a Shrovetide merrymaking, a fire and a regimental departure, all extraordinary occurrences involving elements of ritualized behavior. In *The Cherry Orchard*, the holiday atmosphere is provided by the return of Ranevskaya from Paris and culminates in the ball in act III; but over all looms the most extraordinary occurrence of the lot, the disposal of the estate.

What lends the play its complexity, then, is this peculiar medley of New Comedy motifs and Symbolist devices. The distortion of the comic motifs continually thwarts our expectations: the lovers are not threatened except by their own impotence (Trofimov, Lopakhin), the servants are uppish but of no help to anyone (Yasha, Dunyasha), all the characters are expelled at the end, but their personal norms are not disturbed, since they spring back to their habits, unchanged by the sale of the orchard. This resilience in the face of change brings *The Cherry Orchard* close to the Symbolist concern for the passage of time, the sense of human beings trapped in the involuntary march of moments towards death. But, as Bergson, a favorite ideologue of the Symbolists, insisted, anything living that tries to stand still in fluid time becomes mechanical and thus comic. The shifts from farce to the uncanny in *The Cherry Orchard* occur at just such failures at stopping time.

Jean-Louis Barrault has pointed out that the 'action' of the play is measured not by what occurs on stage but by the pressures without: in act I, the cherry orchard is in danger of being sold; in act II, it is on the verge of being sold; in act III, it is sold; and in act IV, it has been sold.[8] The sale affects all the characters and, because it has been kept off stage, spoken of, intuited, feared, longed-for but never seen, it automatically takes on the quality of Fate or Death in a play by Maeterlinck or Andreyev. The characters are defined by their positions in the temporal flow – are they retarded, do they move with it, do they attempt to outrun it? Those who respond least well to the passage of time, refusing to join it (like Gayev and Firs), or who rush to get ahead of it (like Trofimov) are among the most absurd. This is not to make an ethical judgement of them, as Peter Holland seems to do, but rather to imply their closeness to or remoteness from the comic center of the play. Those who seem most in step with time (such as Lopakhin) do not appear immediately as comic until they are seen in Chekhov's other context, that of displacement, of misfits not only out-of-step with time but also out of place.

The revelation of character Peter Holland speaks of, when response to a natural occurrence like the storm provokes different interpretations of it, takes place consistently and on every level in *The Cherry Orchard*. The characters' attitudes toward the orchard itself or to the passage of time which is symbolized by the orchard's sale define them; every element in the play is perfectly integrated into this scheme, without a loss either of comic effect or symbolic value. Chekhov uses the servants to parody the masters and exaggerate their attitudes. The radiant past nostalgically recalled by Gayev exists on stage in the senile figure of Firs; Lopakhin's go-getting and upward mobility, his social ineptitude, are caricatured by the autodidact Yepik-hodov and the snobbish valet Yasha who longs for Paris but smells like a chicken-coop. The longing for Paris reflects Ranevskaya as well, who is also mirrored by Dunyasha with her hypersensitive nerves, over-elaborate hair-do and penchant for being seduced. Charlotta Ivanova, rootless and without identity (in act III she turns into 'a figure in a grey top-hat and checked trousers') doubles Trofimov, unsettled and dismissive of the past. The servants become a gallery of distorting mirrors that cast back grotesque images of the gentry's behavior, living symbols of *reductio ad absurdum*.[9]

The technique works as well as it does because the characters exist both on the plane of reality and the plane of abstraction. This was remarked at the time of *The Cherry Orchard*'s first production by the critic Nevedomsky, who saw them as simultaneously 'living persons, painted with the colors of vivid reality, and at the same time schemata of that reality, as it were, its foregone conclusions'.[10] These co-existing realms of reality and symbol were further explored by Andrey Bely, who found that instances of reality were so closely scrutinized in the play that one fell through them into the concurrent stream of eternity. He was bemused by the uneasiness provoked by what appeared at first sight to be humdrum characters and situations.

> How terrifying are the moments when Fate soundlessly sneaks up on the weaklings. Everywhere there is the alarming leitmotiv of thunder, everywhere the impending storm-cloud of terror. And yet, it would seem there's good reason to be terrified; after all, there's talk of selling the estate. But terrible are the masks behind which the terror is concealed, eyes goggling in the apertures. How terrible is the governess cavorting around the ruined family, or the valet Yasha, carping about the champagne, or the oafish bookkeeper and the tramp from the forest.[11]

For Bely, as for the brilliant director Meyerkhold, the crystallization of these ambiguities comes in the party scene of act III: on the one hand, it is a tawdry gathering, full of frumps and dolled-up servants, barely staving off the anxiety it was meant to dispel; on the other, it is a wild saraband of scarecrows and animated dummies, a symbol of man's futile activity in the face of inexorable Fate. This is not a matter of *either/or*: Chekhov's mastery enables it to be both those things at once.

Ironically, Peter Holland, in conceding to the famous 'breaking string' a genuine symbolic value, missed the Chekhovian dualism that allows the string both an enigmatic and a realistic status. The moment when it is first heard is perhaps the most Maeterlinckian episode in the play for the characters have fallen silent somewhere on a road, another of those indeterminate locations that is, in actuality, part way between the railroad and the estate, but, symbolically, is part way between past and future, birth and death, being and nothingness. The moment is full of those Symbolist pauses that evoke the hiatuses in existence which Bely identified as horrifying and which provide a link between Chekhov and Beckett[12]: those instants when the characters cease their chatter and leave off their routine time-killing occupations, and hearken to the sound of eternity. But even then, Chekhov cannot resist supplying an explanation for the inexplicable. Shortly before that moment, Yepikhodov had crossed upstage, twanging his guitar, Yepikhodov the awkward, forever stumbling and faltering. Might not the snapped string be one on his guitar? And again at the play's end, when we hear the sound plangently dying away, we have been told by Lopakhin that he left Yepikhodov on the premises as caretaker. Nothing more clearly demonstrates Chekhov's great skill in laying over his symbolic meaning a patina of irreproachable reality, a layering which bespeaks his peculiar genius as a dramatist.

NOTES

1. Quoted in *Theatre* (New York, April 1938), p. 44.
2. Sergey Glagol, 'Probleski novykh veyanyy v iskusstve i moskovskie teatry', in S. Glagol and James Lynch (pseud. of L. Andreyev), *Pod vpechatlennem Khudozhestvennogo Teatra* (Moscow, 1902), p. 162.
3. All translations are my own: *The Cherry Orchard and The Seagull* (Arlington Heights, Ill., 1977) and *Uncle Vanya*, performed at the University of Massachusetts at Amherst, 1979. Ronald Hingley's translations, used by Peter Holland, in trying to create colloquial British dialogue, ignore Chekhov's careful repetitions of phrases and words.
4. *Two Plays by Tchehof: The Seagull, The Cherry Orchard*, trans., with an introduction and notes, by George Calderon (New York, 1912), p. 20.
5. Peter Holland refers to Ostrovsky's 'naturalism', although Zola would hardly admit the Russian playwright as one of his school. The Russians call Ostrovsky's drama *bytoviy*, that is, portraying everyday life, but even this fails to indicate the folk-poetic, melodramatic, romantic overtones in his work. A play of Ostrovsky's

like *Easy Money* may remind us of Henri Becque, but *The Storm* seems closer to Garcia Lorca.

6. Ivan Bunin, *O Chekhove* (New York, 1955), pp. 215–16.

7. See E. M. Sakharova, 'K tvorcheskoy istorii "Vishnevogo sada"' in *Chekhovskie chteniya v Yalte* (Moscow, 1973), pp. 78–97.

8. Jean-Louis Barrault, 'Pourquoi *La Cerisaie*', *Cahiers de la Compagnie Renaud-Barrault*, 6 (July 1954).

9. Chekhov had also used this technique in *Uncle Vanya* in which each doublet presents opposite sides of a single coin: Serebryakov/Waffles = parasitic old husband/sacrificing old husband; Vanya/Astrov = failed but idealistic *intelligent*/failed but cynical *intelligent*; Sonya/Yėlena = unhappy but pragmatic young woman/unhappy but futile young woman; Marina/Mariya Vasilievna = down-to-earth old woman/abstracted old woman. This is highly schematized and within these types there are divergences, but it provides an outline worth elaborating.

10. M. Nevedomsky, 'Simvolizm v posledney drame A. P. Chekhove', *Mir bozhiy*, 8: 2 (1904), 18.

11. Andrey Bely (pseud. of Boris Bugayev), *Arabeski* (1911; Munich, 1969), p. 403.

12. The larger question of Chekhov's relation to Symbolist drama at the turn of the century and his affinities to later writers such as Beckett is treated in my essay, 'Chekhovian Drama, Maeterlinck, and the Russian Symbolists' in *Chekhov's Great Plays*, ed. J.-P. Barricelli (New York University Press, 1981).

Chekhov and the evolving symbol: cues and cautions for the plays in performance

LEIGH WOODS

The debate between Peter Holland and Laurence Senelick about the nature of symbolism in Chekhov's plays is prompted precisely by the playwright's facility as a symbol maker. His symbols succeed to the very degree that they resist precise definitions and elude conventional critical, historical, and psychological categories. When a dramatic symbol is 'open-ended' (in Peter Holland's phrase, see p. 239 above), it becomes subject to disagreement among critics, historians, and directors concerning the playwright's intention in constructing it and its proper function in performance. The debate about whether Chekhov's symbols are 'resistant' or 'irresistible', as Laurence Senelick would have it, testifies to the living force of Chekhov's plays and to a provocative ambiguity that keeps the major works continually on stages all over the world.

Rather than attempt to join in the dispute about Chekhov's intentions as a Symbolist, I should like to offer my own impressionistic responses to his plays as symbolic entities. My exposure to Chekhov's work has been as an actor and director, and practical experience has made me appreciate how strikingly different his use of symbols is in each of the four major plays. In fact, Chekhov's widest divergence from the self-proclaimed Symbolists is in his attempts to alter his use of symbolism to bring it into congruence with the distinct dramaturgy and particular view of life which emerge in each of the major plays. Symbolism, for Chekhov, was not a technique to be applied uniformly to every play, but a resource which should be tailored to the characteristic rhythmic and thematic demands of each individual work. Chekhov's awareness of the adaptability of symbols took some time to grow, and his initial essays at symbolism were less refined than his later ones, even though they approached conventional and doctrinaire 'Symbolism' rather more closely.

His first play was *Platonov*, which seems to have been written in his early twenties, but neither staged nor published during his lifetime. It is unusually verbose, being more than half as long again as any of the other full-length works. A combination of farce and domestic melodrama, its action centers on problems of money and romantic intrigue: the sheer abundance of dialogue and the frequency of long speeches work, in effect, to remove any sense of the symbolic capacity of language which emerges so strongly in the later plays. There is a portentous burst of fireworks to bring down the curtain at the end of act II, and Platonov's eventual murder at the hands of one of his jealous mistresses is foreshadowed by his half-hearted and ridiculous attempt to commit suicide, but such devices are not fashioned into any sustained or coherent expression.

Ivanov, which Chekhov completed in 1887, is much shorter than *Platonov*, although still longer than any of the other full-length plays except *Three Sisters*. It shares the preoccupations with romantic triangles and debts which govern the action of *Platonov*, but it also begins to manifest the subtle, pervasive, and sustained use of symbols which Chekhov was later to refine. Firearms are the most noticeable objects in the play, and they are used by Chekhov to bridge the gap between conventional melodrama and the emerging Symbolism of the 1880s.

But the symbols in *Ivanov* often strike us as literary artifacts, not yet fully assimilated into a naturalistic pattern. For instance, Ivanov likens himself variously to Hamlet, to Lazarus, and to Don Quixote, and he seems to recognize himself and his own unhappy state most penetratingly when he stands before the painting of a dog. All of these symbolic references are drawn from other works of art, and although they succeed admirably in suggesting a self-pitying and self-dramatizing man, they do not find extension into the realm of gesture or of household objects. This failing was not coincidental. Chekhov's initial exposure to Symbolism came from the printed page; and, indeed, none of the Symbolists, in the renunciation of traditional dramaturgy and the search for new forms to counter it, was ever able to refine a compelling dramatic language.

In *The Seagull*, completed in 1896, the symbolism may strike us still as a literary device (see Martin Esslin's argument, especially p. 7 above), although it is much more sustained and ambitious than in *Ivanov*. The lake which is visible during the first two acts may reflect Chekhov's recent reading of Ibsen's *Little Eyolf* and Maeterlinck's *Pelléas and Mélisande*, in both of which lakes assume central symbolic roles. Perhaps, in order to disguise or to qualify his debt to Symbolist works, Chekhov also includes in *The Seagull* a spoof of Symbolism, in the form of Constantin's laughably incantatory, dreamy, and rebellious play. In contrast to such dramaturgy, Chekhov takes care to soften the literary–esthetic cast of his complex of symbols in *The Seagull* by making his four central characters writers and actresses.

It is in the central symbol of the seagull itself that the play shows a lack of dramatic efficacy in comparison with the later works. The bird is associated, at various points in the play, with love, death, creativity, freedom, and innocence, and its contours grow increasingly muddy as it is put in the position of 'explaining' or signifying the relationships between characters and the often contradictory attitudes which these characters have toward themselves. The seagull is a symbol which Chekhov has drawn from outside the setting and action of the play; and his employment of it, particularly in Nina's long confessional speech to Constantin in the final act, suggests some discomfort on his part with regard to the bird's organic link with the central characters and action. Instead of being incorporated into the play, the seagull hovers around its edges, to be invoked or brought on stage in order to signal moments of high passion or significance.

The disparity between the seagull as a central and governing symbol and the cherry orchard of Chekhov's final play could hardly be more marked. The seasons of *The Cherry Orchard* move from spring in the first act to winter in the fourth, and Chekhov captures the orchard first in its bloom and finally in its destruction. The sound of an axe provides the accompaniment to the falling of the final curtain. The organic use of the central image is further reinforced by the nursery as setting for both the first and last acts of the play, and by the clear parallel which this setting suggests between the life cycles of orchard and of characters. The orchard is thought of by Lyubov, Gayev, and Firs as it was in the past, and the manner of its destruction at the end of the play suggests a resonance between its demise and that of its former owners and keepers. We also hear from Firs that the old process of harvesting and preserving the cherries has been lost, out of indifference and over a period of years. Thus robbed of its practical value, the orchard becomes expendable in the mind of the eminently practical Lopakhin, its new landlord.

So total is the process by which the action of *The Cherry Orchard* is immersed in the natural setting and so completely are social changes joined to organic ones, that few symbols of an overt nature are at all evident in act IV. By this time it is as if each character has become so fixed, consistent, and restricted, that any one of his words or gestures can stand for his entire identity. And just as the orchard is stripped away from the landscape, so is the nursery stripped first of its furniture and finally of its inhabitants during the last act, until only the ancient and ill Firs is left alone on the stage.

The peculiar coincidence of unobtrusiveness and ubiquity in the symbol of the cherry orchard signals the ultimate success of Chekhov's dramaturgy. Our appreciation of Maeterlinck's plays, for instance, depends upon the facility with which we grasp the governing symbols of each successive scene and on the esthetic harmony which the central symbols of the plays are able to suggest. Maeterlinck's achievement was original and important, but Chekhov's plays are the more successful both as dramatic and as symbolic entities. Their distinction, as Laurence Senelick argues, lies in their ability to transcend esthetic and critical categories in forms which suggest – while departing from – the most literal correspondence to perceived reality. The two plays which fall between *The Seagull* and *The Cherry Orchard* further demonstrate this paradox at work.

Uncle Vanya and *Three Sisters* contain uses of symbols which are in sharpest contrast to each other. *Uncle Vanya* is the shortest of the major plays, and of the four it is the most sparse in its use of symbols: this bareness makes it seem that the characters have been robbed of their capacity to dream and imagine by a grinding, routinized existence. Their boredom and isolation seem to have stunted their lives, and their world, once so full of natural beauty, according to Dr Astrov, has been leached of its richness and variety. The settings of the play, in the order in which they occur, reflect a shrinking environment: from the garden of the first act to the dining room of the second, still with some tie to the realm of nature and of animal function; to the drawing room of the third act, emptied of any exciting and vivacious people who might animate it; and, finally, to Vanya's small room in the last act.

Against this gathering background of a harsh and blasted landscape, the map of Africa which hangs in Vanya's room becomes a ridiculous emblem of a place very clearly beyond the practical or imaginative grasp of any of the characters in the play. The title of *Uncle Vanya* marks it as the last, after *Platonov* and *Ivanov*, in the line of Chekhov's plays about 'superfluous men'. But in *Uncle Vanya* the title character does not die, and the characters who remain in the country-house at the end of the play are sentenced to an attenuated wasting away – as are those who remain in the diminished estates of *Three Sisters* and *The Cherry Orchard*. There may be some connection between this recurrent concluding image and the process of Chekhov's terminal disease.

In contrast to the spareness of symbol in *Uncle Vanya*, *Three Sisters* is perhaps the most heavily symbol-laden of the entire group. The choric nature of the title may dictate a profusion of symbols. The sisters at the opening are dressed in blue, black, and white, in a visual scheme which seems calculated to represent a spectrum of personality and experience. And in the play as a whole there seems to be a diffusing impulse at work, rather than the 'concentrating' one of *Platonov*, *Ivanov*, and *Uncle Vanya*, or the atmospheric unity which permeates *The Cherry Orchard*. Indeed, the photographs taken of Irina's nameday party near the end of the first act succeed in fixing and reinforcing a palpable image of human diversity. For Irina at this moment it is as if the world of Moscow after which she yearns so strongly has been briefly reconstituted within the narrow confines of a remote military outpost.

Three Sisters also offers a different image of the human condition from that in *Uncle Vanya*. The central characters of both plays are dissatisfied with the terms of their isolated rural existences; but in *Three Sisters*, their imaginations, far from atrophying, begin to work even more feverishly. Instances of such fruitless and compulsive imaginative activity may be seen in Irina's desperate calls for a return to Moscow, which end both the second and third acts, in Masha's obsessive repetitions of a circular scrap of verse, and in Chebutykin's constant resort to his newspaper as the mechanism for fantasy, retreat, and withdrawal.

Through all of this, the need to communicate remains strong among the characters, but the frequency of the references to foreign languages in the play reminds us how regularly attempts at communication are frustrated: Kulygin's Latin becomes a symbol of the clichés and formulas which fill his mind and which succeed in turning his wife against him; Tusenbach, in all other respects the most open and generous of the characters, brags of knowing no German; Natasha, destroyer of the domestic framework of the Prozorov household, speaks a ridiculously fractured French. Andrey states proudly that he and his sisters were taught English, French, German – and that Irina knows Italian, too; but his statement is qualified by his invocation of the pain and rigor to which their father subjected them in the learning of these languages, and by Andrey's own sense of loss at having forgotten them because he never has the chance to practise them. Irina later cries out that she has forgotten the Italian word for 'window', in a lament which echoes her sense of the loss of freedom, initiative, and imagination which the entire family has suffered. Somewhat later, when Chebutykin refers to Irina as his 'little bird', it occurs to us that she has become a bird which can no longer fly.

The very fact that we can pinpoint 'symbols' in such small scraps of dialogue signals the distinctive element in Chekhov's use of symbolism: his ability to synthesize it, as his confidence and control as a playwright grew, with the lineaments of realism. For the purposes of contrast, we have only to compare this impulse, and the course of Chekhov's development as a playwright, with the impulse of the French Symbolists or Maeterlinck, in whose plays language is studiedly 'poetic' and ethereal, and in which a single atmosphere is allowed to predominate, generally at the expense of humor and of the defter forms of irony.

The 'symbol' in Chekhov's plays is nearly always rooted at a personal level, in the chance remarks of characters, in the objects which they handle, or in their distinctive fantasy-lives. The 'realism' which we encounter in his work for the stage is one which has been distilled by a long process of artistic selection and refinement into something which represents universal concerns. The notion of *theatrum mundi* is an old one, but one that flourishes, it seems to me, in the action and *dramatis personae* of Chekhov's last two plays, in particular.

No director should begin to regard Chekhov's four major plays as homogeneous works, nor should he want to employ uniform settings, costumes, or 'moods' in their production. Some of the consequences of this tendency are evident in the humorless productions of Chekhov which often find the stage on both sides of the Atlantic. Let *The Seagull* rest quite distinct from *Uncle*

Vanya in the mind of the director; and when one of the plays is chosen for production let it be because the director finds what is unique and distinctive at work within it.

The curious proximity of the symbols with the surfaces of actuality in Chekhov's plays has been acknowledged and explored in Martin Esslin's paper and by Peter Holland and Laurence Senelick. Let the unanimity of opinion about this essential proximity stand as a warning to designers who would move the plays too far into realms of the figurative and the abstract. It would be ridiculous, for example, to frame Vanya's map of Africa in a stripped, monochromatic interior, and equally ridiculous to draw attention to it as the sole object on the stage. The map assumes its symbolic significance precisely because it is part of a clutter of objects, and that clutter, in turn, stands for the maelstrom in Vanya's mind. In terms of staging, all of the plays make similar 'realistic' scenic demands, and the designer will ignore these at his peril.

Finally, 'symbol-hunting' is a quite satisfactory way to enter into the living spirit of Chekhov's plays. So fine is the craftsmanship of his major dramatic works and so careful the element of selection at work within them, that they stand as analogues to Max Frisch's consideration of the empty stage in Zurich (see pp. 3, 11 above): the Chekhov play script becomes a repository of symbols whose specific significances matter less than does their evocation of a whole and inclusive view of the world.

Index